CU00952225

READERS' GUIDES TO ESSENTIAL CRITIC[

CONSULTANT EDITOR: NICOLAS TREDELL

Published

Thomas P. Adler   Tennessee Williams: *A Streetcar Named Desire/Cat on a Hot Tin Roof*
Pascale Aebischer   Jacobean Drama
Lucie Armitt   George Eliot: *Adam Bede/The Mill on the Floss/Middlemarch*
Simon Avery   Thomas Hardy: *The Mayor of Casterbridge/Jude the Obscure*
Paul Baines   Daniel Defoe: *Robinson Crusoe/Moll Flanders*
Annika Bautz   Jane Austen: *Sense and Sensibility/Pride and Prejudice/Emma*
Matthew Beedham   The Novels of Kazuo Ishiguro
Richard Beynon   D. H. Lawrence: *The Rainbow/Women in Love*
Peter Boxall   Samuel Beckett: *Waiting for Godot/Endgame*
Claire Brennan   The Poetry of Sylvia Plath
Susan Bruce   Shakespeare: *King Lear*
Sandie Byrne   Jane Austen: *Mansfield Park*
Alison Chapman   Elizabeth Gaskell: *Mary Barton/North and South*
Peter Childs   The Fiction of Ian McEwan
Christine Clegg   Vladimir Nabokov: *Lolita*
John Coyle   James Joyce: *Ulysses/A Portrait of the Artist as a Young Man*
Martin Coyle   Shakespeare: *Richard II*
Justin D. Edwards   Postcolonial Literature
Michael Faherty   The Poetry of W. B. Yeats
Sarah Gamble   The Fiction of Angela Carter
Jodi-Anne George   *Beowulf*
Jodi-Anne George   Chaucer: The General Prologue to *The Canterbury Tales*
Jane Goldman   Virginia Woolf: *To the Lighthouse/The Waves*
Huw Griffiths   Shakespeare: *Hamlet*
Vanessa Guignery   The Fiction of Julian Barnes
Louisa Hadley   The Fiction of A. S. Byatt
Geoffrey Harvey   Thomas Hardy: *Tess of the d'Urbervilles*
Paul Hendon   The Poetry of W. H. Auden
Terry Hodgson   The Plays of Tom Stoppard for Stage, Radio, TV and Film
William Hughes   Bram Stoker: *Dracula*
Stuart Hutchinson   Mark Twain: *Tom Sawyer/Huckleberry Finn*
Stuart Hutchinson   Edith Wharton: *The House of Mirth/The Custom of the Country*
Betty Jay   E. M. Forster: *A Passage to India*
Aaron Kelly   Twentieth-Century Irish Literature
Elmer Kennedy-Andrews   Nathaniel Hawthorne: *The Scarlet Letter*
Elmer Kennedy-Andrews   The Poetry of Seamus Heaney
Daniel Lea   George Orwell: *Animal Farm/Nineteen Eighty-Four*
Rachel Lister   Alice Walker: *The Color Purple*
Sara Lodge   Charlotte Brontë: *Jane Eyre*
Philippa Lyon   Twentieth-Century War Poetry
Merja Makinen   The Novels of Jeanette Winterson
Matt McGuire   Contemporary Scottish Literature
Timothy Milnes   Wordsworth: *The Prelude*
Jago Morrison   The Fiction of Chinua Achebe
Carl Plasa   Tony Morrison: *Beloved*

Carl Plasa   Jean Rhys: *Wide Sargasso Sea*
Nicholas Potter   Shakespeare: *Antony and Cleopatra*
Nicholas Potter   Shakespeare: *Othello*
Nicholas Potter   Shakespeare's Late Plays: *Pericles, Cymbeline, The Winter's Tale, The Tempest*
Steven Price   The Plays, Screenplays and Films of David Mamet
Berthold Schoene-Harwood   Mary Shelley: *Frankenstein*
Nicholas Seager   The Rise of the Novel
Nick Selby   T. S. Eliot: *The Waste Land*
Nick Selby   Herman Melville: *Moby Dick*
Nick Selby   The Poetry of Walt Whitman
David Smale   Salman Rushdie: *Midnight's Chidren/The Satanic Verses*
Patsy Stoneman   Emily Brontë: *Wuthering Heights*
Susie Thomas   Hanif Kureishi
Nicolas Tredell   Joseph Conrad: *Heart of Darkness*
Nicolas Tredell   Charles Dickens: *Great Expectations*
Nicolas Tredell   William Faulkner: *The Sound and the Fury/As I Lay Dying*
Nicolas Tredell   F. Scott Fitzgerald: *The Great Gatsby*
Nicolas Tredell   Shakespeare: *A Midsummer Night's Dream*
Nicolas Tredell   Shakespeare: *Macbeth*
Nicolas Tredell   The Fiction of Martin Amis
Matthew Woodcock   Shakespeare: *Henry V*
Gillian Woods   Shakespeare: *Romeo and Juliet*
Angela Wright   Gothic Fiction

Forthcoming
Brian Baker   Science Fiction
Alan Gibbs   Jewish-American Literature since 1945
Sarah Haggarty & Jon Mee   Willam Blake: *Songs of Innocence and Experience*
Keith Hughes   African-American Literature
Britta Martens   The Poetry of Robert Browning
Michael Whitworth   Virginia Woolf: *Mrs Dalloway*

Readers' Guides to Essential Criticism
Series Standing Order ISBN 1–4039–0108–2
(*outside North America only*)

You can receive future titles in this series as they are published by placing a standing order. Please contact your bookseller or, in the case of difficulty, write to us at the address below with your name and address, the title of the series and the ISBN quoted above.

Customer Services Department, Macmillan Distribution Ltd, Houndmills, Basingstoke, Hampshire, RG21 6XS, UK

Tennessee Williams

A Streetcar Named Desire/ Cat on a Hot Tin Roof

THOMAS P. ADLER

Consultant editor: Nicolas Tredell

First published 2013 by
PALGRAVE MACMILLAN

Palgrave Macmillan in the UK is an imprint of Macmillan Publishers Limited,
registered in England, company number 785998, of Houndmills, Basingstoke,
Hampshire RG21 6XS.

Palgrave Macmillan in the US is a division of St Martin's Press LLC,
175 Fifth Avenue, New York, NY 10010.

Palgrave Macmillan is the global academic imprint of the above companies
and has companies and representatives throughout the world.

Palgrave® and Macmillan® are registered trademarks in the United States,
the United Kingdom, Europe and other countries.

ISBN 978–0–230–22868–9   hardback
ISBN 978–0–230–22869–6   paperback

This book is printed on paper suitable for recycling and made from fully
managed and sustained forest sources. Logging, pulping and manufacturing
processes are expected to conform to the environmental regulations of the
country of origin.

A catalogue record for this book is available from the British Library.

A catalog record for this book is available from the Library of Congress.

10   9   8   7   6   5   4   3   2   1
22 21 20 19 18 17 16 15 14 13

Printed and bound by CPI Group (UK) Ltd, Croydon, CR0 4YY

For our grandsons, Simon and William—
and as always to Winnie,
for her patient support

CONTENTS

of masculinity. Includes criticism by John Clum, David Savran, Michael Paller, Dean Shackelford, Roger Gross, Mark Winchell, Georges-Michel Sarotte, and Michael Bibler.

CHAPTER EIGHT   101

Contemporary Critical Theory and *Streetcar*

The poststructuralist and postmodern critics whose work is surveyed in this chapter raise questions about the relationship between text and reader and text and author; of particular concern are issues of authorizing the text, of traces of the author in the text, and of the actor's body as text. Includes criticism by Kathleen Hulley, John Bak, Nicholas Pagan, Philip Kolin, William Kleb, and Laura and Edward Morrow.

CHAPTER NINE   115

Film and Television Adaptations

This chapter foregrounds scholarship about Williams's two dramas as adapted to other media, looking first at the original film version of each and then at the major adaptation of each for the TV screen; some attention is given to the way that film and genre theory have informed this criticism. Includes criticism by Maurice Yacowar, Gene Phillips, Nancy Tischler, Christine Geraghty, Barton Palmer and Robert Bray, Pamela Hanks, and June Schlueter.

CONCLUSION   127

A recapitulation of some of the major currents in Williams scholarship, with an indication of possible avenues of further investigation.

Introduction

LIFE AND ART

Although critics might disagree about the precise ranking of Tennessee Williams among the pantheon of major American dramatists of the twentieth century—along with Eugene O'Neill, Arthur Miller, and Edward Albee—no one disputes that he is the most important playwright to emerge from the South. As such, one of the hallmarks of his works is the conflict between nostalgia for a mythically conceived agrarian South and the critique of a more pragmatic industrialized North. Just as indelible is his kinship, as a gay writer whose homosexuality had to remain hidden on the commercial stages of his time, with all those whom he termed in an early poem 'the strange, the crazed, the queer.'[1] His empathetic connection extended to all outsiders who were somehow marginalized or Other because of either their racial, sexual, or ethnic identity or their artistic gifts—misfits all who became a favored subject throughout his career. As Williams would proclaim in one of his many essays, theatre becomes most vital 'through the unlocking and lighting up and ventilation of the closets, attics, and basements of human behavior and experience.'[2]

Born Thomas Lanier Williams on March 26, 1911 in the Columbus, Mississippi, rectory of his maternal grandfather, an Episcopalian priest, he was the second of three children of incompatible parents, Cornelius Coffin Williams and Edwina Dakin. Sickly as a child, he formed an inordinate attachment to his older sister, Rose, and to their Black nurse, Ozzie. After his boyhood years in Clarksdale, Mississippi, in the heart of the Delta, the family had moved by 1918 to St. Louis, a city Tom always professed to dislike. Early on, Tom began writing short stories; later he enrolled in the University of Missouri at Columbia, though his father forced him to withdraw in 1931 and begin working at the International Shoe Company. He continued his education at Washington University, where he wrote poetry and plays for amateur groups. Williams received his first formal training in playwriting at the University of Iowa, from which he graduated in 1938. In his last year there, he wrote the most overtly sociopolitical play of his career, *Not About Nightingales*, which only reached Broadway in 1999 after being unearthed by London's National Theatre. Heavily expressionistic in style, it introduces several, though by no means all, of the personal attitudes and thematic motifs that would adumbrate the mature Williams: the pervasiveness of human isolation, and a belief in the power of the sustaining dream or illusion and of human sexuality as means of transcending aloneness; an abhorrence of the underdeveloped heart that refuses to reach out and form bonds of human communion with others; a castigation of puritan repression and excessive guilt, along with the need for a nonjudgmental compassion for those whose moral systems are different from one's own; an insistence on the courage to endure in the face of time, that robs one of physical beauty and artistic potency; and a valorization of the artist's near-religious calling to make some sense out of humankind's existential predicament.

After graduating from Iowa, Williams settled initially in New Orleans— where he had his first homosexual experience—before setting out on a peripatetic existence on the road, living for periods in Provincetown on Cape Cod, in Taos, New Mexico, and in Key West, Florida; later in the 1940s, he would travel to London, Paris, and Rome in the company of Frank Merlo, with whom he had a relationship that endured for fourteen years. In 1940, *Battle of Angels*, instead of introducing him to a wide audience as he had hoped, closed in Boston before ever reaching New York; it would, however, be revised as *Orpheus Descending* in 1957 and eventually be revived in a much-heralded expressionistic production in London in the late 1980s. In 1943, Williams's beloved sister Rose, who would be the model for many of his women characters, was subjected to a prefrontal lobotomy that doctors claimed would cure her schizophrenia. The guilt that would haunt him for the rest of his life for not having done anything to prevent the operation provides the impetus for his autobiographical memory play, *The Glass Menagerie*, which opened on Broadway in 1945 with Laurette Taylor in a legendary performance and catapulted Williams to immediate fame. The 'Production Notes' preceding the text form perhaps the most important theoretical statement ever penned by an American playwright (Arthur Miller's famous essay 'Tragedy and the Common Man' (1949) might be a close second). In them, Williams called for a 'new, plastic theatre,'[3] one that, rather than depending primarily on dialogue, drew heavily upon all the multimedia elements of scenic imagery (visual as well as verbal), lighting, sound, and sculptural arrangement of objects and characters to replace the shopworn theatre of 'photographic' realism that too often failed to plumb the depths of experience. The Narrator of the nonrepresentational *Menagerie* confesses to 'a poet's weakness for symbols,'[4] yet Williams in another of his essays would justify their use as 'nothing but the natural speech of drama language' for their economy and ability 'to say a thing more directly and simply and beautifully than it could be said in words.'[5]

Following close upon *Menagerie* came *A Streetcar Named Desire* (1947), Williams's greatest stage success and one of the few undisputed masterpieces of American drama. Set in the 'raffish' city of New Orleans that Williams always loved, it might be said to usher in a new and influential dramaturgical form (that the playwright referred to as 'personal lyricism'), seamlessly blending a naturalistic rendering of character with brilliantly conceived symbolic properties and calling upon expressionistic techniques to reveal the subjective inner reality. Williams followed *Streetcar* with three works that, while lesser, still contributed to his reputation for charting original territory: *Summer and Smoke* (1948), an allegorical modern morality tale whose 1952 revival, directed by Jose Quintero at Circle in the Square, signaled the beginning of the Off Broadway movement; the joyously Dionysian *Rose Tattoo* (1950), famous for providing Anna Magnani with her Oscar-winning film role; and the highly experimental *Camino Real* (1953), deeply imbued with the atmosphere of political suspicion in Cold War America. The late 1940s into the next decade also witnessed the publication of Williams's most characteristic fiction, including stories like 'Desire and the Black Masseur' and 'One Arm' that address sexual subject matter more freely than the theatre allowed, as well as the imagistic 1950 novella, *The Roman Spring of Mrs. Stone*, about the destructive effect of time and aging on art and beauty—which would become a recurrent motif in the later plays.

The mid-1950s began another period of great prominence for Williams, culminating with his picture on the cover of *Time* in 1962 acclaiming him as the world's most eminent living dramatist. Williams expressed the opinion that his second most successful Broadway play, *Cat on a Hot Tin Roof* (1955) 'was in many ways as good as *Streetcar*,' which he considered his 'best play.'[6] From some quarters, however, came the charge that capitulating to what was, at that time, permissible on the stage made him less than candid about his protagonist's sexual 'abnormality.' His justification for the ambiguity gave rise to the most oft-quoted of his interpolated stage directions: 'Some mystery should be left in the revelation of character in a play, just as a great deal of mystery is always left in the revelation of character in life, even in one's own character to himself.'[7] Elizabeth Taylor's performance as the title character brought worldwide renown to the film version of *Cat*, only one of over a dozen Williams dramas that made their way to the screen. Elia Kazan, who had directed both *Streetcar* and *Cat* on stage, also directed Williams's original film script of *Baby Doll* (1956), based on two of his earlier one-act plays—and advertised by a notorious billboard of a scantily clad Caroll Baker in a crib high over Times Square. It was common practice, in fact, for Williams as an inveterate reviser to adapt works into the same or another artistic medium: for instance, among the sources for *Streetcar* are the earlier short plays, *Portrait of a Madonna* and the tellingly titled *Interior: Panic*, while *Cat* is based on the short story 'Three Players of a Summer Game.'[8] Two additional dramas round out the decade: *Suddenly Last Summer* (1957) speaks shockingly about the silencing of sexual difference through the violent death of the homosexual poet who remains offstage; and *Sweet Bird of Youth* (1959), along with continuing the exploration of time and the artist, comments trenchantly on Southern racial demagoguery and the media's handling of celebrity. The death of Williams's father in 1957 drove him into psychoanalysis, while the death of his longtime lover in 1963 plunged him into depression; he became dependent on drugs and alcohol in order to continue working and referred to the 1960s, which ended with several month's confinement in a psychiatric ward, as his 'Stoned Age.'

After an uncharacteristic foray into romantic comedy with *Period of Adjustment* in 1960, Williams produced his final critical and popular success in the wise and radiant work, *The Night of the Iguana* (1961), which is both a summation of some earlier themes—particularly of the necessity for an openness and nonjudgmental compassion toward others, because 'Nothing human disgusts me unless it's unkind, violent,'[9] and for not allowing oneself to become so mired in guilt as to wallow in a despairing passivity—as well as an indication of some he will later come to emphasize, especially the need to go on in a kind of Beckettian endurance in the face of the finality of death. The numerous plays after *Iguana*, many dramaturgically experimental and most dealing with the artist *in extremis*, failed to achieve critical approbation or wide scale appeal. Among them are *In the Bar of a Tokyo Hotel* (1968), *Out Cry* (1971), and *Small Craft Warnings* (1972)—notable for being the first time Williams put an unabashedly gay character on stage—as well as the autobiographical *Vieux Carré* (1977), which treats the Narrator's homosexuality more candidly than *Menagerie* could, and *Clothes for a Summer Hotel* (1980), his last Broadway production before dying in February 1983 by choking on the cap of a medicine bottle. Despite critical disparagement of his later efforts, nothing could negate the enduring body of a half-dozen or so major plays that secured his unchallenged position as one of the masters of the modern theatre. His determination to keep writing, even prolifically so, in the face of adversity reflected the spirit embodied in his private journals and expressed in the closing line of his confessional *Memoirs*: 'high station in life is earned by the gallantry with which appalling experiences are survived with grace.'[10]

THE PERSISTENCE OF *STREETCAR* AND *CAT*

Almost immediately hailed by critical consensus as deserving of permanent spots in the repertoire of classic American theatre, not only did *Streetcar* and *Cat* provide Williams with the longest initial Broadway runs of any of his plays—855 and 694 performances, respectively—but each went on to win the Pulitzer Prize for Drama. A selective sampling of the most often-cited early reviews can help set the scene for the scholarly commentary that only begins to proliferate a decade or more after the plays' initial productions. Both works were accorded rapturous reviews by the influential critic for the daily *New York Times*, Brooks Atkinson, who was particularly supportive of Williams's playwriting career. The essential reasons behind his praise for both works were basically the same: first, 'he is a poet,' not because of his lyricism or any 'fancy writing,' but 'because he is aware of people and of life,' presenting it honestly:[11] and second, because of the utter naturalness of the onstage action so that each work—in a phrase he repeats in the two reviews—'seems not to have been written. It is the quintessence of craft. It is the absolute truth of the theatre.'[12] Atkinson stands amazed that Williams in *Streetcar* can create a harrowing portrait of a tragic character in such a way that it can have both popular appeal and the enduring quality of art, singling out his ability to visualize how he wants his play to look in performance. *Cat* he judges as 'superb' theatre and an even finer drama, partly because it shows Williams breaking free from the 'formula' of the neurotic Southern gentlewoman of his earliest works.

If Atkinson praises the plays for giving the appearance of happening effortlessly, Eric Bentley, himself a stage director, detects a straining after a literary quality in the writing and a too-aesthetic approach to staging as detracting from the all-too-rare 'liveliness' of realistic dialogue in the mouths of carefully observed characters. So in his review of *Streetcar* for the monthly *Harper's Magazine*, he faults Williams for 'seem[ing] to imagine his talent is lyrical' and for the 'bad poetry' of the overall conception,[13] while in his review of *Cat* for *New Republic* he delineates 'Williams's besetting sin [as] fake poeticizing, fake philosophizing, a straining after big statements'[14] about grand abstractions. Both works, nevertheless, embody 'one of the distinctive creations of the American theatre' in their ability to present 'a view of *man's* exterior that is also a view of his interior, the habitat of his body—country of memories and dreams.'[15] Yet he sees a dissociation between the script's reductive dependence upon sexuality as an explanation for behavior ('dirty') and the 'golden'-lit aura of the production given to *Cat*; perhaps, however, precisely because he does have a seasoned director's eye for how the orchestration of characters into tableaux recalls religious iconography, such as the Annunciation, he is disturbed by a potential disconnect between edifying scenic images and the characters' true states of being.

Harold Clurman, longtime critic for *The Nation*, achieved prominence as a director of the Group Theatre, and so, unsurprisingly, he valorizes the role of the actor, crediting him as 'the author of the new meaning that a play acquires on the stage.'[16] Consequently, in discussing *Streetcar*, which he deems a 'beautiful' and 'original' drama that provides a poet's perspective on life, he zeroes in on the complex characters Williams has created, difficult though it might prove for actors to fully realize them upon the stage. Blanche is seen as the 'potential artist' everyone carries within, whose aspirations are denigrated by an environment that victimizes anyone who refuses to conform to societal norms. In Clurman's masterful formulation, Stanley, lionized by a society that deems him a perfect embodiment of the common man, is an energetic bully, 'the unwilling antichrist of our time' who actively thwarts 'a more comprehensive world in which thought and conscience, a broader humanity are expected to evolve from the old Adam.'[17] Walter Kerr, in his likewise character-driven review of *Cat* from the *New York Herald Tribune*, notoriously accused the playwright of being 'elusive and ambiguous' because the 'soul-tied' Brick is also tongue-tied, unable to know himself and unwilling to speak openly of the 'private wounds and secret drives [that] have crippled him,' leaving 'the key' to his innermost being 'mislaid, or deliberately hidden.'[18] The dramatist, Kerr concludes, 'has failed—or refused—to isolate the cause of the corruption in Brick, and the play . . . simply catches something of his sickness.'[19] Kerr's charge occasioned from Williams an unusually full retort: 'Critic says "Evasion," Writer says "Mystery,"' where he asserts that, while there will always remain 'artistically defensible' ambiguities, 'I would never evade it [truth of character] for the sake of evasion, because I was in any way reluctant to reveal what I know of the truth.'[20] (He continues by quoting at length from the Act Two stage direction in the published play underlining his intent to render the 'fiercely charged!—interplay of live human beings' rather than 'the solution of one man's psychological problems,' meaning he must 'observe and probe as clearly and deeply as he *legitimately* can' without resorting to '"pat" conclusions, facile definitions.')[21] Kerr, upon seeing the 1974 revival of *Cat*, which he found 'clearer' and 'more honest,' withdrew his charge, admitting that the answer he sought to an 'unresolved mystery' had always been there in a Brick almost hysterically prone to protesting too much because 'even to have *felt* such an attraction [for another man]' would have destroyed his self-image 'as straight, clean, uncorrupted.'[22]

If Williams answered Kerr via an essay, it appears that Mary McCarthy in her venomous *Partisan Review* attack on *Streetcar* is responding equally as much to one of his essays as to the play itself. McCarthy's description reduces the work to a comic domestic drama, placing it in the category of the unwanted in-law comes to visit. She claims that Williams, dissatisfied with authoring so mundane a story and straining after significance, has grafted onto it an artsy surface, in much the same way that Blanche herself adorned a bleak reality with the 'magic' of a paper lantern, or the way that Joe (sic) Kowalski wafted poetic about the sex act as 'colored lights,' or the way that so many elements of the play, like the bathroom, are endowed with symbolic significance. McCarthy's reductive reading stems from her umbrage at Williams's presenting himself as a serious, totally committed artist in his prepro-duction essay, 'On a Streetcar Named Success,' in which he spoke about the 'spiritual dislocation' that results when a writer is sidetracked from his vocation of creating art by mundane demands on his time; if the artist's life is to be 'very substantial,' then 'the right condition for him is that in which his work is not only convenient but unavoidable.'[23] McCarthy saw this fashioning of himself as 'the rootless, wandering writer' simply as grandstanding, 'careerism' of the worst kind 'rooted in the American pay-dirt.'[24]

On the other hand, William Becker, critiquing the opening of *Cat* for *The Hudson Review*, supports Williams's claim to being considered an art-ist, regarding the stylistic techniques not as excrescences but as integral to a work exemplifying 'the singular dramatic achievement of the post-war decade on Broadway.'[25] Every dramaturgical element—dialogue, setting, characters, action, staging that then becomes a part of the script—is 'harmoniously fused' to forward the play's 'dialectic' between reality and fantasy in Williams's thematizing of truth as the *sine qua non* of human communication and sex as the 'great motivator' of human conflict. Moreover, Becker situates *Cat*, which he considers Williams's 'most powerful' play, within the major traditions of modern theatre: Ibsenite in its narrative construction that only gradually uncovers the past; Chekhovian in its 'rhythms' and lengthy 'digressive' speeches that reveal psychological states and dawning awareness; and even Strindbergian in its tonality.

With Blanche's exit line, which is undoubtedly the most well-known from any American play—'I have always depended on the kindness of strangers'[26]—*Streetcar* has entered into the common culture, and not just of theatergoers. It has become a frequent intertext, in works as various as Pedro Almodóvar's 1990 prize-winning film, *All about My Mother*, and Stephanie Grant's well-received 2008 novel, *Map of Ireland*. Although it is not developed enough to be considered an intertext, there is even reference to *Cat* and the click that comes after drinking in Haruki Murakami's first novel, *Hear the Wind Sing* (1979). And shortly after the all-Black production of *Cat* starring James Earl Jones became a sought-after ticket on both sides of the Atlantic, in 2010 *Streetcar*, in an Orientalist, Japanese-infused production directed by Lee Breuer, became the first American play ever to appear on the stage of Paris's *Comédie-Française* in its more than three-hundred-year history.[27] If any other proof of his undiminished stature and continuing pertinence is needed, it surely resides in the fact that no other American dramatist has had so many of his significant works for the stage revived so frequently, while generating such multifaceted, if, at times, diametrically opposed, responses by audiences and scholars alike, as Williams.

In the chapters that follow, it has been my intention, whenever possible, to focus the discussion on the texts of both *Streetcar* and *Cat*, as well as to bring the critics into conversation with one another. The first aim has been achieved except in the case of two chapters where the material does not lend itself to that goal: Chapter 7, which is predominantly about *Cat*; and Chapter 8, which almost exclusively concerns *Streetcar*. My second goal has been accomplished throughout by arranging the material not chronologically but according to topics, and then putting the relevant critics and their viewpoints into dialogue with each other. After Chapter 1, which I devote largely to a consideration of the performance texts and production history—with special emphasis on the collaborative creative process that Williams and Elia Kazan engaged in initially to bring the plays to the stage—the material falls mainly into three groups. The first looks at the broader cultural milieu out of which Williams wrote, including the geography, history, and myth of the South, along with classical and Christian mythology and iconography as they are alluded to and reworked in the plays (Chapter 2); and the sociopolitical background more peculiar to America in the post-World War II period, with the rise of consumerism, the paranoia of the Cold War era, and the way that existentialist philosophy enters into the debate about the individual and conformity to forces outside the self (Chapter 3).

The second group of two chapters—what will perhaps be of central interest to many users of this book—considers the traditional academic scholarship that Williams's two classic dramas have generated. Chapter 4 presents major critics from both sides of the Atlantic employing a variety of different analytic methodologies, but with a heavy debt to biographical and New Criticism, as they explore the chief constituents of Williams's dramaturgy, most especially characterization, visual symbolism and the handling of stage space, and thematic motifs. Chapter 5 narrows the focus slightly to zero in on how scholars have categorized Williams's fundamental style as either realistic or expressionistic (or a blending of the two), particular instances of stage symbolism, and, finally, the somewhat daunting question of whether or not Williams has succeeded in writing tragic drama.

The third group, this time of three chapters, explores a variety of recent Williams scholarship about sexualized and textualized bodies: about feminist approaches that consider the sexual politics of the desiring woman who transgresses the mores of a patriarchal power structure that tries to contain her (Chapter 6); about queer theoretical strategies that explore how Williams brings gay sexuality out of the closet and onto the stage, through making the male body the object of the erotic gaze and challenging traditional notions of heteronormativity

(Chapter 7); and contemporary poststructuralist criticism, raising issues of the relationship between author, text, and reader and the construction of meaning (Chapter 8). Rounding out the book is a section (Chapter 9) devoted to the critical commentaries about the major film and television adaptations of both *Streetcar* and *Cat* and their emphasis on how the handling of sexuality is adjusted in the transition from stage to screen, followed by a brief conclusion reflecting upon the main currents of thought pursued in the earlier chapters and offering some ideas about possibilities for future scholarly inquiry.

CHAPTER ONE

Producing Performance Texts

KAZAN ON *STREETCAR* AND *CAT*

From the mid-1940s through the 1950s, the dramatist/director/stage designer triumvirate formed by Tennessee Williams, Elia Kazan, and Jo Mielziner was not only one of the most creative and productive teams that the American theatre had ever known but, more importantly, one of the most influential in establishing a production style blending naturalism and expressionism, poetic lyricism and gritty realism, that would be a dominating force in theatre staging for years to come. For his part, Williams—despite some sense of what he called 'psychic violation' over acceding to Kazan's suggestions for revising *Cat on a Hot Tin Roof*—had the greatest admiration for the man he called 'the most brilliant director we have,' one who 'brings to bear an intensely creative imagination,' who 'magnified [any] play in a good way.'[1] He cherished the director for recognizing the centrality of a prodigious work habit as the very essence of the playwright's being:

■ But my work—I don't think anyone has ever known, with the exception of Elia Kazan, how desperately much it meant to me and accordingly treated it—or should I say its writer—with the necessary sympathy of feeling.[2] □

If one thinks of directing a dramatic text as an interpretive act, then the resulting stage production might be seen as an example of analytic criticism much like a scholarly essay. Kazan's 'Notebook'—a series of ruminations, initially intended for his eyes only, published in 1963—provides a unique insight into the creative process of moving Williams's *Streetcar* from page to stage, beginning with brief attention to the play's overall genre, theme, style, and structure before zeroing in on the characters. Kazan considers the work a 'poetic tragedy,' charting the 'dissolution of a person of worth' (Blanche) victimized by an antagonist who represents the 'basic animal cynicism of today' (Stanley).[3] And so the theme—much in keeping with Williams's own assertion when he articulates it as 'the ravishment of the tender, the sensitive, the delicate, by the savage and brutal forces of modern society':[4]

■ is a message from the dark interior. This little twisted, pathetic, confused bit of light and culture puts out a cry. It is snuffed out by the crude forces of violence, insensibility, and vulgarity which exist in our South—and this is the cry of the play.[5] □

Since so much of the play probes Blanche's interiority, the overall production will need to be stylized, lyrical rather than strictly naturalistic in nature. Furthermore, to see how that subjectivity plays out, to convey how she adopts a series of performative roles or masks, each episode will have to center on one of the way stations in Blanche's journey seeking security, only to see it end in destruction: from her arrival, hoping to 'find a place' to belong, through rejection and exclusion by her sister Stella and brother-in-law and a 'temporary salvation' when she believes she has found solace in Mitch, to desertion and 'dissolution' as she is 'disposed of' by a society that finds her anachronistic and superfluous.[6] Finally, the conflict that eventuates in her exile is triangular in nature, as Stella, its 'apex,' must choose between Blanche and Stanley. (A subsidiary triangle structuring the work, that Kazan implicitly acknowledges, exists between Blanche, Mitch, and his mother.)

In order to interpret the characters, Kazan employs the Stanislavskian method of discovering the 'spine' or overriding motive for each of them. For Blanche, it is to 'find protection'; for Stella, to 'hold onto Stanley'; for Stanley, to 'keep things his way'; and for Mitch to 'get away from his mother.'[7] Kazan's reading of Blanche, despite its relative brevity, will govern all later interpretations of her. He understands her as an anachronistic holdover of a culture largely passed away, who yet cannot escape its impossibly idealized notions that demand the woman deny her physical side rather than integrate her need for 'human contact' through sexuality, causing a 'fatal inner contradiction.'[8] If by the end of the play the audience is to experience the sense that 'something extraordinary' has been irrevocably lost, she must, however, be the 'heavy' at the beginning, flawed by her airs of superiority and refinement, despite her real aloneness that Kazan links to the Blues music. Her desperation, 'an artistic intensification of all women,' is what universalizes *Streetcar*; Blanche's special relation to all women is that she is at that critical point where *the one thing above all else that she is dependent on: her attraction for men, is beginning to go.'*[9]

Stella is also seen as dependent, but hers is a willed dependency rather than a socially constructed one. Her escape to 'sensual stupor' in the arms of Stanley has brought a measure of psychic health denied to Blanche, yet it has come at the cost of his crudeness and abusiveness, and Blanche loses no time in playing on her latent dissatisfaction. Although Stella ultimately chooses husband over sister, she nevertheless begins to question the accommodations she herself has made, so that, after the baby's birth and Blanche's departure, she will 'never' be able to regard Stanley in quite the same way again. Kazan calls the cynically hedonistic Stanley (orally fixated on food, drink, and sex) the 'hoodlum aristocrat' who is 'supremely indifferent to everything except his own pleasure and comfort.'[10] Unsure of his ability to hang on to what he has, he is the great leveler who resorts to violence in the face of Blanche's threat to his territorial domain; as Kazan encapsulates him, 'He conquers with his penis.'[11] Mitch, too, has a violence about him, suppressed but ready to erupt, stemming from a hatred of his mother who has made him dependent upon her. His clumsiness around Blanche, who offers him a last chance to exert his manhood, evidences just how 'damn full of violent desire'[12] he is for women.

No such extensive director's notes are available for *Cat*, and so one must rely on the brief remarks in Kazan's autobiography (1988), which have less to do with character analysis than with the crucial alterations to the production design and style that Mielziner undertook at the urging of the director, who considered the work's 'great merit [as] its brilliant rhetoric and its theatricality ... the glory of the author's language.'[13] If Williams originally envisioned a realistically conceived plantation bed/sitting room that honored the convention of the fourth wall, Kazan decided, despite the dramatist's initial objections, that the characters' long monologues should be delivered from 'the edge of the forestage ... looking that audience straight in the eye.'[14] This would necessitate that Mielziner design a stripped-down set, a raked platform stage dominated by a big double bed, that 'made it impossible to be played any way except as [Kazan] preferred: ... Dear Tennessee was stuck with my vision, like it or not.'[15] Kazan goes on to insist that the plot alterations he requested in Act Three and to which Williams ultimately acquiesced because he 'passionately' longed for 'success'— such as bringing Big Daddy back on stage—'had nothing to do with making the play more commercial'; and he claimed to feel 'hurt' when the printed version put the onus on the director, somehow blaming him for sacrificing art to commerce:

> He'd published the third act he said he preferred to the one I'd influenced him to write. I thought his book made me out to be something of a villain corrupting a 'pure artist.' I especially resented Tennessee's calling 'my' third act—which I didn't write, plan, or edit—the 'commercial' third act. I'd had no such purpose in mind.[16]

READING KAZAN'S PRODUCTIONS: DAVID RICHARD JONES, BRENDA MURPHY, AND MARIAN PRICE

In order to establish Kazan's claim to the honorific 'great' because of his ability to attune himself to the differing sensibilities of the playwrights with whom he works, David Jones, in *Great Directors at Work* (1986), uses *Streetcar* as a case in point, drawing heavily upon Kazan's own 'Notebook.' Arguing that Kazan, rather than Williams himself, was almost entirely responsible, along with making other changes in dialogue and stage business, for giving final shape to Scenes 5 and 9 as the play went into production, Jones presents him as largely committed to moving an audience through the truth of human behavior, with theatrical style designed to serve that end; under him, the play would take on its three part structure based on the seasonal movement of spring, summer, fall. As a follower of the Stanislavsky method, as filtered through his own work with the Group Theatre, character revelation is the goal, and the character's dominant action, or through line, provides the work with its spine(s), as seen in Kazan's preparatory notes. Jones contributes to the discussion what he calls the 'bipolarity' of Stanley and Blanche:

■ The two principal characters are this play's symbols and spirits. They are aware that their tensions symbolize a cultural warfare—Stanley always sees the columns behind Blanche; she thinks Stanley represents the world she can no longer protect herself from. When Williams was writing the early drafts, he gave the play titles that expressed Blanche's personality (*Blanche's Chair in the Moon*, *The Moth*), substituted others suggestive of Stanley (*The Primary Colors*, *The Poker Night*), and finally settled on a neutral title referring to place.[17] □

Rather than 'neutral,' perhaps 'inclusive' would have been a better choice of word, since 'desire' is the domain of both characters. Working from this concept of 'bipolarity,' Jones attends to the play's oppositions and ambivalences that Kazan needed to keep in balance—in a way that Thomas Hart Benton's famous painting of the poker scene, by emphasizing the seamier side of Blanche, failed to do. In particular, he underscores how Kazan shifts the audience's sympathies, originally with Stanley but later (Scenes 5 and 6) moving to Blanche. Initially, Stanley is humorous and spirited, brutish yet 'boyish,' a despiser of pretense and of anyone putting on airs. He is belligerent and quick to retaliate when someone challenges his superiority, especially in the sexual arena. Blanche's performance, meanwhile, fluctuates between the feminine archetypes of tiger, virgin, and vamp; a creature of the Southern tradition, her sexuality has been thwarted, and she has developed a kind of attraction to violence that may harm her—which Kazan thought true of her creator's cruising as well. Already at the beginning, the incipient madness that will overtake her is present; and the expressionistic theatrical style Kazan fosters to reveal both the subjective interior and the objective social environment (a hallmark of this director's style) charts her breakdown. Jones finds in this what he calls Kazan's 'larger topic': the 'progression from psychological disintegration to social madness that can destroy an already fragile mind.'[18] Thus Jones explores at length the rape scene as staged by Kazan in which Blanche is confronting 'real evil': 'rape is a horrifying personal inversion, the failure of two individuals and the cultures they represent to achieve understanding.'[19]

The most detailed investigation of the collaborative interplay between Williams and Kazan is to be found in Brenda Murphy's 1992 book. The period of their collaboration during the late 1940s and early 50s marked the beginning of a shift from a playwright's theatre, when the dramatic text was sacrosanct, to one where directorial choices and input were much more crucial in determining what audiences saw upon the stage. These two men, together with their frequent set designer, were largely responsible, from Murphy's point of view, for ushering in what she calls an American style of 'subjective realism,' sometimes termed the era of 'gauze' because of Mielziner's penchant for using transparent scrims to simulate the haziness of characteriologic interiority. So Murphy thoroughly glosses both the printed and acting versions of the *Streetcar* texts, not only to indicate what alterations Williams made at the suggestion of his director, but also to raise the issue of the extent to which the playwright felt he might have been compromising his artistic integrity during the production process. Most tellingly, one of the great virtues of Murphy's monograph is her ability to help the readers see what the plays looked like in performance, helping them recreate in their mind's eye the visual stage picture, including the language of gestures and props— what she repeatedly terms Kazan's 'kinesic' effects that encode character and meaning. From the director's point of view, to go from text to production was to go from something inert to something 'living.'

The working relationship between playwright and director during the production of *Streetcar* was much less fraught with tension and dissension than the process of bringing *Cat* to the stage would later be. As is apparent from his 'Notebook,' Kazan bought into Williams's insistence that *Streetcar* eschews any easy division between a good Blanche and an evil Stanley in favor of a tragedy of 'misunderstanding' springing from one character's inability to see life from the perspective of another; consequently, they were able to agree on around a hundred revisions in the dialogue during the preopening phase. In the process, the work is shaped for each of the four central figures into a tragedy of loss: of Blanche's fragile hold on reality as she retreats into a protective fantasy at the end, so that one of the many roles she played as an illusionist will be permanently fixed; of Stanley's sexual supremacy as he throws over the unwavering devotion of Stella; of Stella's complete faith in Stanley as she experiences guilt over the betrayal of her sister; and of Mitch's better nature as Stanley brings him down to his level of physical violence and distrust. The production style would be a 'middle ground' between representational and presentational, between traditional realism in its quasi-naturalistic handling of the social environment and milieu and a quite innovative theatricalism in its more expressionistic moments that open up Blanche's disintegrating psyche to the audience's view.

■ Kazan agreed with Williams's opinion that conventional realism would be inadequate for the play, but he did not oppose realism simply to expressionism as Williams did. Instead, Kazan was to find a middle ground between the epistemological assumption that the action on stage was empirical fact and the assumption that it was a character's subjective perception.[20] □

So Kazan embedded certain aural and visual codes into the performance: the music of polka, Blues piano and jazz trumpet, oftentimes heightening the aura of sexuality; the use of the follow-spot on Blanche; the clothing of contrasting colors to suggest strength and delicacy; Stanley's incessant oral fixations to indicate his hedonism; and the props that accompany Blanche, her trunk and purse and cologne. On the other hand, Murphy argues that Williams really did feel 'violated' as an artist by the concessions that he made to Kazan in bringing *Cat* to the stage, and that the most compelling reason for including the 'Note of Explanation' in the first printed edition was to enable the dramatist to reclaim 'ownership' of his work as a literary text. Granted, Williams had approved all of the changes, perhaps because of being convinced that without them the play would never reach a wide audience. Yet he still felt uneasy. Reading Williams's 'Note' inserted between the two versions of Act Three in *Cat on a Hot Tin Roof* gives the impression that the major changes between his initial conception of the play and what was finally seen on Broadway resided mainly in the handling of Maggie, Brick, and Big Daddy. Yet, as Murphy makes potently clear, just as important was the way that the overall design concept of the play veered away from Williams's original scene description. Insofar as the characters are concerned, there were admittedly alterations. The emphasis on Maggie shifts from her using her strength to dominate Brick and relying on wiliness out of greed to her being somewhat more gentle and sympathetic, contributing to the work's emphasis on human communion. Brick, meanwhile, goes from being physically violent and coolly passive to more actively admiring of Maggie's determination for renewing him through a child. Big Daddy's language is made less sexually graphic and his concern for helping Brick face his demons more palpably compassionate, while his confirmation of the 'life' within Maggie in the face of awareness of his own impending death is heightened. Although Kazan placed increasing emphasis on Big Daddy's easy camaraderie with the Black servants and field-hands, Williams's original insistence on Big Daddy's great tolerance for his homosexual forebears is, however, sadly diluted; whereas initially he had valorized their sexual relationship even over what was, according to Brick, his perfectly pure friendship with Skipper, the details about Straw and Ochello's love are largely submerged in the reworking. Williams's central expression of the nature of the bond between the 'old bachelors' is, in fact, confined mostly to the extra-dramatic 'Notes for Designers' that precedes the play text, indicating that the stage set must 'evoke some ghosts; it is gently and poetically haunted by a relationship that must have involved a tenderness which was uncommon.'[21]

But Kazan well understood that if he could control the overall design of the play, he could wrest the play away from its belonging primarily to the dramatist. He did this, as recounted in the director's autobiography, by picking up and expanding upon Williams's notion that the long speeches by the three central figures should be like 'recitatives.' With the interludes of direct address, including four by Big Daddy, Kazan intended that *Cat* would generate much greater intimacy with its audiences. His ally in this was Mielziner, whose final design concept veered radically from Williams's suggestion that the bed/sitting room have the aura of a Victorian home in the Far East, such as the one Robert Louis Stevenson inhabited in Samoa. (Williams's 'Notes' did, however, end with an admonition that 'the set should be far less realistic than I have so far implied,' with walls 'dissolv[ing] mysteriously into air' and a ceiling open to the sky.[22]) Part of Murphy's accomplishment, then, is that through reading her extensive commentary one gets a much clearer picture of how the play worked on stage than one ever could through simply reading any of the printed texts. Though Williams may not have liked what was done to his authority as author in the process, and vowed that he would never let it happen again, the resultant production repaid him through critical acclaim and audience acceptance.

If Murphy argues that Williams's 'Note' between the two versions of Act Three focusing on character motivation told only half the story (and perhaps the less important half at that), Marian Price places greater emphasis on Williams's insistence that both the original and revised versions of the final act appear in the printed play as a basis for her 1995 essay's reading of *Cat* as the dramatist's psycho-autobiography. The play marked a watershed for two reasons: first, the three works immediately preceding it, *Summer and Smoke*, *The Rose Tattoo*, and most especially *Camino Real*, occasioned disappointment in both critics and audiences after the enormous achievement of *Streetcar*; and second, Williams had not yet been able to negotiate the tacit restrictions of the commercial theatre when it came to openly handling homosexual subject matter that prevented his being 'true' to his sexual identity. And so, in her allegorical approach to *Cat*, Price proposes that the characters be seen as 'warring sides' of the contest between success and idealism within the playwright's personality, Maggie representing 'artistic survival at any cost' and Brick 'the immobilized artist,' with the unseen Skipper standing for 'suppressed truths.'[23] The alterations he made between the acts, then, provide less evidence for capitulation to Kazan's demands, while his later denunciation of these changes speaks to Williams's residual guilt for having privileged commerce over art, for having failed to out himself, and for having betrayed the support he received from the mostly closeted gay community, particularly 'the debt he owed to Frank Merlo' his longtime lover[24]—though Price neglects to mention Williams's openly appreciative dedication to *Rose Tattoo*: 'To Frank in Return for Sicily.'[25] As Price expresses it, the 'confinement of his art to heterosexual characters was tantamount to hanging up on a lover.'[26]

Price notes that already in the original version of *Cat's* third act, there exist indications of Williams's admiration for Maggie's tenacity in pursuing success, and the revision only adds to her attractiveness. When Brick, who is so outspoken in his disgust with mendacity, makes the dubious ethical choice in the new version to support his wife in her lie about being pregnant and submits to her regime to rehabilitate him, he appears no longer to blame her for Skipper's death. Price regards this alteration as crucial to moving *Cat* away from more philosophic issues like mortality and existential dread and in the direction of the domestic problem play about the nurturing woman saving the psychologically troubled man (like Robert Anderson's *Tea and Sympathy* (1953) which Kazan had also directed) that audiences at the time found reassuringly palatable:

> ■ It is this change, far more than the sweetening of Maggie, that signifies Williams's decision to sacrifice Idealism for Success. In the instant that Skipper is abandoned, the playwright snaps the slender thread that tied the play to his homosexual world and the friends and lovers who peopled it. Accompanying this loss is the loss of a broader thematic vision.[27] □

On the surface, Williams might be charged with acting in 'bad faith' in adopting these changes, and Price finds evidence that he was perpetually ambivalent about them and deeply bifurcated in his motivation. Williams admittedly regarded his daily regimen of writing as a way to keep at bay the fear of death—a fear initially embodied in Big Daddy until, in the new third act, he sees 'life' in Maggie—so Brick's temporary impotence would be symbolically like losing the ability to write. Thus, if the restorative sex act that a manipulative Maggie demands of Brick to secure their hold upon the plantation is seen as somehow equivalent to the act of writing, she becomes akin to the artist's amanuensis who remains 'self-interested' while being helpful, making Brick's submission to her a ceding of autonomy to another (in Williams's case, Kazan). So Williams's compromising his artistic vision on the road to success will continue to haunt him, more especially so since Brick's escape from passivity and paralysis may have been achieved only at the great personal cost of denying his true self.

MULTIPLE *CATS*: WILLIAM SACKSTEDER AND BRIAN PARKER

The alterations that Williams acceded to have occasioned some critical studies whose primary purpose is to contrast the variant texts. Had William Sacksteder written his article dating from the mid-1960s a decade later, he would have needed to entitle it 'The Four Cats,' as by that time there was yet another authorized revision of the play's text being used for performance (the 1974 version, as Price mentions in passing). As it is, the word 'Three' in his original title is somewhat misleading, for, even though Williams had no involvement in writing the screen adaptation for the film version of *Cat*, Sacksteder speaks of it as if he did, only clarifying in his footnotes that James Poe and Richard Brooks shared total credit for it. Added to that, the film (what he calls *Cat 3*) actually incarnates material that Sacksteder prefers. He admires particularly the film's use of the father–son tension as a psychological 'surrogate' for the 'pathology' of homosexuality in the stage version; the handling of space as Brick and Maggie go back up the stairs to the intimacy of the bedroom, where Brick throws the pillow on to the bed; and the implication that Maggie in taking Brick to bed is now initiating an act of redemption rather than a less noble fulfillment of purely mercenary motives. So actually only two *Cats* exist (or, more precisely, two third acts) that can be attributed to Williams: his initial conception and the revision prompted by Kazan.

Governing his assessment of *Cat* in its various embodiments is Sacksteder's conviction that the work's overarching conflict resides in Maggie's determination to get Brick to come to bed with her, which subsumes issues of restoring Brick's sense of self-worth, solidifying the marriage, and providing an heir to console Big Daddy as he approaches death. Occurring on a day celebrating a birthday and featuring a bed as the focal stage property, the play partakes of the comic mode in drama—as perhaps best exemplified by Shakespeare's romantic comedies—though Williams's handling allows for greater ambiguity in the final outcome. With this in mind, *Cat* as originally conceived ends pessimistically, for Maggie's calculated lie that she is pregnant brings her down to the level of Gooper and, especially, Mae, the putative inheritors, and makes her bedding of Brick, in Sacksteder's estimation, 'rape rather than seduction or creation.'[28] The play is seen as ending pretty much where it began, with the playwright tied too strongly to a naturalistic conception of drama rather than allowing himself to follow his powerful instincts that Maggie is the heroine and should be featured as such. Williams's capitulation to Kazan's desires produces only an inferior compromise, albeit one that is more affirmative: Brick now admires Maggie, confirming her lie that is a birthday offering to Big Daddy, so that Maggie in taking her husband to bed will now more nearly 'seduce, if not redeem.'[29] Even so, Sacksteder rejects this revision as dramaturgically weak.

Like Sacksteder before him, Brian Parker, in his 2000 essay, also focuses on Act Three of *Cat*, but from the prism of Big Daddy rather than of Maggie. As a leading scholarly expert in the drafts and archival material surrounding *Cat*, Parker grounds his discussion in a lengthy narrative passage from Williams's writings wherein he hypothesizes how Big Daddy might be brought back on stage by placing him up on the mansion's belvedere, shotgun in hand, potentially to harm himself. Though thankfully never used, these musings end with, for Parker, a crucial commentary by Williams on his 'tragic intention in the play' that 'Kazan's alterations weaken': Big Daddy, though *in extremis*, 'has it still in his power not to squeal like a pig but to keep a tight mouth about it,' while Brick's acquiescence to Maggie shows 'that love is possible, not *proven* or *disproven*, but possible.'[30] After stating his own preference for the play as Williams originally conceived it without Big Daddy's return in Act Three—as well establishing the fact that Kazan influenced the writing of it fairly early in the drafting process, while it was still titled *Place of Stone* after the original epigraph from Yeats rather than the final one from Dylan Thomas—Parker turns his attention to the overtly sexual groping of Maggie by Big Daddy and the notorious elephant joke that first surfaced during the Philadelphia tryout. The groping would be replaced by a stare, and the story temporarily excised in later reprinted versions, only to return in the final authorized 1974–75 revival that boasted a somewhat 'enigmatic ending' and was published by New Directions as the standard text. Parker understands that Kazan saw the joke as an opportunity for 'male bonding' between father and son, but neither he nor any other commentator on the play has ever noticed what is quite obviously Big Daddy's intention in telling the story: as a cautionary tale to encourage Brick to realize the importance of exercising his virility and fathering a child. Kazan also interpolated much, sometimes excessive, stage business (character movement inside, the storm outside) to bolster 'the symbolic environment and social commentary'[31] that had also been apparent in a number of other works he directed. Finally, however, Parker opts for Williams's initial, less sentimental version without Big Daddy on stage during Act Three, claiming his presence 'catered to the macho sensibility of Kazan' rather than to 'the austere compassion'[32] of Williams that it violated.

PRODUCTION HISTORIES: PHILIP KOLIN AND GEORGE CRANDELL

Writing production histories of Shakespearean texts, to name just the most prominent example, is a common scholarly endeavor. Relatively few American plays, however, have been accorded this attention, and so Philip Kolin's volume in Cambridge's Plays in Production series not only attests to *Streetcar's* acceptance as a classic American drama, but also establishes how a record of the particulars about past performances can help theatre practitioners imaginatively reimagine the play text for the present and future and, more pertinent to our purposes, help establish the agenda among academics for further (re)interpretations of the literary text. For Kolin's own intention, as one of *Streetcar's* most knowledgeable and prolific scholars, is to situate the work on stage not simply from a theatrical but from a literary/theoretical point of view as well, bringing in Karl Marx and Michel Foucault, race and ethnicity, androgyny and the female gaze as he explores how the play's 'sexual politics' have been 'interrogated' and 'destabilized,' 'radicalized' and 'renegotiated' during half a century in various media (theatre, film, ballet, television, opera). Beginning with the first landmark production, one of the central issues has always been achieving a proper balance between two such protean characters as Blanche (played over the years by Jessica Tandy, Uta Hagen, Vivien Leigh, Arletty, Tallulah Bankhead, Faye Dunaway, Claire Bloom, Blythe Danner, Ann-Margret, Jessica Lange, Frances McDormand, and later Glenn Close, Natasha Richardson, and Cate Blanchett) and Stanley (played by Marlon Brando, Anthony Quinn, Jon Voight, Treat Williams, Aidan Quinn, and Alec Baldwin, among others). In directing the premiere, Kazan, as Kolin notes, tipped the balance in favor of the proletarian Stanley in a swaggering and brutish if sensitive and even humorous performance that raised Brando to iconic status. In the film version of a few years later, sanitized to remove any hint of homosexuality yet still adult enough to be seen as helping inaugurate an American art cinema, the T-shirted 'male anatomy' is gazed upon as 'the object of desire.'[33] Blanche's guilt-haunted character has been conceived of and directed in ways to bring out numerous ambiguities: from the refined tragic victim of the double standard, vulnerable and shimmering like a fragile moth, constantly theatricalizing herself in sometimes nefarious ways; to the hysteric, neurotic sexual predator, the sensualist who somehow achieves sanctification in madness.

If some of the American productions, particularly those boasting Black or interracial casts, or those that foreground urban violence, have unearthed a decidedly sociological dimension, it is in reporting on two dozen international productions that Kolin can discover evidences of considerably more politicized *Streetcars* than the original one. In Rome, the 1949 staging by film director Luchino Visconti—which Williams preferred over all other European versions—emphasized a morally decadent New Orleans (and, by extension, America) as the site of class struggle, with the laborer Stanley pitted against the elitist Blanche. That same year in Paris, Jean Cocteau scandalized audiences by adding a 'black presence' in the form of half-naked belly dancers, symbolic of Stanley's sexuality, to create an atmosphere of racial fear, while the Swedish director Ingmar Bergman returned to a heightened emphasis on the role of art and illusion by placing a movie theatre, called Desire, or the Pleasure Garden, showing a film entitled *Night in Paradise* directly upon the stage. In post-occupation Japan in 1953, Blanche was simultaneously the intruder on the territory of others and the one violated, just as Japan had been violated by the imperialist Americans.

Increased awareness of Blanche's potential for being seen as a 'poisoned disrupter' and an aggressor attracted to the Other is just one of the ways that production history might aid scholarly theorization, by showing how greater contextualization of race, gender, and ethnicity within the play has helped alter the ideological assumptions associated with more traditional readings. As Kolin writes:

■ revivals of *Streetcar* (1956–98) on the English-speaking stage illustrate how later decades and tastes renegotiated the performance of the script and how that script consequently evolved through productions. One major change involved the ways in which Williams's characters were transformed from the social models Kazan envisioned and enshrined in the 1940s: Blanche became far less willowy and more assertive in the 1980s and 1990s and Stanley was more sly, subtle, not nearly as much in control. In revivals, Mielziner's expressionistic scrims were exchanged for much more realistic and provocative sets, including the experience of *Streetcar* in theatres in the round.[34] □

Kolin devotes a half-dozen pages of his monograph to explicating *Belle Reprieve*, a 1991 queer/camp deconstruction of Williams's classic developed by members of two British theatre cooperatives, Split Britches and Bloolips, that specialize in transgressive, gender-bending stage events. Devised by Bette Bourne, Paul Shaw, Peggy Shaw, and Lois Weaver, the play casts a man in drag as Blanche, a 'butch lesbian' as Stanley, and a fairy parading as a man in the role of Mitch. Irreverently blending snippets of dialogue and scenic elements from *Streetcar* along with elements of the music hall such as vaudeville routines, bawdy songs, and tap dances, it parodies and/or 'inverts' stereotypical ideas about sexuality and makes explicit certain notions of gender identity that were left, in Kolin's words, 'latent' or 'opaque' in its source. Paradoxically, if *Belle Reprieve* had a salutary, if unintentional, effect it was to demonstrate just how misguided any production of Williams's text that presented Blanche as a man in drag would be.[35] An analogous take-off of *Cat* is found in Ryan Landry's 2004 avowedly gay *Pussy on the House*, which, in the words of one reviewer, 'is drop-dead funny' while still 'hew[ing] closely to Tennessee Williams's humane melodrama.'[36] Complete with a drag queen Maggie and a 'heartbreaking Brick, drowning in sniffed glue and grief,' it adds a 'second-act flashback in which the dead "Skippah" gets his paws around a tall glass of 80-proof.'[37]

No extensive stage history of Williams's *Cat* has been published, and understandably so given the rarity of this kind of scholarly undertaking by American academics; however, George Crandell devotes sections of his 1998 biographical/bibliographical essay to 'Chief Productions' in the theatre and on film, starting with a brief commentary rehearsing the different versions and the critics' 'strong preference' for Williams's original. From his remarks, one can cull a list of major actors who have performed the three central roles: Barbara Bel Geddes, Elizabeth Taylor, Kim Stanley, Natalie Wood, Elizabeth Ashley, Kathleen Turner (Maggie); Ben Gazzara, Paul Newman, Max von Sydow, Robert Wagner, Keir Dullea, Ian Charleson, and Tommy Lee Jones (Brick); and Burl Ives, Laurence Olivier, Leo McKern, Fred Gwynne, Eric Porter, and Charles Durning (Big Daddy). Although Crandell mentions European stagings in Sweden—directed by Ingmar Bergman—France, and Ireland, he is most informative, though lacking the detail and richness of Kolin, about English-language productions after the highly successful 1955 Broadway run. Because of censorship by the Lord Chamberlain, the 1958 English premiere, employing Williams's original third act, could only open in a private club. The American Shakespeare Theatre's 1974 revival of *Cat*, seen first in Stratford, Connecticut, and then in New York, was notable for 'incorporate[ing] changes Williams made to the script combining elements from both the original and Broadway versions,'[38] while the 1988 London production directed by Howard Davies returned to using the initial third act, as did the New York revival of two years later that Davies also directed.

It is not until a decade after Crandell's study, with James Earl Jones and Terrence Howard starring, respectively, as Big Daddy and Brick and Phylicia Rashad as Big Mama in an all-Black staging, opening first in New York in 2008 and a year later in London's West End, that a potentially significant reinterpretation or re-visioning of the work (like those that *Streetcar* invited) might be attempted. Directed by Debbie Allen, the text restored the salty language that Williams had been forced to sacrifice to the puritanical bent of theatergoers in the 1950s, while the staging twice interpolated the presence of a Black saxophonist playing mournful tunes. But although, as historians have documented, there were Black plantation owners who themselves owned slaves, the production seemed, by deliberate choice, not to shed any new perspective on issues of race (or, for that matter, of gender and [homo]sexuality). As an astute reviewer commented: 'Race plays as much or as little role in this revival as you want it to. When the incredible Jones uses the word "nigger," to describe his boyhood self, you can feel how hard Big Daddy has worked to rise above all epithets to become himself.'[39] Unlike scholarly theorizing about *Streetcar*, then, it appears more likely that academic writing about *Cat* will continue to remain firmly grounded in the literary text rather than in innovative, even daring, reconceptualizations of the play in performance. As this chapter has demonstrated, the nature of all theatrical production has meant that Williams's artistic vision, as initially articulated in the dramatic texts, has been refined—in ways that may either diminish or enhance it—by the directors and designers and actors who have collaborated in bringing these two works to the stage. As the next chapter will make clear, Williams's vision is also imbued with the cultural currency of history, religion, and literature that he absorbed and internalized and that then became an integral part of the fabric of his dramas.

CHAPTER TWO

Mythic Patterns—Southern, Classical, and Christian

THE GEOGRAPHY OF THE SOUTH: KENNETH HOLDITCH AND KIMBALL KING

Put simply, among writers of the American South, Tennessee Williams is to the drama what William Faulkner is to the novel. But whereas Faulkner created the mythical Yoknapatawpha County, several actual locales in the South have long been associated with Williams. There are, first, towns or regions in Mississippi: Columbus where he was born, Clarksdale where he spent much of his childhood years, and the Delta, setting for *Cat on a Hot Tin Roof*. Next, there is New Orleans, the city he most loved, in whose French Quarter he lived for long stretches of time, and where *A Streetcar Named Desire* is set. Finally, there is Key West, Florida, where he had a home with a writing studio to which he often retreated from his forays around the world. Yet along with these geographical places, there is for Williams a nostalgically remembered South of myth and tradition that proves every bit as vital in adumbrating his major plays. As Esther Merle Jackson has written in her 1965 book:

> ■ As a Southerner, Tennessee Williams has had advantages of consequence: the symbolism of the South, a region separated from the mainstream of the American society by an intricate complex of political, cultural, and economic factors, has greatly enriched the language of the arts.... Its primordial interpretation of man's struggle in an unfriendly universe has produced a highly developed iconography.[1] □

In a number of essays (1985–2002), Kenneth Holditch has demonstrated how Williams employs specific Southern locales that he knew firsthand in numerous major works. Suggesting that the South itself was second only to 'his family and his sexual orientation'[2] in the influence it exerted upon him, Holditch argues that Williams imbibed the particular qualities and general atmosphere of certain places, especially of the Mississippi Delta and New Orleans, the city he came to think of as his 'spiritual home,' and then recreated them so potently in his works that, for his audiences, these imaginative constructs became the reality, their mental image. Despite this, the South for Williams remained a dichotomous force: his romanticization of the 'old South' was always accompanied by an unflinching critique of the flaws of the 'new.'

The Delta, a crescent-shaped piece of land dotted with fertile plantations stretching from below Memphis south to Yazoo City, Mississippi, was home to a multicultural populace and the birthplace of the Blues, imbued with the dark forces of slavery, sexuality, and violence. At the heart of the Delta in Coahoma County was Clarksdale, Mississippi, where the young Tom Williams lived in his grandfather's Episcopal rectory for several years near the end of the War and briefly again in the early 1920s. Residing in an opulent mansion were the Cutrer sisters, Blanche and Stella, one of whom married a man who drowned in nearby Moon Lake. One of Tom's schoolmates was Brick Gotcher, who broke his leg attempting to jump over a statue, and among the planters he knew and heard of were models for Big Daddy.[3]

He first visited the New Orleans that he came to favor above all other cities—and where he adopted the name Tennessee and wrote over half of the works for which he is best remembered—in the mid-1930s, inhabiting different addresses there for much of the rest of his life. He treasured the city for the bohemianism and freedom of the French Quarter (or Vieux Carré), with its openness to artists and eccentrics and its charming architecture, 'rattletrap streetcar,' and cathedral garden with Christ and his outstretched arms, as well as for the classier Garden District, with its mansions and old-money stratification. To explain how Williams saw the symbolic potentialities of adjusting a particular location to his desired end, Holditch corrects the widely accepted but mistaken notion that the streetcar named Cemeteries ran on Royal Street along with the one named Desire (whereas it actually ran on Canal six blocks away) and then continues:

■ He placed the play at 632 Elysian Fields, then as now an ordinary building unlike that in his stage directions. It seems likely that he merely transferred the number from his own address at the time (632 St. Peter), to Elysian Fields, a street name that suited his artistic purposes. Desire to Cemeteries to Elysian Fields: life to death to the afterlife.[4] □

Broadening his focus from the specific locations that Holditch pinpoints, Kimball King's 1995 essay situates the dramatist at a pivotal point, straddling the Agrarian Movement that had come into prominence by the time Williams began his career and the more activist politics of the Civil

Rights movement that would emerge soon after the playwright's classic Broadway offerings. As King writes:

■ The plays of Williams reflect many of the characteristics of Southern writers noted by literary critics in the modernist era, beginning in the twenties and thirties, and they anticipate the postmodern dilemma in an era begun by integration and the growth of the formerly despised middle classes. Nearly every play Williams wrote reflected traditional topics which were extolled or satirized by Southern writing: agrarianism vs. urbanism, the New South vs. the Antebellum, and the chevalier vs. the upstart.[5] □

Williams, because of his 'aristocratic connections,' can be seen as clinging to the 'prevailing romantic' viewpoint of the White writer in the South that extolled the history of a civilized past over the 'base realities' of the present. Nevertheless, King positions him among those who most harshly deconstructed the idyllic myth in order to reveal the hypocrisy lying at the base of the South's most cherished values: a paternalism mired in greed that succeeds through the enslavement of Blacks; an idealization of women that subjugates and restricts personal expression—fostering a double standard of behavior and rendering them economically dependent; and a religious fundamentalism that fails to recognize moral evil in the original sin of slavery and racism, locating it instead in what it considers expressions of aberrant sexuality.

King adopts Hugh Holman's categories of the three geographic regions of the South and pinpoints their representations in Williams's works. The Tidewater, the locale of the large plantations, is made manifest in the Belle Reve of Blanche's youth and the fertile farm overseen by Big Daddy. Receiving the bulk of King's attention is the area called the Piedmont; harboring the small towns where class stratification and the prejudicial attitudes of narrow-minded people are most prevalent, the playwright reimagines it from his boyhood as the Two River County of such paradigmatic works as *Battle of Angels/Orpheus Descending*. Finally, there is the Deep South, the Gulf Coast and, in particular, New Orleans, where gentility and bohemianism intersect and, sometimes uneasily, coexist. Although Williams deplores the 'exclusionary' ethos and consequent 'denial' of diversity in the Old South, he manages to maintain a careful balance, King believes, by undercutting the eccentricities without falling prey to the condescension of the outsider.

THE MYTHOLOGY OF THE SOUTH: JACOB ADLER, THOMAS PORTER, AND ROBERT BRAY

Two important chapters defining how Williams employs the Southern myth serve as something like bookends to the scholarly inquiry about the topic during the decade of the 1960s. In a seminal essay from 1961, Jacob H. Adler focuses on the way that a romanticization of a lost tradition perpetuates a dividedness and lack of harmony in both self and society that is overcome only with the greatest difficulty, if at all. The oppositions between culture and power, between a retreat into the past and acceptance of moral responsibility in the present, and between an attenuated decadence and an emerging violence, consequently lie at the base of Williams's vision of the South. As Adler writes:

■ Thus Williams depicts a stale poetico-idealistic culture, refusing to face reality, yet still partly beautiful; and unable to achieve, or to attract, power, until reality is faced. And he warns that waiting too long to come to terms with reality can result, when reality is faced, in a complete denial of the ideal, in a failure to attract genuine power, and in a comparatively trivial fulfillment. On the other hand, the South's genuine power, both intellectual and physical, is dissipated because it can find no valid ideal—or is psychologically cut off from pursuing such an ideal, if found.[6] □

Adler is much prone to allegorical readings; and so Blanche is not only an individual but a type representative of the South. Clinging to a past ideal of purity and refinement, of qualities associated with the soul, and yet sexually promiscuous, acceding to the demands of the flesh and the body, she cannot integrate or reconcile these opposites, and so she dissipates her power. Like the South, she 'violently betrays the code while desperately trying to maintain it.'[7] Stanley, on the other hand, is the 'foreigner' who brings to the South vitality and exuberance that it has lost. Because, however, this power is excessively violent, audiences are made to regret the passing of those values that Blanche embodies, while at the same time recognizing the decadence and futility that make that passing 'inevitable.'

In his brief remarks on *Cat*, Adler suggests a shift in focus to financial power as sought by a Southerner of lower-class origin, Maggie, who willingly deserts any semblance of culture in order to stoop to the acquisitive tactics of a mercenary family. Likewise, for both Big Daddy and Brick achieving power cannot exist apart from sex. Even though Big Daddy's power emanates from money, without his sexual drive the 'tremendous aggrandizement could not have existed,'[8] while for Brick only the embrace of 'normal sexuality' can bring about the inheritance of the family wealth. Yet Adler makes no mention of the original sin of slavery on which the plantation was founded and thrived; nor does he comment on the irony that the patrimony that will be passed on to Brick through Big Daddy is an inheritance that derives ultimately not from a heterosexual marriage but from the union of the gay lovers, Straw and Ochello.

At the end of the decade, in his 1969 monograph *Myth and Modern American Drama*, Thomas Porter provides a considerably fuller articulation of the ideas earlier sketched out by Adler. The narrative of the dying-out of the Old South—epitomized for the popular imagination by Margaret Mitchell's novel, *Gone With the Wind* (1936), which by the end of the 1940s had sold six million copies—set forth a comprehensive myth of gracious living, personal honor, and the importance of family on the antebellum plantation. But, according to Porter, Williams is at pains to show the 'inadequacy' of that myth, and of an uncritical notion of the plantation: its white-columned mansion may have been the site of chivalric virtues and of fancy dress balls and courtship rituals, but it was also the site of patrician violence and a double standard and of the domestic dependency and submissiveness of the mistress of the house, as well as of slave quarters and cotton fields worked, as a falsified myth would have it, by devoted field-hands—who, in actuality, were treated much worse than the sentimentalized tales designed to comfort the White oppressors would have it. Yet the Southern past, with its code of honor and graceful manners, would survive in the imagination even after the agrarian ideal was checked by the progress of a more urban and mechanized society. A heroine born and bred at a time when this culture is on the wane, like Blanche, is bound to suffer from an almost inherent schizophrenia—torn between being the fragile and modest damsel and a flighty temptress in need of security—but then so, too, will Stanley, a creature of the present and the future, display a tendency to align a sexual voraciousness and domination with a certain degree of sensitivity. But as Blanche moves from the expansiveness and spaciousness of Belle Reve ever more into the confined and, by contrast, squalid world of the Kowalski flat, she reveals the 'idiosyncrasies of the Southern heroine in profusion,'[9] maintaining her faith in the old order and clinging to the illusion of her refined youth while simultaneously being dissembling and deceitful.

Perhaps the most original aspect of Porter's analysis is his consideration of *Streetcar's* plot as an inverted version of the Civil War romance, in which the foreign invader who comes from the outside into the secure society is roundly defeated and sent packing—although an 'emotional and conceptual ambiguity' perhaps arises because the violence of Stanley's rape may leave room for a sympathetic acknowledgement of the superiority of the South's virtues:

■ The antebellum way of life that Blanche represents exerts its wonted fascination. Moreover, Stanley's reactions reflect the standard charges leveled against the Yankee army in the romance: destruction of property, looting, and rape. Stanley smashes dishes, rummages through Blanche's trunk and finally rapes her. These actions swing the sympathies of the audience to the Southern belle. On the other hand, the structure makes a different comment because Blanche is cast in the role of invader. As far as Stanley's world is concerned, she is the outsider, the disruptive influence.[10] □

Porter concludes by suggesting that Williams's own ambivalence toward the conflict, which is reflected in Stella's being repeatedly torn between the forces at play, parallels an irresolvable tension in the mind of the Southerner. Since Williams is himself a Southerner, it means that he writes from inside the myth, and thus has neither 'the resources' necessary to resolve the tensions in the myth, nor can he fully 'escape the excesses [i.e. conflict between Puritanism and hedonism, penchant for violence, etc.] of the syndrome he is investigating.'[11]

Robert Bray, in his 1993 Marxist-shaded sociocultural approach to *Streetcar*, advances the examination begun by Adler and Porter into the mythic conflict between the Old South and the New. He claims, however, to find in Williams a much more ideologically based position and so examines the play's political subtext that he feels has not been afforded adequate attention. Williams's own discontent with the South's shift from an agrarian to a mechanized mercantile economy is reflected in the desperate but ultimately futile clinging to the past by a heroine bound up in a mythic sense of Southern history who, 'in her progressively parasitic attachment to the Kowalski household ... ironically becomes more and more dependent on that which she so vehemently disdains.'[12] Arguing that the post-World War II economy was defined largely by an emphasis on the commodity value of material objects, Bray formulates *Streetcar's* central conflict as grounded in 'an evolving social system changing from one means of production to another'[13] with the transfer of property from Blanche to Stanley, as the mountains of papers from her trunk having to do with the ownership of a moribund Belle Reve are conferred upon a more vital upstart.

Power resides in property; and so Blanche, divested of her claim to Belle Reve, now invades Stanley's territory in Elysian Fields, a more democratic domain than the socially and racially stratified plantation of the past. While emotionally Williams (and his audience) may side with Blanche, intellectually they will recognize Stanley as the 'survivor,' the representative of the new proletarian ruling class superseding Blanche's family that stood for the exploitative bourgeoisie of the postbellum South. Calling upon Huey Long as his hero, Stanley espouses a quasi-socialist cause voiced in the rhetoric of populism.

■ Blanche may be seen as the ultimate outsider, positioned outside of time, social order and place. Furthermore, the society that she represents, southern plantation, gives way to the mechanistic grit and grind of the factory, and her psychological death at the play's end must be seen as a victory for the oppressors and the new order that they represent. In this play, at least, the proletariat becomes the ruling class. Thus, since economic and class conflict serve as the basis for much of Marxist ideology, and for *Streetcar*'s conflicts as well, Williams, it would appear, infused his play with ideological considerations.[14] □

Thus, in Bray's reading, Stella becomes the synthesis in the Marxian dialectic. Her adaptability, her choice of economic security in marriage to Stanley over the weakness and indolence of an outmoded aristocratic class, render her the means through which the old blood line will be simultaneously diluted and reinvigorated. Just as the plantation served as a symbol of the past, Stanley and Stella's baby stands for the way that the 'working class' ethos will be carried on into the future.

CLASSICAL AND CHRISTIAN MYTH: LEONARD QUIRINO, GEORGE CRANDELL, AND JUDITH THOMPSON

Leonard Quirino's 'The Cards Indicate a Voyage ...' (1980) provides something of a counter-argument to Bray by proposing an alternative frame of reference. Along with commenting on the voyage through the cleansing waters of Lethe before entering the Elysian Fields that is evoked by *Streetcar*'s opening lines, as well as Blanche's reference to the Pleiades (the seven nymphs who must flee Orion in the same way she must attempt to ward off Stanley's attack), Quirino finds a classical analogue for the plot of *Streetcar* in the tale of Tereus's rape of his visiting sister-in-law Philomela. Whereas in the myth, however, Tereus's wife Procne takes her revenge by feeding his son to him, in Williams's play Stella sides with Stanley by disbelieving Blanche's report. Furthermore, Quirino links Stanley and his poker-playing buddies to the cave-dwelling Cyclopes, the blacksmiths for Vulcan, whose brute, amoral, 'strength is unhampered by Culture or intellect.'[15] But Quirino's larger project is to interrogate what he sees as the too-limited sociocultural readings of the drama in favor of focusing on larger symbolic and archetypal patterns: the moth as soul, incarnated in the body or flesh; the game as signifying luck, chance, or destiny; and the journey through life. As he writes:

■ Too many critics have made oversimplified sociologically oriented inter-pretations of the conflict in *Streetcar* as a representation of Williams's nostalgia for vanished, decadent southern aristocracy and his horror of vital industrial proletarianism. Other critics ... claim that his presen-tation of social conditions is ambivalent and confusing. But Williams, little interested in sociology ..., does not use Blanche's pretentious cultural standards –which he exposes as pitiful—to measure Belle Reve against Elysian Fields; rather, he emphasizes the uninhabitability of both for his supremely romantic heroine to the extent that she symbolizes the soul.[16] □

In pursuing his project, Quirino arrives at a pessimistic reading of Williams as a neo-Darwinian, for spirit must always be enfleshed in matter, and in a *de*volution the apes will inherit the earth. On her voyage through life, the moth-like Blanche may be yearning for the stars (Stella) but becomes mired in the horribly earthy (Stanley), since all quests for the ideal in a flight from disillusionment with reality inevitably end in frustration. Although it is true, as Quirino says, that the soul is fettered within the sexually desiring body, he seems seriously to misstate Williams's distaste for the absolute necessity of the flesh as the only possible avenue or means through which human beings can achieve any sort of communion, if not transcendence: 'Williams' intention was to portray the impossibility of ideally consummating any union in which the body is involved.'[17] So Williams's quarrel, according to Quirino, was with the fact of base matter itself, the dust out of which the body that imprisons the soul was created.

To support his position, Quirino looks at the poker-playing that structures the work, making the stud game the chief analogue of life. From that perspective, everything resides in luck, in that Stanley, as the master player and Darwinian survivor, controls all. Cruelty and brute vitality become the order of the day, the norm of human existence; and the tragedy acted out in *Streetcar* is 'the futility of attempting to flee the apes.'[18] In such a world, all of the positive values associated with the archetypal symbolism of water are rendered impotent, as the 'brutally fittest rule' and life is reduced to a rhythm of 'tumescence and detumescence, desire and death.'[19]

Taking his cue from the appearance of the trade name Echo Spring as the brand of Brick's preferred liquor in *Cat*, George Crandell's 1999 essay turns to the myth of Narcissus, who stared at his self-image in a pool until he was transformed into a flower after death, to explain Brick's psychological disorder. Seeing Brick as the drama's focal character and a microcosmic representation of the alienated mid-century man who feels he can live unconnected from others, Crandell's analysis is more existentially based than the social commentary of others who are looking at the play's mythic patterns, though it does entail societal ramifications:

■ Brick's narcissism anticipates ... what Christopher Lasch later describes as 'the culture of narcissism,' a society characterized by self-interested individuals, people largely indifferent to the past, the future, the needs of others, and a culture—in its pursuit of immediate gratification—unwittingly intent upon self-destruction. What Williams describes realistically in terms of a narcissistic personality is at the same time a prophetic image of an American cultural phenomenon emerging in the post-war decades and becoming widely apparent by the mid-1970s.[20] □

Crandell structures his discussion by employing several of the medically agreed-upon criteria for defining the narcissistic personality. First, Brick feels he deserves to be the center of attention, because of his former athletic prowess and his status as favorite son of Big Daddy and Big Mama. Second, he fantasizes about an ideal love from the past—though his morality is too conventional to acknowledge the homosexual nature of his sexual desire for Skipper. Third, he needs constant sympathy and attention from those around him, their admiration serving as a means of validating his self-importance. Fourth, in his self-obsession he lacks empathy for the feelings of others, refusing to listen to them, and becomes enraged at their criticism of him. And, fifth, he takes advantage of others, focused solely on recapturing a youth he thought would be eternal and lacking concern for connectedness with others in the future.

One of Crandell's most intriguing moves is the way that he links the myth of Narcissus to the issue of *Cat's* two endings. Whereas Williams's original third act coincided with Ovid's rendition of the narrative up through Narcissus's death after pining away in self-adoration, the Broadway version of the third act reflects the closure original to Ovid's tale, with Narcissus metamorphosed by being transformed into a beautiful flower. And since, as Crandell comments, the artist, too, is like the mythical figure in his need for approbation from the audience, perhaps that makes more understandable Williams's reasons for acceding to the changes in Brick that Kazan felt would bring the play greater popularity.

Throughout her 1987 book *Tennessee Williams' Plays*, Judith Thompson's aim is to be exhaustive in pointing out the multitude of allusions to classical and biblical myths and later literary texts, as well as the archetypal patterns and ritual actions that inform Williams's dramaturgical practice—an analytical strategy whose results run the risk of seeming over-determined but can reward by being richly suggestive. She finds in *Streetcar* the underlying pattern of the journey or quest motif, and reads it from dual perspectives: Blanche as stripped of a largely illusory memory of an idyllic past and plunged into a nightmarish present (and future); and Blanche as the intruder into a hostile new world, only to be expunged as a scapegoat. Thompson is particularly astute at elucidating innumerable parallels and patterns of repetition: Blanche suffers the death of both Belle Reve and Allan; for Blanche to see the foreplay to Stanley and Stella's lovemaking is like coming upon Allan and the older man together; aspects of Blanche's relationship with Allan are reenacted in different ways with each of the men in the play—Mitch, Stanley, the paperboy, Shep Huntleigh, and the Doctor; Mitch's rejection of Blanche (she is 'Not straight') replicates hers of Allan (he 'disgust[s]' her); if Stanley's rape of Blanche is a 'demonic' marriage, the 'kindness' she finds with the Doctor is a 'mock' marriage; Stanley's 'antithesis' is Shep, an 'ironic Savior'—though one might question whether Williams intended him as representative of the *deus absconditus*, the 'Judeo-Christian God who remains incommunicado in the modern world of disbelief.'[21]

Thompson detects numerous classical allusions. The curse on the royal house of Greek tragedy is like the 'epic fornications' that bring down the antebellum Belle Reve, and fate or fortune appears in the game of poker. The guilt-haunted Blanche is pursued by the Furies, her alcoholism sending her into a Lethean oblivion, and she finds not the happy underworld of the Elysian Fields, but the fearsome Tartarus. She is Psyche and Persephone, as well as Pentheus to Stanley's Dionysus, while Stella is Astarte, and Shep is Midas. In terms of biblical myth, Blanche is both Eve who falls into carnality to become the Whore of Babylon and Cain who slays the innocent, as well as Delilah to Mitch's Samson. Shep Huntleigh, on the other hand, is the Good Shepherd. Literary references abound as well, and not just to Poe and Browning and the Rosenkavalier and his Sophie. Stanley is Yeats's 'rough beast,' while the newsboy is the Prince from *The Arabian Nights*. Blanche is both the Lady of Shalott and the Ancient Mariner, condemned to retell her tale, as well as a 'reformed' Scheherazade, the witch from Hansel and Gretel, and Marguerite to Mitch's Armand.

Blanche's baths, as most commentators have noted, are rites of purification, though other everyday versions of sacred rituals, like the uneaten or interrupted meal (a secular communion) that Williams was fond of, go unnoticed here. More attention on Thompson's part to the way that Williams sometimes ironizes or inverts his religious symbolism might have led, in fact, to a less determined emphasis on the 'comic mode' of the play's ending. For she perhaps reads the image of the reunion of Stanley with wife and child too uncritically or unquestioningly. A scrutiny of the religious iconography here reveals it to be not a Holy Family, but rather a family rendered unholy by Stanley's lustful groping for Stella's breast. This, taken together with Stella's nagging sense that Stanley has lied to her about Blanche and that her future lies with her son rather than her husband, color and mute Stanley's 'victory,' calling into question just how sanguine Williams wants audiences to be over the fact that the status quo is seemingly restored and 'the miracle of new life ... ensures that Stanley's brutish nature will prevail.'[22]

In her chapter on *Cat*, Thompson demonstrates how a consideration of myth and ritual can help to bring the differences between Williams's original conception of Act Three and the text as revised for the Broadway premiere into sharp relief. Relying upon Northrop Frye's generic distinctions in *Anatomy of Criticism* (1957) and Frazer's detailing of the myth of the Fisher-King in *The Golden Bough* (1911–15), Thompson finds that the Broadway version falls within the comic mode, celebrating resurrection, fertility, and new life, as Brick, under the aegis of Maggie, undergoes a transformation and renewal. In a play that exhibits only limited Christian religious iconography, Maggie's announcement of life beginning that will perpetuate Big Daddy's line is likened to the Annunciation, just as her name recalls St. Margaret, the patroness of childbirth who chose martyrdom rather than giving up her chastity.[23] (It should perhaps be noted that Brick's offstage shower is more redolent of the locker room after an athletic contest than a rite of purification like Blanche's frequent baths. And his injured body, unlike that of other physically attractive males in Williams, is never associated with being crucified or wounded like St. Sebastian the martyr.) Although any sense of such a fairy-tale resolution was 'defeated' in Williams's original version, the generic mode there had been ironic rather than tragic: Brick, though he may father a child, does not undergo rebirth but remains a 'dismembered' Fisher-King—whose emotional impotence Thompson contrasts with the stoicism and self-awareness of Hemingway's Jake Barnes in *The Sun Also Rises* (1926)—and the play's ending actually mocks the fertility ritual, since the heterosexual relationships between Big Daddy and Big Mama and Gooper and Mae are lustful rather than loving; founded upon greed and hypocrisy. Marriage and family are here presented as severely flawed institutions, making the Pollitt family a 'microcosm of a corrupt society and culture.'[24] This reading of Williams's initial ending reduces Maggie to being a 'survivor' rather than a purveyor of life, while the antiheroic Brick, a victim of the societal homophobia he has 'internalized', which prevents him from admitting his sexual nature, exhibits neither the moral sensibility nor remorse (though he is not unhaunted by guilt, as Thompson argues) that would open him up to tragedy; instead, his moral cowardice renders him 'pathetic.' Any tragedy, instead, is that of the society itself for its willfully benighted attitude towards homosexuality.

Along the way, Thompson explicates the full panoply of classical references, allusions, and analogies. Brick, like the Aristophanic forbears for whom male homosexual love is the most 'enduring,' yearns for the Platonic ideal of psychic completion that finding his soulmate would secure. He is Apollo—albeit in a 'debased' form since he does not honor the truth—the injured hunter who caused the accidental death of Hyacinthus, afterward resurrected as a flower. He is Hippolytus, who 'scorned' the love of Aphrodite to pursue the chaste Artemis. He is, as well, Timmus, Adonis, Attis, Osiris, the last named the fertility god who was dismembered by his brother Set, whose sister and consort, Isis, in turn magically 'reconstituted' his body and then conceived a son, Horus, with his 'reanimated corpse.' If Maggie is Isis, Ishtar, Aphrodite, and Cybele, she is also Diana and Artemis, forced into chastity and aggressive sexual pursuit and archer/slayer (of Skipper). Finally, Jack Straw and Peter Ochello, who, unlike Brick, are willing to openly declare and live out their homosexual love, are seen as paralleling Castor and Pollux—though the centrality of their relationship is perhaps unnecessarily downplayed by Williams's decision to present it largely through the extra-dramatic set description at the beginning of the play. Thompson concludes that:

■ The play presents with such subtlety its favorable attitudes toward the Straw–Ochello relationship that they are easily dismissed as irrelevant— an aside, a footnote—to the play's central theme. ... [This] obscures its significance as a viable alternative to the corruption depicted as inherent in heterosexual love, in American society, and, by extension, in modern Western culture, all of which are represented as spawning only continuing cycles of greed, lovelessness, and mendacity.[25] □

Along with the broad overarching cultural and intellectual currents that these scholars see as impinging upon Williams and becoming an integral part of the way that he perceived and presented human experience was the pervasive climate—social, political, philosophical—of the time in which he lived and wrote. These historical contexts that helped shape his world view will be taken up in the chapter that follows.

CHAPTER THREE

Political, Social, and Cultural Contexts

SELF AND SOCIETY IN THE POSTWAR YEARS: PAUL HURLEY AND LARRY BLADES

When Williams cast his only ballot ever in a presidential election in 1932, he voted for the Socialist candidate Norman Thomas, testifying to his 'interest in the discovery of a new social system ..., an enlightened form of socialism, I would suppose.' And in an essay that appeared between *Streetcar* and *Cat*, he asserted 'I don't think any writer has much purpose back of him unless he feels bitterly the inequities of the society he lives in'—although he does go on to disavow any 'acquaintance with political and social dialectics. If you ask what my politics are, I am a Humanitarian.'[1] His political stance tends to be practical rather than theoretically oriented, and so it comes as no surprise that in the narrative sections providing the social and historical background of even so personal a play as *The Glass Menagerie* he will reference everyday facts like the economic hardships of the Depression, the labor unrest of the frustrated masses, and the mood of isolationism in the face of events in Spain and Germany that portend the coming conflagration. In spite of this, critics for a long time chose to speak of Williams as if he were an apolitical writer. Gradually, however— particularly in light of increasing accessibility to the writings from his apprenticeship years in the 1930s—a corrective to this viewpoint would emerge, so that by the mid-1990s there was widespread understanding of how Williams reacted to the social climate of his times: not only in his public life by his long-ago vote for Thomas and his much-later vocal support for George McGovern, as well as his denunciation of the military-industrial complex and the Vietnam War; but also in his plays that would explore such issues as the dissociation between culture and power and the complicity of art with social evil, patriarchal repression and exclusion of minorities (sexual and other), imperialist domination abroad and government thought-control at home, and

36

institutional hypocrisy and apocalyptic violence.[2] As Robert Corber suggests in his recuperation of the political stance of gay male writers such as Williams, they enlisted a plethora of current-day issues, from consumerism and the accumulation of capital to the rise of the organization man, from changes in the power dynamic of the domestic sphere to the plight of those who, because of race, gender, or economic class, were disenfranchised from the American dream of upward mobility.[3] The critical literature on *Streetcar* and *Cat* addresses specifically several intellectual and political currents that had a strong bearing on Williams's thinking: burgeoning attention to the civil rights of individuals and minorities; the anti-Communist paranoia of the Cold War; research on human sexuality and its impact on individual and societal morality; and the development of existentialist thought as it relates to personal freedom and identity formation.

In an early (1964) and wide-ranging treatment of Williams as a sociopolitical dramatist, Paul Hurley proposes that he is intensely attuned to what are regarded as 'typically American values'[4] or characteristics. Employing *Cat* as particularly illustrative, this translates into a critique of the way that hypocrisy and lies, materialism, consumerism and greed, getting ahead in the world and conforming to group mores can all warp and corrupt the individual. Reading the play very much as Arthur Miller had in his 1957 essay 'The Shadow of the Gods,' Hurley sees Williams as musing over whether the Darwinian 'necessity for continuing life'[5] is absolutely paramount, even when it would mean a loss in dignity for the individual and a diminution for society as a whole. Or, as Miller put it, does society have 'the right ... to renew itself even when it is, in fact, unworthy?'[6] If, as Hurley insists, Williams is employing homosexuality metaphorically in order to convey the notion of 'difference,' then the playwright is castigating society for its lack of toleration and its promotion of sameness.

Seen in this light, Brick's idealization of his relationship with Skipper runs counter to society's values, and so causes in him a feeling of alienation; furthermore, on the level of personal culpability, Brick allows Skipper to die rather than permit him to sully his ideal by suggesting it was anything other than a 'pure' friendship. It is fear of society's suspicion and of being ostracized for difference that caused Brick to fail in his responsibility to his friend, a kind of denial of shared humanity resulting in 'spiritual cripple[dness].' Society would judge any physical relationship between the two men as 'not in the service of life'[7] because it cannot generate new life, so on that basis alone society would place a higher value on the marriage between Brick and Maggie. Yet, curiously, though it would promote the survival of the nation and the race—and thus warrant an American audience's assent to Maggie's lie of pregnancy—the marriage itself might well be loveless.

In essence, Hurley views Maggie's relationship with Brick as an imbalanced one, the strong dominating the weak. According to him, what motivates Maggie is a kind of animal lust after sex, money, and property, and not love: 'What Maggie loves is her husband's weakness; she loves her power over him in the way a lioness loves her prey.'[8] Hurley refuses to entertain the notion that when Maggie speaks of her determination to 'take hold' of Brick and 'gently with love hand your life back to you, like something gold you let go of,'[9] she may, in fact, be thinking first of him, offering him her necessary greater strength so that he can bury his disgust with himself and regain something of the self-respect he lost in his rejection of Skipper (much like the chance that Blanche believes Mitch offers, if only momentarily, to her). Yet Hurley does not acknowledge any potentially admirable side to Maggie. Returning to the issue of the individual defending his or her actions and ideals rather than adhering to society's mores that may constrain and diminish the individual, Hurley concludes:

■ Maggie and Big Daddy may see the world steadily (if not whole), without illusion, but they have also committed the Williamsian sin of having *accepted* that world as final and irrevocable. Brick may be too weak to temper his vision of an ideal world with acceptance and understanding of the real one, but Maggie and Big Daddy refuse even to entertain the possibility of an ideal world or to give much sympathy to those who do.[10] □

For Hurley, then, Williams's chief contribution to political thought resides in his interrogation of the precise workings of the social contract in the matter of personal choice versus group values, of whether one can ever hope to balance truth-to-self and one's ideals with conformity to the standards of a community in which all must coexist—but which the individual may regard as thwarting freedom and growth.

In another exploration of the young male protagonist up against the pressure to conform and succeed, Larry Blades, writing against the backdrop of a socioeconomic milieu nearly a half-century later than Hurley's, focuses in a 2009 essay on Stanley Kowalski's experience in the armed services. Situating his discussion in the context of the conventional Hollywood treatment of the returning veteran (in films from the late 1940s such as *The Best Years of Our Lives*, *Till the End of Time*, and *All My Sons*, the last adapted from Miller's first successful play), Blades argues that in *Streetcar* Williams 'inverts' the expected outcome and tenor of such likeminded works. Instead of presenting the veteran coming home from World War II as someone who, oftentimes with the help of a nurturing woman, manages to reintegrate himself responsibly into a community that moves mutually toward fulfillment of the American Dream, Williams's more pessimistic model posits an embittered returnee who brings back with him all the aggression and brutality of the battlefield and then 'finds meaning in a violent assertion of his individual self and his antisocial urges.'[11]

Although Williams strategically positions several references to Stanley's involvement before the opening of the play's action with the Army Corps of Engineers, these have not been systematically examined; to remedy this, Blades employs the writings of famed journalist Ernie Pyle to describe their stressful duties in deactivating minefields, providing water, and mapping locations, often under fire. All of these tensions would only have been exacerbated during the fierce battle at Salerno—where victory came on the day Williams chooses for Blanche's calamitous birthday celebration, September 15. A foray into the history of the Corps, founded, significantly, by the heroic Polish fighter Thaddeus Kosciusko, reveals a commitment to freedom and equality that Williams plays off in an ironic fashion through Stanley's Darwinian tactics. Even though Blanche may not have understood that Stanley was a noncommissioned officer, his status as returned soldier may have given him higher cachet than his ethnicity and class would otherwise warrant in her eyes. Determined to be top dog, Stanley will control and dominate by the act of rape, his physical brutality an outgrowth, in Blades' eyes, of the violence of the military campaign. So Stanley, rather than being the exemplar of Pyles's ideal soldier who supported his country during war time and came home to submerge his own goals to benefit the larger common good, falls more into the category of the essentialist individual as promulgated by Henry Luce: the jingoistic loner ready to flex his muscles in order to forward an 'imperialist agenda' for postwar America.

As Blades hints in the subtitle to his essay ('Stanley as the Decommissioned Warrior under Stress'), he also employs the current understanding of post-traumatic stress syndrome as a lens through which to examine Stanley. Detailing such symptoms as dependence upon alcohol, antisocial and histrionic behavior, and marking anniversaries of traumatic wartime events, along with finding comfort in the camaraderie of those, like Mitch, who shared his war experience, allows Blades to argue that Stanley should be seen as rendered just as 'fragile' by his past experience in the military as Blanche had been by her discovery that her husband Allan was gay. This makes *Streetcar* even more resonant for contemporary audiences who have lived through, and must welcome soldiers home from later wars in Kuwait and Iraq. Praising what he calls 'Williams's keen psychological insight,' Blades writes:

■ Stanley's military experiences and his subsequent return to a confusing and conflicted civilian world are every bit as important to his development as Blanche's upbringing, encounters with dying relatives, and aborted marriage are to hers. Both characters have suffered devastating pain and trauma and are thus vulnerable to the intrusion of destructive experiences from the past.[12] □

Yet Blades does not specifically hint that this fragility could just as compellingly have been attributed to the insecurities and vulnerabilities attendant upon the soldier's returning to face a workforce and a domestic scene/nuclear family that had functioned without him and changed drastically during his absence. For, despite Stella's insistence that Stanley will get ahead better than his buddies, and his own rhetoric of superiority, his economic situation is precarious; and his need for forgetfulness and reassurance is assuaged only in his demanding, and sometimes rough, sexual domination in the marriage bed.

RACE, CLASS, AND ETHNICITY: LIONEL KELLY, GEORGE CRANDELL, AND MARY BREWER

Two widely disseminated artifacts from popular culture might help throw into relief by way of illustration the issues of ethnicity and race raised in *Streetcar*. The first praises unity and melting-pot assimilation: a *'Victory Liberty Loan'* poster designed by Howard Chandler Christy and dating from 1919 that lists, in its honor roll under the heading of 'Americans All' the family names DuBois, Kowalski, and Gonzales, along with the more predictable ones of Smith, O'Brien, and Levy. The second underscores separation and exclusion: a highly prized 1955 photograph by Robert Frank entitled *Trolley—New Orleans*, which shows, arranged sequentially in the window seats from front to back, an adult White male, an adult White female, a White boy and girl, an adult Black male, and an adult Black female—the Whites all dressed in Sunday best, while the Blacks wear working attire. While the first of these is gender neutral and the second gender specific, neither tells anything about sexual attitudes in Williams's time; that was left to *Sexual Activity in the Human Male* by Alfred C. Kinsey, Wardell B. Pomeroy, and Clyde E. Martin, which was published early in 1948 within weeks of *Streetcar's* opening and became an enormous best-seller. Kinsey's experiential inquiry, by revealing that many practices once thought the province of only a small minority were actually indulged in by a large proportion of the population, threw into question the previously sharp distinction between 'normal' and 'abnormal.' For Williams, this only served to confirm the multitudinous varieties of human sexual expression and affection and the need for a nonjudgmental attitude toward others where matters of gender and sexuality were concerned.

In 'The White Goddess, Ethnicity, and the Politics of Desire' (1992), Lionel Kelly demonstrates how the racial, ethnic, and class dynamics of *Streetcar* belie or call into question the '*easy intermingling*' that Williams, in his opening stage directions, claims is a hallmark of social relationships in New Orleans's French Quarter. Through successive analyses of the Negro Woman, of Stanley, and of Blanche, Kelly shows that the Elysian Fields in this reworking of the underworld, rather than being an Edenic site of communal harmony amidst the economically disempowered, is actually a squalid lapsed paradise of deprivation and decay masked by the '*raffish charm*' Williams himself found so appealing. In a play featuring symbolically and metaphorically named characters, the fact that the Negro Woman is left unnamed helps to ameliorate any claim to a cosmopolitan toleration of difference in any of its multiple forms; in fact, the presence of the African-American, whom audiences cannot ignore but who seems to have little purpose other than to add local color, creates an 'effect [that] is shocking in a writer of Williams's stature.'[13] In the arena of ethnic division, however, Kelly finds the work much more substantive.

For into this world divided between Whites and Blacks, Stanley's intrusion as the ethnic immigrant and economic *arriviste* displaces the racial issue and recasts the terms of debate: the focus is now on the 'parvenu aggressor' challenging the claims of a southern aristocracy, of territorial rights against inherited property. His aim is to dominate, without any regard for prior claims, hoping to achieve mastery even through verbal means. In one of his most original insights, Kelly points to the bipolarity of Stanley's language: idiomatic expressions coexisting with a vocabulary that apes the 'verbal dignity' of the social classes which can lay claim to an Old World pedigree. Yet the ultimate brutality of Stanley's male sexual domination will be underlined in the last word spoken by him or anyone else in the play: 'stud.'

Unlike Stanley's verbal tirades, Blanche's poetic language is what connects her with the White Goddess of Kelly's title, borrowed here from Robert Graves's 1948 book about the Moon Goddess or the inspirational Muse; in fact, Williams consciously makes use of several names associated with astral bodies: 'Moon Lake Casino,' 'The Evening Star,' 'Stella' (though unaccountably, Kelly does not remind readers of one of Williams's discarded titles for the play, 'Blanche's Chair in the Moon'). Like the mother of all things living, who both creates and destroys, Blanche is a 'primitive force' whose link with death is seen in her prompting Allan's suicide—whose homosexuality becomes 'inscribed' as 'a perversion of generative lust issuing in death'[14]—just as Blanche's nymphomania is seen as 'a perversion of predatory sexuality,' her desire misdirected and ultimately becoming self-annihilating. Although Kelly is incorrect in asserting that the white coats worn by Doctor and Matron who usher Blanche offstage to the asylum that will be her final Elysian Fields are specified in Williams's text, they become 'images of erasure'[15] of Blanche's personality, that in any event has always been an exercise in ritualized performativity.

■ Blanche's fading star [is] erased from the scene of ethnic vitality by Kowalski's claimant American nationalism. At the same time, the myth of national union is questioned as Blanche's dream gives way not to the power of the North, but to the demands of the immigrant in the figure of Kowalski. Blanche's case may also be read as a version of that history freely inscribed in post-Civil War narrative realizations of the difficulties of unionist accommodation.[16] □

So Kelly reads Blanche's exit from the stage metaphorically, in national and public rather than purely local and personal terms.

Several critics have responded pejoratively to Williams's handling of race in *Streetcar*, since the lone Black figure, the Negro Woman, is, as Kelly noted, silenced by remaining nameless and virtually without dialogue. George Crandell's 1997 essay, however, finds a more potent African-American presence in the play, arguing that Stanley is encoded as the racialized Other. While it is true that, in general, Black characters in Williams's theatre exist mostly on the margins, fulfilling subservient positions and even bearing less-than-flattering names,[17] the perceived absence or gap should not be taken to signify disinterest; rather, Williams reveals 'a fascination with the fearful and desirable prospect of miscegenation.'[18] Crandell intimates a paradigm for Williams's notion of Blackness in some of the short fiction (such as 'Big Black: A Mississippi Idyll' and 'Ten Minute Stop') where the 'racial Other'—perhaps reflecting nineteenth-century attitudes—portrayed African-Americans as strong in physique, deficient in intellect, and beset with uncontrollable sexual urges that made them animalistic.

Variations of these features, Crandell claims, are displaced onto Stanley: he is inarticulate, sexually potent, brutal yet desirable; Blanche even refers to him in bestial terms, calling him an 'ape.' Furthermore, of Polish descent, his ethnic status was lower than the Irish, who were often likened to Blacks. Drawing upon Toni Morrison's assertion that immigrant groups measured Americanness in opposition to Blackness, if he is to erase Blanche's reinscription of him and assimilate fully as White, Stanley must deny his Polish heritage, though for audiences he continues to occupy the boundary uniting Black and White. Crandell judges this a strategic intervention on Williams's part:

■ Perhaps a sensitivity to the expectations of Broadway audiences in 1947 and a fear of commercial failure prompted Williams to misrepresent the topic of miscegenation in the form of an ethnic rather than a racial liaison in *A Streetcar Named Desire*. By the means of a racialized discourse, linking a descendent of Polish immigrants with imagery traditionally associated with black characters, Williams nevertheless overtly broaches the topic of miscegenation in a play ostensibly without an Africanist presence.[19] □

Although Mary Brewer, in *Staging Whiteness* (2005), identifies *Streetcar* as a 'text of sameness and otherness'[20] and one permeated by an African-American aesthetic (jazz and the Blues), she resists the tendency necessarily to inscribe Stanley as Black because of a stereotypical notion of 'primitive' Black masculinity/sexuality that he might seem to embody, as Crandell apparently felt prone to do. Rather, Stanley's Whiteness has been 'diluted' by his Polish ancestry, which admittedly renders him 'dangerously different' and a 'destabilizing presence,' leading to Brewer's preference to categorize him as a 'variegated white.' She centers her analysis, therefore, on the means by which he might be able to reassert or reconstruct his identity as a White male in a post-World War II society, an identity that he has allowed to be challenged in a number of ways. First, he rents a flat rather than owns property (a White prerogative and signifier). And, as if that were not enough, the locale of the Kowalski apartment is the seedy and economically lower class French Quarter, a space that because of its racial 'intermingling' is identified as Other 'compared to normative U.S. society'[21] and so adaptable to his presence. Second, Stanley's sexual potency, compared to the White phallocentric patriarchy that spawned Blanche and inculcated her class sensibilities and racial attitudes, is tenuous and threatened in two ways. Not only does Stanley (from a Lacanian perspective that would permit either gender to be the locus of the phallus) by suffering emasculation and infantilization at the hands of Blanche's tactics as a tease and threat to supremacy in his home find himself subject to 'fear of feminine difference,'[22] but, furthermore, validation of his masculine superiority is made dependent upon how he is perceived in the eyes of others; in short, he 'requires the reciprocal gaze of the White woman to cement his identification with U. S. man.'[23]

   Thus challenged, Stanley can only (re)establish his White masculinity through the act of rape, which in effect will be a 'symbolic castration' of Blanche who (again in Lacan's terms) had temporarily seized phallic power from him. In this way, Brewer suggests a differently nuanced motivation and outcome for Stanley's physical violation of his sister-in-law:

■ Stanley and Blanche's opposed epistemological stances are molded by their racial and gender differences. Until the rape, Blanche's Whiteness allows her to enforce the male-constructed rules by which race-gendered identities are verified. Only by reversing the dualism of nature and culture, by allowing Stanley's enactment of primitive man to achieve Blanche's subordination, does the 'truth' of race become contingent once again on a masculine action.[24] □

EXISTENTIALISM, AUTHENTICITY, AND THE COLD WAR: BRUCE MCCONACHIE, JOHN BAK, AND RITA COLANZI

In his essay 'Something Wild ...,' first published as a newspaper article two years before *Streetcar's* premiere and reprinted as the introduction to a collection of plays two years after, Williams terms theatre art 'benevolent anarchy,' emphasizing its "social function" [as] an irritant.'[25] In a statement alluding directly to the House Un-American Activities Committee (HUAC) witch hunt and racial and ethnic prejudice, he goes on to deliver a decidedly political declaration:

■ Today we are living in a world which is threatened by totalitarianism. The Fascist and the Communist states have thrown us into a panic of reaction. Reactionary opinion descends like a ton of bricks on the head of any artist who speaks out against the current of prescribed ideas. We are all under wraps of one kind or another, trembling before the specter of investigating committees and even with Buchenwald in the back of our heads when we consider whether or not we dare to say we were for Henry Wallace. *Yes, it is as bad as that.*[26] □

During the Red scare, gays were particularly subjected to being ferreted out as security risks, since the sexual deviant was regarded as an easy target for blackmail. And artists, especially writers and directors in the film industry and theatre profession, came under suspicion as well—and many were blacklisted—for their supposed leftist sympathies. So it is not surprising that this culture of fear during the Cold War that promoted hiding in the closet—and not just the homosexual one—affects both Williams's life and works. Reportedly, he composed a letter to the State Department protesting its refusal to grant a passport to his fellow playwright, Arthur Miller, but never mailed it because of the 'atmosphere of intimidation.'[27] In the drama of the 1950s, references to the tactics of the McCarthy era are not always as explicit as the analogy drawn in Miller's own 1953 play *The Crucible*, and so, as Brenda Murphy cautions, one must be attuned to 'the persistent subtext ... in which political, social, and moral issues were engaged and debated with intensity and passion.'[28]

Bruce McConachie's 1998 essay moves from more specific manifestations of repression in Cold War America (such as widespread surveillance and homophobia) to what he sees as Williams's larger philosophical concern over who holds the authority to legislate the truth, issuing a challenge to 'fact-based language as the only mode of truth telling.'[29] Even those who have read *Cat* superficially as primarily a Southern gothic romance, with its pillared plantation, home to a wealthy patriarch, subservient Blacks, and sexually frustrated women, have seen in it elements of the grotesque, particularly in its exaggerated minor characters, often treated parodically for comic effect. Yet in his generic approach to the play as an example of what might be called 'The Theatre of the Grotesque,' McConachie understands the term in the broadest manner possible, so that it includes, among other things, the notions of 'monstrosity' (as seen in the set's consumerist shrine of entertainment center/liquor cabinet); an irresolution of situations and contradictions; an indecisiveness about meaning and ethical uncertainty; a simultaneous attraction and repulsion for its characters; a Bakhtinian polyvocality that fosters relativity rather than certainty; and a refusal to allow the audience any 'stable subject position.'[30] According to his reading, Williams deploys the theatrical grotesque for its political usefulness, either 'to challenge the cultural imperialism of the North'[31] or to endorse more tolerance for 'sexual deviance' by societal authorities.

The second section of McConachie's article contrasts Williams's original vision of the play, replete with all its grotesqueries, with the conception it received at the hands of its director Kazan, who wanted to remold it into the form of a melodramatic liberal tragedy à la Lillian Hellman and Miller, one that would move toward the revelation of a guilty secret, resulting either (tragically) in the downfall of its protagonist or (melodramatically) in a regenerative moment at play's end. Kazan's direction would mix the sculptural arrangement of characters in unironic tableaux conveying mythic or iconic overtones together with the presentational method, almost expressionistic in its handling, of the characters' direct address to the audience. Such a revisioning of the work intended to undergird a hegemonic 'culture of liberal containment'[32] has the effect of blunting Williams's refusal to pigeonhole characters according to conventional sexual categories and demonizes what the Kinsey report had tried to normalize, seeing homosexuality instead as a threat to national unity and familial institutions.

A third segment of the essay applies Emile Benveniste's linguistic theory of utterance as either *histoire* (that is, speech marked by its objectivity and reliability in conveying the truth) or *discours* (that is, speech acts as subjective and open to multiple perceptions/interpretations), with Williams favoring the second over the first. In this regard, McConachie probably overemphasizes Williams's likeness to the late modernist playwright Harold Pinter, with his emphasis on incomplete exposition and the unverifiability of the past, suggesting that many of the stories characters tell in *Cat*, such as Maggie's about the bowl parade and Big Daddy's about the incident with the beggar in Morocco, must be taken with a grain of salt. Nevertheless, what is clear in a world steeped in 'mendacity' is that *histoire* is under suspicion, for those in society who claim to possess the literal truth—doctor, preacher, lawyer—and who are most homophobic and hold the narrowest belief in patriarchal power can finally not be trusted. Calling into question the audience's assumption that realistic drama provides them with an objective perspective, McConachie argues that:

■ Williams's reliance on *discours* and his undercutting of *histoire* during *Cat*, however, repositions the audience as subjective interlopers with incomplete information, a repositioning that heightens the grotesquerie of the play. The dominance of personal narrative and the impossibility of objective knowledge in *Cat* call into question the reliability of hegemonic forms of cold-war information.[33] □

Such a position renders it impossible for Brick—or his creator—to swear with certainty if he is now or has ever been a homosexual, as several of the play's critics, especially Walter Kerr, seemed to demand.

In a complex and multifaceted essay of 2004 on existential thought as it impinges on Williams's *Cat*, John Bak, employing a masculinist studies approach, limits his discussion to a consideration of the anguish involved in exercising the choice to take action rather than live inauthentically. Bak's range of references includes not only Jean-Paul Sartre but Simone de Beauvoir and Alfred Kinsey as well, as he explores Williams's challenge to how Cold War politics, in response to what it perceived as a feminization of the American male, constructed an essentialist notion of masculinity as exclusively heterosexist. In what Bak regards as a 'politically subversive' move, the dramatist—unlike the hegemonic society that defines what is 'normal' in terms of a heterosexual/homosexual binary and then stigmatizes everything that falls outside the privileged side of it—leaves Brick's sexuality at best ambiguous and uncertain, making him yet another example of what Bak terms *Homo americanus*, that 'species of queer heterosexual males who have haunted the pages'[34] of canonical American literature.

The ideal of Cold War heteromasculinity, promulgated by the government, by organized religion, by business and industry, and even by Hollywood in its popular myths, had already been threatened by the research of Alfred Kinsey, which showed that 40 percent of American males had participated in at least one homosexual activity, though only 4 percent would name themselves as gay. The fact of this preponderance of male–male desire problematized the question of identity: if masculinity is performative, what could and could not be tolerated without having a destabilizing effect upon the norm? Heterosexist and even homophobic language would be adulated, whereas effeminacy would be suspect. Homosocial bonding, oftentimes heavily charged erotically, would be acceptable, whereas blatantly homosexual acts would not. Consequently, 'In expressing mutual appetites for male exclusivity and masculinist iconology but lacking the performative heterosexual to anchor them, Brick is a Kinseyan male through and through—a sociosexual conundrum, a Cold War signifier without a signified.'[35] As Bak asserts, it is this landscape of suspicion and demonization that the playwright is attacking:

■ it is Williams' distaste for a society which first determines someone's private identity and then systematically marginalizes those who do not fit its model of normalized sociosexual behavior that mostly drives the play's sociopolitical engines. Certainly Brick had never desired Skipper sexually— at least not consciously—but his desire for Skipper socially over all other things now makes him equally susceptible to being labeled a homosexual. ... At a time when evidence of an alternative family was perhaps what America most needed, Cold War society (both Brick's and Williams's) privileged the recapitulation of the nuclear family, the backbone of consumerist American society.[36] □

In terms of Sartre's philosophy, where one's meaning or essence is not a given but can only be created through the choices one makes, in order to live authentically Brick faces the existential anguish of defining himself in his own terms rather than having an identity imposed upon him. His freedom becomes a burden when it is circumscribed by how others insist on seeing him according to their categories of sexuality. In such an atmosphere of suspicion, if he is to 'prove' his identity as heterosexual, Brick is pressured into adopting a posture of homophobia in order to accommodate homosocial bonds—which he deems pure—while reviling homosexual activity.

    Bak examines Maggie within the framework of de Beauvoir's 'second sex,' wherein the woman, though largely defined passively by forces outside herself, still has an 'independently formed essence' insofar as her 'sexuality inevitably play[s] a role in establishing [that] essence.'[37] Being dependent on Brick for her own self-definition forces her to define him, in turn, as the 'heteromasculine patriarch.' Childless in a play where much is made both literally and figuratively of the contrast between fertility and sterility, she must therefore define herself in 'opposition' to Mae who, along with Gooper, reads Brick as psychologically impotent based on their eavesdropping (for which read HUAC-like surveillance) through the bedroom walls. As part of Williams's agenda to condemn the Cold War mentality that defines a person's identity by the absence of some performative act, Maggie comes in for harsh criticism from Bak as a base Machiavel, 'manipulate[ing[society's unwritten handbook of male–male conduct'[38] in order to convince Skipper he is gay. Finally, given Brick's dilemma in a society that reduces the individual's freedom to choose for himself by legislating what is and is not a normative identity, Maggie is, nevertheless, able to direct him into heterosexual performativity. Brick's existential burden is to prove that society is wrong in the label it appends to him or, failing that, accede to a definition of gender identity imposed from without that does not coincide with his private determination of self. In either case, society (and thus the audience, with 'its own ambivalent attitudes toward male–male desire'[39]) comes under Williams's indictment.

Citing Williams's explicitly stated interest in the works of Albert Camus and Sartre, intensified by his stay in Paris the year after *Streetcar* premiered, Rita Colanzi sets out, in a 1992 essay which is wider-ranging than Bak's, to explore how the playwright both adopts and complicates the concept of 'bad faith' that he found in Sartrean existentialism. According to Sartre, our awareness of nothingness leads us to see ourselves as Other, or as a thing, a 'being-in-itself,' but this only serves to render us incomplete or lacking in meaning. The sole way to counter this condition of bad faith is to accept the responsibility for making ourselves by creating our own essence through the act of choosing. In short, we have existence (the *that* we are) which is only 'insubstantial,' while we must create our essence (the *what* we are) for ourselves. Consequently, when the characters in Williams's dramas 'seek to flee the anguish of their nothingness by defining themselves as fixed, unchanging objects or things,'[40] they live in bad faith.

This bad faith may take any one of several forms in Williams. Some characters, menaced by the awareness of temporality, or loss of beauty, or, ultimately, mortality, may attempt to run away; in this category, Colanzi would place Blanche and Big Daddy. Others might try to hide from nothingness either by accepting the 'mislabeling' imposed by others or by deceiving the self; here Colanzi locates Maggie, the tenacious cat who pursues a security she will never achieve in order to escape the necessity for confronting the anguish of being always alone. Still others might give themselves an aura of 'respectability,' adopting a mask they know to be false; such a one is Blanche, the performer who miscasts herself in a number of roles, such as pure Southern lady. Finally, others might try to escape nothingness by anesthetizing themselves through mechanisms like alcohol or drugs or sensuality; this group would include Stella, whom Colanzi mentions, but also Brick, whom she does not.

Colanzi claims that such a Sartrean existentialist reading of Williams is incompatible with a Freudian deterministic one, which she finds a deficient approach to understanding his characters. For whereas Freud would 'absolve' them from the responsibility of making choices, Sartre would insist that, though trapped in a meaningless existence, they are not just victims of the id or of the unconscious. And, yet, Colanzi argues that Williams provides a more nuanced and 'ambivalent' understanding about the notion of bad faith than Sartre does, 'reveal[ing] himself to be sympathetic towards those who cannot confront their existential anguish and ... unwilling to denounce them completely.'[41] As a case in point, she offers the example of Blanche: while the ideal might well be to live with the horrors revealed by the naked light bulb of reality, unshaded by the lantern of illusion, the dramatist still proposes that her magic and lies might be forgivable, even preferable, as true to the heart. Generalizing from Blanche's condition, Colanzi concludes by using a recurrent image of captivity from the plays for the refusal to embrace a responsible self:

> ■ Williams does not take as firm a position in regard to bad faith as does Sartre. While rejecting the posture, he admits a need for and an attraction to illusion, the lie to oneself, or the act of bad faith. He bids the caged bird fly, and yet, at times, cautions it to remain imprisoned.[42] □

The post-World War II period, in short, because of a confluence of pressure points that could more easily be met by a capitulation to society's definition of the 'right,' placed an inordinate burden on those who tried to act authentically, in good rather than bad faith. The currency of these and other ideas circulating at the time Williams was writing forms an essential part of the background against which his plays must be read. Although perhaps not specifically acknowledging or even alluding to this rich cultural context, the work of the academic scholars and critics who take center stage in the next chapter is informed by an awareness of these ideas, while placing a heavy emphasis upon explicating characters and thematic motifs within the two masterworks.

CHAPTER FOUR

Williams and Literary Canonicity

EARLY ACADEMIC VOICES: NANCY TISCHLER, ARTHUR GANZ, AND BENJAMIN NELSON

Until fairly recently, dramatic literature was marginalized or, at best, only grudgingly accepted as an object of serious academic inquiry within English and critical theory departments, existing under the veil of such sobriquets as the 'ugly stepchild' or 'unwanted bastard child' among American literary genres.[1] As C. W. E. Bigsby has remarked in *Modern American Drama 1945–1990* (1992), 'Any account of American drama must begin by noting the casual disregard with which it has been treated by the critical establishment.'[2] In an essay dating from 1989, Susan Harris Smith put forth a number of reasons that might explain this dismissive attitude: the visual nature of a medium meant initially for performance and popular consumption; the collaborative nature of theatre art that might occlude identifying a single author; and drama's proclivity to take 'an adversarial and critical position toward dominant ideologies' and to resist 'existing proscriptions about the style and function of literature.'[3] So ingrained is this antitheatrical prejudice that the flagship journal *American Literature* has published only a handful of articles on drama. Its first notice of Tennessee Williams in 1979 takes the form of a rather self-evident argument that his dramas leech over into the fictional mode in his stage directions, wherein the playwright 'tells' information to readers of the text rather than 'shows' an audience characters in action. Using Williams as a case in point to dispel the long-held notion of drama as 'a uniquely unmediated vision,'[4] Nancy Cluck likens him to the novelist as narrator—'omniscient' in revealing characters' thoughts or explicating themes, 'disguised' in creating patterns of image and symbol—calling especially upon the famously 'intrusive' stage direction in Act Two of *Cat* about the essential 'mystery' of human personality in order to demonstrate that 'the distinction between drama and prose fiction is artistically clouded in the plays of Tennessee Williams.'[5]

An over-emphasis on widespread critical disregard, however, paints a somewhat distorted picture of the position that Williams's plays came to hold fairly rapidly both within the academy and within the canon of American literature. On the occasion of his death in 1983, a remembrance in a mass-market magazine would place him firmly among the nation's canonical authors:

> ■ His earthy characters journey over a landscape that pulses with the strife-torn dualities of human nature. ... God and the Devil, love and death, the flesh and the spirit, innocence and corruption, light and darkness, the eternal Cain and the eternal Abel. In the American tradition, this links him to three 19th century moral symbolists: Hawthorne, Poe and Melville.[6] □

And fortuitously, his emergence as a major dramatist in works like *Menagerie, Streetcar*, and *Cat* preceded by only a few years the appearance of the first journals devoted exclusively to drama[7]—a heady convergence between a body of dramatic literature crying out for substantive explication, a new generation of literary specialists committed to theatre art, and outlets ready to disseminate their insights to scholars and students.

Nancy Tischler, whose 1961 book *Tennessee Williams: Rebellious Puritan* establishes the parameters for much successive Williams criticism, positions him as a romantic writer set on taking his personal experiences and objectifying them for his audiences. As such, writing becomes 'a form of psychotherapy' through which he reveals his 'tormented personality'[8] in characters who are 'alter egos.' That torment arises, in part, from the tension within his family upbringing between the Cavalier spirit of sex and violence (represented by his father Cornelius's ancestry) and a Puritan repressiveness (inherited from his prudish mother Edwina, daughter of an Episcopalian rector—who himself was, however, extraordinarily tolerant). This tension appears in terms of appetite versus soul, intellect versus intuition, reality versus fantasy, and, for the Mississippi Delta Southerner, an idealization of a mythicized agrarian past versus an encroaching present that is mechanized and urbanized. Tischler finds her book's subtitle, *Rebellious Puritan*, in an appellation Williams applied to himself, indicating that he would be chomping against the bit of restrictive conventional mores, so that finally no subject would be 'off limits' to his pen. Drawing heavily upon Kazan's notebook entries, production history, and the initial critical reception, Tischler sees *Streetcar* as a well-plotted (each scene is 'like a one act play'[9]) epic drama, in essence a 'parable' about the North's 'destruction' of a refined and 'civilized' South. The three central characters form a triangle, with Stella at the 'apex' as the 'key figure' over whom Blanche and Stanley are in contention. Since Stanley may have prevented Stella from falling prey to a Southern decadence and desuetude in a relationship of socially sanctioned sexuality, to Tischler's mind she is 'wrong in loving him but still right in living with him.'[10] Although Tischler's assertion that Blanche 'desires' to be forcibly violated at Stanley's hands is questionable at best, her sexual proclivities do challenge the patriarchal tradition and so their gratification seems to garner the playwright's 'intellectual enthusiasm,' even if Williams's attitude toward sex remains for Tischler annoyingly ambiguous. Blanche, however, with her nymphomania and neuroses, is regarded as more a case study in psychopathology than a tragic figure.

In Tischler's reading of *Cat*, Big Daddy, because of his integrity (admittedly laced with crude if life-affirming humor), is the heroic figure in a work that focuses centrally upon the father–son relationship and the way that hurting the other may be, sometimes even must be, an integral component of demonstrating love and bringing the other to see the truth. As such, Tischler sees it as an autobiographical reflection of a renewed understanding and acceptance between Tennessee and his father Cornelius after years of estrangement. While still centering upon female aggression (in Maggie) and male passivity (in Brick), *Cat* is lauded here as a mature work featuring normally sensuous human beings, displaying a 'healthy' ability to handle 'perversion and idealism sensibly and honestly without any apparent need to shock.'[11] Although Tischler calls Brick puritanical in his attitude toward homosexuality, he is seen as having loved Skipper in a way that he could never love Maggie; consequently, his too-sudden change in the revised third act seems a violation of Williams's artistic integrity: Brick will still hold Maggie responsible for soiling the purity of his friendship and will remain in denial of the true nature of Skipper's love for him, while his and Maggie's going to bed to conceive the child does not guarantee a 'sensual paradise' for them. Tischler is particularly thorough in delineating the work's themes, including the inability to communicate, the destruction of youthful idealism, a family's predatory treatment of its more sensitive members, and the way that the life-lie (à la Pirandello) can be creative. But mostly she detects in the play:

> ■ a maturer view of the possible combinations of love and lust: ideal love of friends ..., love of parent for child ..., lust between the sexes (which Gooper and Mae experience ...), and love-lust between the sexes (which Big Mama feels for Big Daddy and Maggie feels for Brick). The last of these combines sex with respect and devotion. It is certainly a more ideal possibility than Stella's surrender to Stanley... .[12] □

And yet, the possibility for the highest forms of love is oftentimes thwarted in Williams by a 'malignant universe.' Tischler, however, can still zero in on, even be prescient about, what emphatically will remain the central ethical tenet of his entire oeuvre: the need to face down one's own personal demons and respond sympathetically to the other person, understanding that this may demand a relativistic notion of what is right. If apathy toward the other is damnation, then salvation can only come through positive action.

In a 1962 article that echoes Tischler's emphasis on rebellion against repression (and that could well have been called 'The Puritan and the Lawrentian'), Arthur Ganz proposes that Williams, rather than be considered a 'psychologist' peculiarly adept at character portrayal, is actually a 'moralist'—and this despite the violence and sensationalism prevalent in his works. His 'moral system,' centered in the notion that 'the rejection of life is the greatest crime,'[13] finds its chief source in D. H. Lawrence, from whom he inherited, in Ganz's view, a belief in the necessity for 'awakening life' in those who had repressed it and 'a rationale for the sexual obsessions that dominate his work,' although the playwright 'betrayed' his influence in 'extending the approval of Lawrentian doctrine to areas of sexual experience beyond the normal.'[14] This ethic, however, comes into conflict with an innate Puritanism:

■ Williams is passionately committed to the great Romantic dictum inherent in his neo-Lawrentian point of view, that the natural equals the good, that the great natural instincts that well up out of the subconscious depths of men—and particularly the sexual instinct, whatever form it may take—are to be trusted absolutely. But Williams is too strong a moralist, far too permeated with a sense of sin to be able to accept such an idea with equanimity.[15] □

As evidence of this, Ganz claims that Williams was never able to look upon homosexual activity unambiguously, but always with both 'sympathy' and 'revulsion'; painfully aware of the torment and despair it causes, he must 'censure what he wishes to exalt.'[16]

The chief pattern of action that Ganz traces in Williams's plays occurs when a character rejects life, as Blanche in *Streetcar* does when her cruel taunting of Allan leads him to commit suicide; for this, she must atone by undergoing punishment at the hands of Stanley. By destroying her, he becomes the avenger of Allan, and yet his cruelty toward her replicates Blanche's toward her husband, whom Ganz thinks she could potentially have saved. But the moral imperative of sin being followed by retribution is complete, with the sound of the Varsouviana that signaled Blanche's guilt being heard again as she is led off by the Doctor to the asylum. From Ganz's perspective, however, Williams's morality becomes confused and upended when, as in *Cat*, his protagonist is a man, which means that Brick, the rejecter of Skipper, is simultaneously the 'martyred' homosexual victim. Forced into homophobia and denial by a bigoted society, Brick, then, 'cannot openly [be] punish[ed] for failing to be an honest homosexual'[17]—a punishment in the form of castration/impotence (symbolized by the athletic injury) that would have occurred were it not for a determined Maggie's regenerative activity that saves him. In fact, the entire tenor of *Cat*, through Big Daddy's tolerant respect and admiration for the 'idyllically conceived' love of Straw and Ochello that blessed him with the land, is toward 'acceptance' rather than stigmatization of homosexuality. What results in *Cat*, therefore, is an ethically uncomfortable situation 'when we cannot tell whether the central figure [is] innocent or guilty.'[18]

Benjamin Nelson, in his 1961 book *Tennessee Williams: The Man and His Work*, shares with Ganz and other early critics a concern over how to respond to the sensationalistic aspects of Williams's plays; this is apparent, for example, when he writes:

> ■ *Cat on a Hot Tin Roof*, while illustrating some of his glaring inadequacies—the obsession with sex, ... the tendency toward sensationalism, the 'psychoanalyzation' of a character or situation—at the same time manifests his great strengths. And to dismiss these qualities because of disagreement with his choice of subject matter or his view of man and the universe, is to treat his work unfairly.[19] □

Nelson's treatment of *Streetcar* is representative of much early criticism in its focus on two questions: where do the dramatist's sympathies lie? And is Blanche a tragic heroine? Recognizing that both on stage and page Stanley can appear an attractive character, Nelson builds the case for him and then proceeds to dismantle it. Stanley is virile and vital, the representative of the normal American male building up the new working class after the War, shrewd and not given to impractical dreams. So in his conflict with Blanche, an anachronism from a romantic past and intruder into his domain, he might rightly be seen as 'deservedly victorious.' Yet he can only dominate through brute force. A narcissist concerned solely with his own pleasure, he rapes to satisfy his 'illusion' that he is the supreme animal, undercutting Blanche's air of superiority. Although unable to integrate her sensual side, Blanche gallantly maintains her code, certain that 'truth and beauty are the only light in a bleak universe.'[20] In spite of this, Nelson senses an 'insufficiency' in the work: even though Blanche, with all her complexes, succeeds in being more than a psychological case study, she is still lacking in tragic stature since she does not 'grow from her ordeal and so there is no exaltation.'[21] In suggesting, however, that she admits to no responsibility for her brokenness, Nelson ignores her awareness of having failed by rejecting Allan, the obverse of the compassionate response that Williams implicitly sets up as a value in an otherwise pessimistic universe.

Because he finds a positive emphasis on love and hope in the face of death and a skillful employment of the symbols of the cool moon (for Brick) and the hot cat (for Maggie) in *Cat on a Hot Tin Roof*, Nelson deems it a more satisfying drama, though one still marred by its preoccupation with the more sensationalistic side of sexuality and some too explicit overstatement of its big themes and concepts. Problematic, too, are the rendering of Brick as little more than a case study, and Williams's evasiveness in the handling of Brick and Skipper's relationship. Yet Nelson brings some originality to his interpretation of that relationship, saying the 'unnaturalness is not in the homosexuality but in the idealization of Skipper':[22] to erect an ideal so untainted that no one could ever approach it is to fail in understanding that if something is perfect, it is also not human. Big Daddy, through a love that must lacerate his son in order to help him, and Maggie, through a love so determined that she will resort to a life-lie to save her distant husband, affirm staunchly 'moral' positions. If Nelson perhaps gives too absurdist a tint to Williams's overriding ideology, he nonetheless sees Maggie and Big Daddy as 'wrench[ing] life' from literal and metaphorical death.

TRANSATLANTIC PERSPECTIVES: C. W. E. BIGSBY AND THOMAS ADLER

The preeminent British scholar of American drama, C. W. E. Bigsby, is recognized as the world's leading expert on Arthur Miller, although he has written substantive overviews of Williams's career as well. Trained as a specialist in American Studies, he tries to elucidate overarching patterns that he discerns within an author's work, with frequent attention to the sociocultural milieu and allusions to other classic writers (in his treatment of Williams, to Hawthorne and Melville, to Fitzgerald, Hemingway, and Faulkner). The metanarrative that he pursues in *A Critical Introduction to Twentieth-Century American Drama* (vol. 2; 1984) is that 'Williams was the protagonist of all of his plays,' and that his 'essential theme' centers on how he 'used [his] art as a desperate means of shaping [his] experiences into an acceptable form.'[23] This theatricalizing of personal experience, which involves a blurring of the distinction between life and art, reality and fiction, truth and 'lies,' the literal and the poetic, takes on added complications for Williams who, as the alienated outsider because of his homosexuality, must suppress or hold back part of the actual truth and resort to performativity—a tissue of lies—in order to achieve imaginative truth. This bifurcation between vulnerability and strength, the compulsion to hide and the courage to reveal, plays itself out in various forms in Williams's characters, and can result as well in a bifurcated response on the part of audiences which are pulled in two directions at once. And yet Williams, by incorporating so much of his personality—of the 'betrayal and redemption, torment and consolation' of a sexuality that 'provided the grammar of his drama'—within his creative endeavors, accomplished something truly distinctive. As Bigsby puts it in *Modern American Drama*:

■ The shock of *Streetcar* when it was first staged lay in the fact that, outside of O'Neill's work, this was the first American play in which sexuality was at the core of the lives of all its principal characters, a sexuality with the power to redeem or destroy, to compound or negate the forces which bore on those caught in a moment of social change.[24] □

As a consequence, the playwright himself, as well as his audience, might be both attracted and repelled by Stanley; even Stella is aware of the 'deeper humanity' that she alone seems able to call forth from her husband. There exists a similar doubleness in the response of Blanche and Stanley toward what they regard as negative about the other: 'Blanche is powerfully attracted by the social crudity and masculine directness which she simultaneously despises, as Stanley is fascinated by [the] aristocratic arrogance and neurotic sexuality which he affects to hold in contempt.'[25] If Bigsby finally reads Stanley as ending in a state of bafflement, incapable of fully comprehending either himself or how what he has wrought has come about, Blanche, who always 'inhabit[ed] a no-man's land'[26] between 'systems' she was unable to negotiate, seems not only to have lost but to *be* lost in a larger sense as well. Unlike Stella, who fled to a marriage of passionate intensity, Blanche thought marriage to Allan would recapture qualities of civility and grace she associated with the past, only to find that his sensitivity was a 'cover,' just as Mitch (whom Bigsby terms a 'gross parody' of Allan) finally belies an innate brutishness akin to Stanley's. Seeking 'to generate a space which she can inhabit without fear,'[27] Blanche attempts to refashion herself by donning a succession of masks, creating and producing a drama in which she performs the central role, and even resorting to a rarified, archaic language, but all to no avail since a destiny of 'defeat' is the core of her being. Little wonder that Bigsby concludes: 'Offered a choice between decadence and brutality the audience can hardly enter into an alliance with either.'[28]

Bigsby centers most of his discussion of *Cat* on Brick, whose problem he sees as something deeper than homosexuality. Granted, Brick is 'deeply conventional,' and so unable to dissociate himself from the societally imposed 'rigid categories' that govern acceptable sexual mores and generate fear of abnormality and transgressive behavior in oneself. Having failed to respond to Skipper in 'human need,' he has adopted a death-like posture of retreat and passivity, as if to 'ally' himself with his dead friend. This, however, is perhaps symptomatic of a more generalized attempt to prevent being 'pull[ed] into the world of sexual and emotional maturity with its ... profound ambivalences.'[29] What faces Brick, in short, is the appeal of 'arrested development' versus being implicated in the 'corrosive materialism' that defines the world of mendacity, of greed and power grabs, that he rails against. Succumbing to Maggie's entreaties that he father a child to inherit the land is tantamount, then, to 'enrol[ling himself] in the materiality of which the play is so distrustful.'[30] Nevertheless, Bigsby can still find 'optimism' in Maggie's supportive strength of her husband—a counter to his initial failure with Skipper.

Writing from the perspective of a moral aesthetician who focuses on the author's ethical ideas as they are embodied in dramatic structure, characters, and especially visual symbolism and scenic imagery, the American academic Thomas Adler, in his 1990 monograph, approaches *Streetcar* through an eclectic mix of critical approaches: formalist, generic, psychoanalytic, sociocultural, mythic, feminist, and thematic. Situating Williams's play in the post-World War II period—with its sense of displacement and alienation in the face of consumerism and the demand for conformity in a dehumanized workplace—Adler analyzes the play's structure as a working-out of the journey motif: Blanche is viewed as the archetypal outcast, a desperate 'wanderer seeking some kind of human connection'[31] and being either accepted or rebuffed as she goes from initial desperation into the final loneliness of madness. In its patterning of arrival and departure, from late spring through early fall, in its sense of loss and general coarsening of life, and in its moral symbolism and elegiac tone, the play replicates the usual structure and tone of one of Williams's major influences, Anton Chekhov. Stylistically, the play marks a movement away from a language-bound drama and a foray into expressionism to dramatize the heroine's 'nightmarish disintegration' through visual and aural distortions that reveal Blanche's subjective condition.

The bulk of Adler's comprehensive study is given over to analysis of the four central characters, grounded in psychoanalytic and therapeutic literature. Blanche is running not only from the deaths of her ancestors, but mostly from her condemnation of her gay husband that precipitated his suicide. Though absent from the stage, he is not silenced, since Blanche is haunted by the sound of the Varsouviana polka and the gunshot. A succession of liaisons—perhaps to assuage her conscience—is troubling for someone who sees sexual desire as inimical to the ideal of Southern womanhood fostered within her, and so has turned her into a hysteric. The symptoms of her neurosis, which psychologists attribute to the unrealistic expectations of a paternalistic society, include exhibitionism, seductiveness, hyperemotionality, and an embrace of a fantasy life, all exaggerated to the point of a travesty of femininity as a means of compensating for powerlessness. As Bigsby had emphasized, Blanche fictionalizes both herself, by refashioning her identity through role-playing, and the world around her, by (re)setting the stage; and, like any artist, she needs an audience to 'believe' in her, thinking she has found that in Mitch. But when he learns of her sullied past, he rejects her as she did Allan, and all of his pent-up sexuality comes out in a violence hardly different from Stanley's, as he attempts to force himself upon her and tears the paper lantern, symbol of the fragile Blanche herself, off the revealing light.

If Blanche is a creature of fantasy, Stanley is a creature of hard fact, displaying symptoms of machoism, which therapists see as the male version of female hysteria. A returning veteran whose economic station remains uncertain and whose participation in homosocial rituals like poker and bowling substitute for expressions of feeling, Stanley hides insecurities beneath a surface of virility that can easily descend into brutishness. Although audiences might at first see this red-blooded American 'agent of democratization [as] inherently attractive,'[32] toward his docile wife, Stella, he is verbally and physically abusive; if some regard her as having made a healthy adjustment from plantation to urban flat, her life is still one of enslavement and dependency— though she continues to hold a sexual power over the needy Stanley. Blanche's pretensions make him self-conscious over his lack of refinement and those material things that he is unable to provide his wife; seemingly defiant of any moral norm, he retaliates against the threat Blanche poses to his dominance by becoming a smasher of material things and violator of Blanche (metaphorically by tearing off the paper lantern, literally by raping her body). Even in her subsequent retreat into madness (the ultimate movement into illusion/art) Blanche retains a sufficient hold on reality to realize that the Doctor, whose appearance is accompanied by ominous strains of the Varsouviana, is not the rescuer of her dreams. Rather than focus on her potentiality as tragic, Adler proposes that in *Streetcar* Williams might be issuing a jeremiad warning of the audience's potential tragedy, apparently condemned to a general coarsening and loss of values in modern society.

On a mythic level, Adler sees *Streetcar* as playing out not only the conflict between the morally flawed Old South built on the original sin of slavery and the New North of proletarian pragmatism, but also that of the biblical fall from innocence. If the hope of recapturing an Edenic past partakes more of nostalgic fiction than realizable possibility, it was still a wedge against a demeaning pessimism. In that context, many of Williams's secular rituals evoke hints of the sacred, couched as they are in overtly religious symbolism. Blanche's birthday dinner interrupted by

Stanley's violent outburst is like an uneaten communion, while his rape of her is like a desecrated marriage ceremony. And if the concluding sculptural arrangement of father, mother, and child in swaddling blanket is more an unholy family because of Stanley's lustful groping, the iconography associated with Blanche strikes a more positive note:

■ Williams appropriately employs clothing to mirror the spiritual transformation his heroine has undergone. Blanche emerges radiant from the last of her ritual expiatory baths, clothed in a 'Della Robbia blue [jacket], the blue of the robe in the old Madonna pictures';[33] she hears the ringing of the 'clean' cathedral bells and *'fingers the bunch of grapes'* [that] are the source of the wine that becomes Christ's cleansing blood during the Eucharist and that iconographically suggest wisdom in Renaissance paintings of the Madonna and Child. Blanche leaves the stage a violated Madonna, blessed by whatever saving grace insanity/illusion can provide.[34] □

Adler concludes his consideration by recapitulating many of the themes (some of them delineated earlier by Tischler) that have been implicit throughout his discussion, including: mutability, and the attempt to thwart time by recapturing the past; the supremacy of an ethic of mutuality and nonjudgmental compassion toward the Other which may require a relaxing of moral absolutes and social mores that reject difference as abnormal; the need to integrate rather than fragment seemingly incompatible aspects of human nature; and the potentiality of art as a saving grace in an inhuman and inhumane world.

Although Adler has not written a monograph on *Cat* that parallels his on *Streetcar*, over a period of years he has considered the later play in a number of book chapters and articles. While he begins by making a point similar to Ganz's, that the action of both works is propelled by a prior decision by Blanche and Brick to fail to respond to another person's cry for help, he draws a sharp distinction: whereas Blanche's hearing of the Varsouviana haunts her with the memory of her guilt that even the gunshot sound cannot silence, Brick's hearing of the click when inebriated brings a much desired oblivion from his 'moral culpability' in hanging up on Skipper. Adler approaches his analysis of *Cat* primarily through attention to visual as well as aural image patterns and the strategic handling of stage space. Brick enters hobbling in on a crutch as the injured athlete leaving an area redolent of the homosocial/homoerotic locker room/shower. The crutch symbolizes not only the loss of phallic power and the artificial escape mechanism of alcohol, but also the choice to retreat into self rather than depend on human contact and communication—as he will later need to do when he must accept Big Daddy's hand to rise from the floor, or Maggie's determination to restore his self-respect. Blessed by Big Daddy after her 'announcement' that she is pregnant (a lie that, in a household rife with 'mendacity,' she will make true), Maggie finds completion, even paradoxically emancipation, in her 'freely chosen' vocation as the wife who will return her husband to full manhood: 'Her definition and completion as a woman can come only from her success in making [Brick] whole.'[35] And so what had begun as a death day—with Big Daddy needing to come to terms with the death from cancer that symbolizes the avariciousness eating away at the Pollitts—ends as a birthday, both for a regenerated Brick and the putative baby.

The plantation's bed/sitting room is a private domestic space, frequently invaded by others but also eavesdropped on and under surveillance from the outside balcony veranda by the grotesque despoilers out to inherit the land and all too consumed with the sexual goings-on inside (shades, almost certainly, of the Cold War witch hunts that ferreted out security risks). Dominated by a massive double bed, it is the site for discussions about hegemonically sanctioned heterosexual marriage and procreation. As Adler writes, 'The pained subtext' of the play 'might very well be, then, that of the latent homosexual forced by societal pressures and family expectations to "cure" his sexual orientation through a heterosexual union.'[36] Yet Williams is also able, in a move subversive for the commercial theatre of his time, to 'open the door on the closet and stage the homosexual bedroom,'[37] for the room was once the domain of the gay lovers, Straw and Ochello, whose relationship is revered with tolerance and tenderness by Big Daddy. Not only was their 'marriage' built on an unselfish 'mutuality' and respect exceeding that found in the heterosexual marriages of either Big Daddy and Big Mama or Gooper and Mae, but it was the source of the financial patrimony and ethical values inherited by Big Daddy. So among Williams's most notable accomplishments in *Cat* is that of rendering the 'homosocial economy as normative.'[38]

OTHER ACADEMIC VOICES: FELICIA LONDRE AND MARC ROBINSON

In comments that are almost an aside to her larger focus on *Streetcar*, Felicia Londre, in a 1997 essay 'A Streetcar Running Fifty Years,' goes further than either Ganz or Adler in delineating explicit comparisons between that play and *Cat*, which she terms the dramatist's 'most perfectly crafted work.'[39] She points out that Blanche and Brick, who become guilty alcoholics after rejecting homosexual lovers, are both attempting to defy time and recapture some golden age of innocence. While both Blanche and Maggie have had to develop hardness in order to survive, Stanley and Big Daddy are marked by 'ebullience and vulgarity.'[40] The marriage bed is a focal point in the setting of each, while the offstage bathroom serves as refuge for Blanche and Brick; finally, each play incorporates an interrupted birthday celebration and concludes with an image of a baby, either real or putative. Londre's remarks on *Cat* provide, moreover, tantalizing hints about two aspects that warrant further development: first, what she calls, in her 1979 monograph on Williams, the 'vocabulary of gamesmanship,'[41] with reference to literal games like the croquet outside and Brick's sports endeavors, as well as the metaphoric game of strategy that is being played by Maggie and Mae in their attempts to gain the family estate; and, second, her reference to the spatial design, with the interplay between the bed/sitting room inside and the metaphorical blue sky and fireworks and storm without, stage effects that critics have sometimes found melodramatic and distracting.

Londre's starting point in discussing Williams presents him as a writer ruled by a series of opposing forces: White (associated with Blanche's name) and Black (the dramatist himself claimed at one point to have felt racially Other); privacy and exposure; purveyor of the sordid and yet seeker after purity. Her approach to *Streetcar*, along with clarifying that 'Belle Reve' means not 'beautiful dream' but 'beautiful shore,' raises the seldom-considered issue of Blanche's impact as an agent of change on the people around her. She makes Mitch question his acceptance of the excessive machoism of his male friends. She causes Eunice to rethink her tolerance for the males' animal crudity. And she raises Stella's awareness of her own situation and the impossibility of a united family within it. For a more detailed handling of Williams's quintessential work than Londre accomplishes in her 1979 monograph, one must look to her *Cambridge Companion* piece of twenty years later. This article is notable because, were one editing a definitive edition of the play and seeking an appropriate introductory essay for students and general readers, Londre's would be a wise choice—inclusive though brief, steeped in the scholarship yet eminently readable, and incorporating salient quotations from Williams, such as his remark that in the paperboy Blanche discovers 'her fantasy of how Allan would have approached a young boy.'[42] Admittedly 'indebted to decades of scholarship and theatrical productions,'[43] her essay, while not laying claim to great originality, is extremely comprehensive, artfully integrating a scene-by-scene analysis of the playtext with stage history and critical commentary. She considers the work a 'compendium' of his dramatic practice, inviting her to address verbal, structural, visual, and thematic components; in the last regard, Londre emphasizes, as others have, the way that the wounded individual searches for human contact in an inhospitable and time-bound universe.

In a play that reflects changing gender roles in a postwar world and a more generalized feeling of 'confusion' socially and metaphysically, Blanche's 'desire' is seen not just in sexual terms but as a devout wish for 'rest' from any false hope of redemption or any paradisal end, the only possibility being madness. Her desperate journey is expressed in a work that is episodic in structure and simultaneously objective and subjective in technique, particularly in its sound and transparent scenic elements. The stage space is one of 'ill-defined boundaries,' with Blanche trying to take control of the territory of the bathroom, associated with recurrent images of water and heat and the site of ritual purification, only to have it violated as her person itself will be. Londre places more emphasis than most on what Kazan had identified as Stanley's orality, and notes how he recalls Blanche's epithet 'pig' for him in Scene 3 when he later hears in Scene 11 her use of the word 'swine,' which becomes the last straw provoking the physical rape. Blanche, who squirms under the physical touch of others, is seen as a player queen, but one who actively divests herself of role playing in her remembrance of turning away Allan, so that Mitch at that point 'is not just witnessing another performance.'[44] In a play whose most 'obvious thematic value' Londre claims, is 'illusion in opposition to reality,'[45] the tearing of the paper lantern marks the 'definitive retreat into illusion,'[46] not only of Blanche but of Stella as well, since she must now live with the delusion of Stanley's truthfulness that she defensively embraces. If Stanley's actions toward Stella and Mitch have long since made the audience reconsider its initial favorable response to him, the concluding color imagery associated with purity and Blanche's agency in controlling her own destiny 'salvage [some] dignity'[47] and generate for her the audience's sympathy at the end.

Unlike Londre, Marc Robinson, in *The Other American Drama* (1994), tends not to draw comparisons between *Streetcar* and *Cat*, partly because the clichéd generalizations that can result about such things as the 'Williams woman' or the 'misunderstood outcast' run the risk of reductionism. He attempts to offer a corrective to some other common critical practices as well: to exercises in psychobiography that 'turn drama into case study ... with Williams himself as patient,'[48] or to symbolic readings that draw such restrictive one-to-one correspondences as to flatten out complexities. What he refuses to deny is that Williams, from a position of 'outsiderhood,' writes with a liberating 'emotional truthfulness' and 'frankness' about intense erotic encounters between the sexes. Robinson's contention (perhaps too narrow) that 'Williams's chief contribution to twentieth-century drama looks unremarkable from our perspective. He wrote character-centered drama,'[49] controls how he approaches the plays, oftentimes to the exclusion of such elements as stagecraft or theme. He characterizes Blanche as a creature of artfully adopted illusions as well as of sustaining ideals that ultimately elevate her. As Bigsby and Adler had both argued, she is theatrical in assuming many roles, although Robinson insists that she never 'believe[s] in the parts she plays,' trusting that the 'effort' required in masquerade can itself 'make her feel better' and prevent 'actual pain.'[50] She desires not to escape, but rather to experience more intensely the penance she seeks for transgressions committed earlier, so that paradoxically her 'dignity' and 'stature' grow even as her lies are 'exposed.' Thus, at her seemingly most abject, straitjacketed as mad, she believes the world's 'limitations are more ruinous than her own' and exits 'too proud and smart ever to cut herself down to its size.'[51] Even her poeticized language is designed not to prettify or 'gussy up the suffering, but instead to restore its true dimensions and feel through language its full horrors.'[52] Finally, she has faith in her stabilizing ideals and 'moral beliefs,' even as she admits her failure to live up to them. Her outcry for magic, which necessarily distorts a reality that has become too limited, represents that of the dramatist who once said '"Blanche is me"' and 'developed his own theatrical magic to bring him closer to the hidden parts of minds and manners.'[53]

If, in discussing *Streetcar*, Robinson focuses almost exclusively on Blanche, in analyzing *Cat* he ranges more widely than just Maggie, a creature of self-constructed defiance against the status quo in a domain where she feels 'useless.' Neither mother nor daughter, she is confined and marginalized and needs to gain control over her space—something even the breathless volubility of her language denotes. Because telling the truth does not achieve her ends, she must resort to an untruth (albeit, one she will 'will' into being); adapting means succumbing to the family's mores. Robinson judges *Cat* a 'cynical' and 'pessimistic' work, reading Maggie not as assured but rather as fearful of what is to come at play's end. Robinson is especially astute about the use that Williams makes of 'fleshly life' in *Cat*: not only is the audience fascinated at watching the physical bodies of Maggie and Brick, hers languorously sensual, his coolly assured, but these are played off against the 'corpulently proportioned' Pollitts with those annoying and unattractive children underfoot. Finally, there is the dying body of Big Daddy, whose 'vulnerability' opens the floodgates of greed. Yet Robinson cautions against imposing symbolic readings upon sick or injured bodies:

■ Illness in Williams isn't always a symbol of more abstruse problems. ... [His] characters ask only to be looked at for who they are, not for what they represent. Searching for the deeper meanings of these conditions, we risk making the suffering less of a private matter—and so cheapen even as we try to ennoble it. A character's pain may acquire stature in symbolic readings, but the character himself becomes irrelevant, overshadowed by politics or philosophy.[54] □

Clearly, Robinson advocates a more cautious, balanced agenda, typified by the best of Williams scholarship. Even those critics like Bigsby, Adler, and Londre, whose readings of the plays attempt to be most comprehensive, can, however, oftentimes only touch upon rather than explore in any depth certain elements of Williams's artistry. These matters of form and style, of stage symbolism, and of dramatic genre have generated an extensive body of work that deserves a consideration of its own, to which we now turn.

CHAPTER FIVE

Dramatic Form, Style, and Genre

THE MATTER OF FORM: ESTHER JACKSON, MARY ANN CORRIGAN, AND ANNE FLECHE

When Jo Mielziner undertook to create the set designs for Tennessee Williams's plays, he understood that he was involved in a grand experiment to dramatize human consciousness on the stage. As he wrote: 'My use of translucent and transparent scenic interior walls was not just another trick. It was a true reflection of the contemporary playwright's interest in—and at times obsession with—the exploration of the inner man.'[1] In essence, Williams's visionary stagecraft brought about a revolution akin to Henry James's use of the first-person point of view or Virginia Woolf's experimentation with subjectivity in narrative fiction. Trying to define better the precise nature of Williams's dramaturgical method, one critic has even drawn on Woolf's own writings to speak of the playwright's development of an 'androgynous form,' one that marries characters presented in a realistic manner to effect great psychological probity (the masculine technical element) with a nonrealistically handled poeticized stage space that impacts kinesthetically on a multiplicity of the audience's senses (the feminine stylistic element) in order to rejuvenate what Williams came to see as a worn-out naturalistic mode that valorized surface verisimilitude over inner truth.[2]

In her seminal 1965 study of Williams's dramaturgy, Esther Jackson canonizes him as 'the chief architect of form in American drama,'[3] going on to explore systematically the constitutive elements of his practice: an expansion of realism into expressionism to convey subjective experience better; a heavy dependence upon a symbology of language (both words and sounds) and stage props; the adoption of a poetic, almost cinematic structure, with the play proceeding as a 'montage' of images that express a 'philosophical' content; a 'sculptural' patterning of characters and objects upon the stage; and the use of verbal and pictorial elements from myths that are classical, Christian, and geographical/regional in origin. The 'distinctive' production style of *Streetcar*, for instance, is a compendium that 'borrow[s] heavily from the common forms of American life: from cinema, newspaper, and magazine; from television and billboards; and from illustrations and advertisements,'[4] while its angle of vision, like that of *Cat*, expresses the consciousness of its protagonist, so that the former presents experience as seen from the point of view of Blanche, just as the latter does from the 'angle' of Brick—which, though Jackson does not pursue this, has ramifications for who should be seen as the central character of the respective plays. Moreover, such a form captures the conflicting truths characteristic of a modernist reading of the epistemological difficulties inherent in 'human understanding' which, along with the salvific effect of 'human love,' becomes one of the dramatist's persistent emphases. While the structure of *Streetcar* recalls for Jackson the progression of images one finds in film, that of *Cat* harkens back to the more 'incantatory' beginnings of drama, with its stylized speeches that confer an 'aural' identity upon the chief characters, punctuated by expressive choral background sounds.

If, from the perspective of classical mythology, both Blanche and Brick are seen as guilty transgressors in the line of Orestes, from that of Christian iconography both are suffering sinners who made wrong choices that must be expiated to find redemption. Whatever ambiguous salvation Blanche may achieve is signaled by the birth of Stella's child, while Brick's salvation seems more elusive. For he is one of Williams's 'emotional, spiritual, and moral cripples,' whose condition as symbolic of modern man raises unsettling questions:

■ The answer given by Williams reflects the gradual usurpation of the pagan idea of tragedy by the Christian concept of human worth. For the Christian concept holds every man a sinner, redeemable only through love. Similarly, it insists, as does Williams, that all men are anti-heroic; that these figures, no more than others, are guilty of the human condition.[5] □

Jackson's remarks explicating the plight of Blanche as antiheroic remain slight: suffering over her responsibility in the death of her husband, she becomes fragmented, descending into a kind of hell from which there is no 'clear' release. Her account of Brick as antihero is fuller, couching him in existentialist terms: caught up in the illusion of youth rendered false by the passage of time and history, his outer condition of withdrawal from human contact, sexual and otherwise, reflects an inner psychic or spiritual malaise, the 'nausea' or 'sickness-unto-death' of alienated modern man whom he comes to symbolize. This renders *Cat* ultimately metaphysical and ontological in its concerns.

In a now-classic 1976 essay, 'Realism and Theatricalism in *A Streetcar Named Desire*,' Mary Ann Corrigan analyzes how, by blending the methods of traditional realistic drama with stylistic devices that openly employ stage artifice, Williams perfectly melds form to content in order to produce a 'great' play. Corrigan's article serves as a primer, not only for students but for all later commentators who elaborate her argument. Though she does not neglect those visual and aural elements associated with the symbolic distortions of expressionism used to reveal the interior mentality, she goes beyond them to include other of what Williams would term the 'plastic' properties of the theatre. Thus she discusses the transparent walls that allow *Streetcar's* urban life outside the apartment to be seen from within; the white clothing whose insubstantiality foretells Blanche's end; the 'tilted perspective' and garishness of Van Gogh's *The Night Café* (1888) that references the 'moral degeneracy' of the chief player at the Poker Night; and the rhythm of the honky-tonk piano that is Stanley's music. But Corrigan focuses her attention on those menacing elements that objectify Blanche's disorientation and disintegration: the fearsome sounds; the images of death; the violence in the alley.

For Corrigan, Blanche's struggle resides in the contention between the sexually desiring female and the ideal Southern belle; the song lyric, 'It wouldn't be make believe, if you believed in me,' extols the 'capacity of imagination to transform facts.'[6] Corrigan finds this inner tension externalized in the conflict between Stanley, for whom the naked light bulb signifies 'what is *real* and, therefore, what is *true*,'[7] and his victim, for whom imagination, symbolized by the paper lantern, may hold a higher truth. Yet Blanche, who remains sufficiently aware of her situation to break the mirror when she sees her reflection in it, is left with no final retreat but madness. The real measure of Williams's genius is that he does not revert to symbolic theatrics willy-nilly, but calls upon them only when he realizes that strict realism is no longer adequate to his end:

■ When Williams can no longer convey the disintegration of her mind by depicting only objective reality, he resorts to distortion of verisimilitude in order to present subjective reality. Blanche does not mechanically move from one extreme to the other; she suffers and undergoes—on stage.[8] □

Williams's nimble technique of how this might be achieved provides a textbook example for others dramatists to follow.

Whereas Corrigan, through the lens of New Criticism, resolves the question of how to define *Streetcar's* stylistic departure from strict realism by settling upon the designation 'theatricalism,' Anne Fleche's 1997 book, *Mimetic Disillusion: Eugene O'Neill, Tennessee Williams, and U. S. Dramatic Realism*, looking at the issue from the vantage point of poststructuralist theory, opts instead for 'Expressionism'—restricting the term even somewhat more to optical or visual elements.[9] Fleche describes the form against which Williams rebelled in terms of the popular reformist realism of 1930s American theatre, with its emphasis on ameliorating the problems of the working class and ushering in a better world. If art need no longer be socially efficacious as it was for his immediate predecessors, there still remains the question of 'how we assign meaning to what we perceive.'[10] Submitting that Williams's plays—which 'break radically with speech' and are 'less novelistic than verselike'—pose considerable difficulties for the reader, Fleche believes that poststructuralism with its 'positive rethinking of the relation between reality and representation as the very sources of writing and dramatic innovation'[11] will enable her to articulate insights about *Streetcar* that could not have been made before.

Much of Fleche's discussion hinges upon Williams's experimentation in the use of theatrical space. In dramatic realism, with its linear structure moving toward closure, space tends to be stable and continuous, and the bourgeois audience voyeuristically experiences the 'hidden behavior' of characters for whom sexuality's end is procreation that helps rein in disorder. The typical middle-class audience, therefore, did not expect to experience abnormal sexuality in their playgoing, and so Williams of necessity must embrace an expressionistic form that, through optical means, destabilizes space and distorts temporality in order to provide a counterweight to thwarting those expectations. In realism conceived in post-Derridian terms, mimesis can only exist 'without reference to truth';[12] Williams, however, continues to insist that truth can be apprehended, but in the new medium he creates it is *emotion* that now supplies that truth and that propels the action forward. Whereas previously the playwright had required legends on a screen in order to verbalize feelings (in, for example, his original conception of *Glass Menagerie*), here Blanche's dialogue itself, by resorting at times to brief, staccato-like outbursts, externalizes her feelings.

Blanche's opening line, with the names of the streetcar 'Desire' and the destinations 'Cemeteries' and 'Elysian Fields,' seems to invite an allegorical reading of the play, yet Fleche believes such a 'reading seems false because allegorical language resists being pinned down by realistic analysis—it's always only half the story,'[13] and, furthermore, that if the work's integrity is to be ensured, a 'moralistic reading' of the work would need to see Blanche's violation as the 'inevitable' end of an erring woman. More telling and the crux of Fleche's discussion is the manner in which Williams is able, through the scenic device of disappearing walls, to 'relativize' space, rendering the outside the inside in order to make visual the 'restless discourse' of the desiring individual. Unlike Corrigan, however, Fleche does not believe that all of the expressionistic devices are intended to objectify Blanche's subjectivity; instead of the 'lurid images' all being products of Blanche's mind, they also function as indicators of how the brutish urban scene creates a generalized feeling of paranoia. At the end of the play, however, Williams must revert to realism as a means of curtailing Blanche's power: closure entails confinement in madness. The reassertion of normalcy is indicated in two ways. First, Blanche's gentleman caller, the Doctor, is 'particularized,' a realistic character who can 'contain' her 'expressionistic fit.' And, second, Stanley and Stella are redeployed to embody 'healthy' heterosexual desire. Yet, in spite of imposing a 'reassuring form over subjective disorder,' there remains the uneasy sense that 'beneath the appearance of order, something nameless'[14] has been sacrificed—specifically those qualities embodied in Blanche that Williams holds most dear. Perceiving that realism's 'mimetic assumptions have tended to close off possibilities for social criticism that lie precisely in the fantastic' enabled Williams to recuperate it as a viable form:

■ Williams's flights of fantasy are never reducible to the individual unconscious, say, or to any other conventional 'expressionistic' alienation from the real. On the contrary, he puts the real/fantastic in suspense, bringing it continually into question. Williams's approach shares with poststructuralism its positive rethinking of the relation between reality and representation as the very sources of writing and dramatic innovation.[15] □

PATTERNS OF SYMBOLISM: HENRY SCHVEY, JOSEPH RIDDELL, AND RICHARD VOWLES

Critics have long read Williams's plays as if they were closer in nature to poetry than to other forms of narrative, explicating visual and verbal imagery of considerable consequence (Blanche's paper lantern, Brick's crutch). As will be seen, they have unearthed sources for Williams's symbolism in works of pictorial art, in elements of nature, and even in philosophical systems.[16] Henry Schvey, asserting that as late as 1980 only inadequate attention had been paid to the scenic pictures in Williams, uses as his jumping-off point the likeness between the Scene Three setting of *Streetcar* and Vincent Van Gogh's painting *The Night Café* in order to pursue three avenues of inquiry: an examination of the Van Gogh-like stage set; a fuller explication of the play's color symbolism; and a consideration of the basis for Williams's system of signs and symbology in Renaissance art. Schvey suggests that the audience reaction at first observing Scene Three is likely to be 'silent absorption' as if they were looking at a *tableau vivant*, since Williams employs color and shape expressionistically to objectify emotional states. Just as Van Gogh used a dark palette, Williams's choice of vivid dark colors is portentous, since the battle between Blanche and Stanley unfolds in 'an atmosphere of barbaric, jungle-like violence.'[17]

More generally, the color contrasts throughout the play pit Stanley's vibrant harsh hues against Blanche's shimmering whites and pastels— but not always. So while Stanley tosses the white radio out the window just as he will later expel Blanche from the Kowalski apartment, Blanche at one point dons a red satin robe; and even her white apparel might be seen as ironic, given her sexual past. Blanche, nevertheless, throws off her 'sensual side' for a kind of 'spiritual rebirth,' trading the red robe for a suit of Della Robbia blue—the color most associated with her at the close of the play. Water symbolism, of course, abounds: from Blanche's repeated warm baths (and Stanley's enforced cold shower); through the song about the 'captive maid' rescued from the 'sky-blue water'—though Schvey sees her as captured once again at the end by the Doctor and Nurse; to her desire for a clean burial at sea. And Schvey notes links other than just the blue clothing between Blanche as 'tragic heroine' (which he takes for granted) and representations of the Virgin in Renaissance painting: her sign is Virgo, and Stanley refers to her sarcastically as a 'lily'—the traditional symbol of Mary's purity; the rhinestone tiara she wears might call up Mary in her role as Queen of Heaven, and the 'tragic radiance' Williams says she exudes might be like the aureole surrounding the body of the Virgin. Led off defeated at the end, Blanche finally is akin to the Mater Dolorosa, or sorrowing mother.

However, the baby in Stella's arms, swaddled in a blue blanket, in Schvey's eyes points to and even confirms imagistically that new life has somehow sprung from Blanche's 'symbolic death.' Although he does not make precisely clear the causal connection between the child's birth and Blanche's 'heroic transcendence,' Schvey concludes that:

■ Through a careful consideration of the play's pictorial elements, it has become clear that the end of this play is not so much a 'descent into hell' as an expression of spiritual purification through suffering.[18] □

In 'A Streetcar Named Desire—Nietzsche Descending,' an intricately argued essay from 1963, Joseph Riddell uses the Apollonian/Dionysian dyad as elaborated by Friedrich Nietzsche to posit that Streetcar ultimately fails because the play's 'welter of symbols—both linguistic and theatrical'[19] actually contradict, rather than support, Williams's 'undigested' and 'over-abundant intellectualism'; in short, the drama finally 'is torn asunder ... by overextended symbolism and an excess of self-consciousness.'[20] To Riddell's way of thinking, Apollo versus Dionysus, rational order versus creative energy, and repressive form versus vital chaos play themselves out on virtually every level and in every imaginable element of the work, beginning with the realistic surface covering over a symbolic sub-structure. When a dialectical relationship is not maintained between these dichotomous tensions—as in the case of a plot that valorizes the 'creative impulse' over 'civilized decorum' because of Williams's overt critique of society's suffocating mores—the result is 'a thesis play of sorts and a series of violent if symbolic actions.'[21] The play's setting places into contention the 'raw,' temporal reality of the urban scene and the impressionistically conceived lyrical fantasy of a more primitive 'Elysian Fields,' while the aural component pits cathedral bells and a romantic waltz against jazz, polka, and Blues. About Blanche's famous speech in Scene Four designed to undercut Stanley in her sister's eyes, Riddell remarks:

> ■ There is implicit in Blanche's remarks—made against the background of the inevitable train whistle, while Stanley stands in the wings—the call of history and progress, and the Apollonian illusion of reconciliation through culture, the arts, beauty. Against this rhetoric Williams juxta-poses the action of Stanley as a reminder of the necessary vitality in any creative dream, the incipient animal within the human.[22] □

Because the characters tend to become symbolic, realism gives way to allegory; instead of characters whose universality arises from their being carefully individualized, they are portrayed as 'pure essence,' some 'primordial idea.' Blanche, hailing from 'Laurel' (the orchard of Apollo) is, like her name, 'pallid,' a person who must shade the light; she symbolizes a society that could only become civilized by denying the elemental self and the desiring animal impulses to arrive at a Christian morality that ends by victimizing her, whereas Stanley's freely indulged hedonistic appetites attain through the agency of Stella's passionate love a well-nigh spiritual quality. So the rape, while an act of realistic violence, is simultaneously a 'symbolic ravishing of the Apollonian by the Dionysian self.'[23] Blanche exits on the arm of a psychoanalyst, high priest of a modern culture that elevates the rational as the greatest good but that Williams unalterably rejects—yet one to which, in his muddled, heavily symbolic 'anti-intellectualism,' he offers no 'plausible' alternative but some vague notion of 'love.'

In an early (1958) impressionistic essay, 'Tennessee Williams: The World of his Imagery,' Richard Vowles discerns a symbolic pattern that he believes runs fairly continuously throughout the first two decades of Williams's work, thereby contributing 'continuity' in action and meaning. Starting from the premise that Williams's commercial success during the 1950s, as well as his seemingly narrow focus on Southern manners, had lessened 'critical approbation' of his plays, Vowles traces the recurrent presence of what he terms a '*liquid principle*,' water or its lack, that reveals a definite artistry at work. Water—appearing in one form as the intense humidity of the semitropical South—not only lends both an element of sacred ritual and a structural flow and rhythm or 'fluid bustle' to the plays but (particularly in Williams's fiction) was metaphorically associated with sexuality. Vowles's reading of the sound of water at the opening of *Cat on a Hot Tin Roof*—a play about 'the shadowy no-man's land between hetero-and-homosexuality'[24]—is especially novel. For when Brick enters from the shower to tell Maggie that she should know he cannot hear her when the water's running he is actually voicing the 'sexual deviation' that separates them. This brilliantly suggestive verbal imagery is paralleled by a fluidity in the handling of formal elements like plot, seen in the way characters move on and off the stage, and even in their oftentimes overlapping speeches; the manner in which naturalistic dialogue blends with choral moments (sometimes background noises) and ritual-like recitatives is, Vowles feels, wave-like. The liquid symbol bodies forth even the flow of emotion and feeling among characters:

■ *An almost liquid warmth of human sympathies!* Maternity, memory, passion, the multiplicity of love, the achievement of flow, all of these are fused in the controlling metaphor of fluidity which constitutes Williams's idea of the theatre. To it may be attributed both Williams's flexibility and resilience in the modern theatre.[25] □

TRAGEDY—OR SOMETHING ELSE? ROBERT HEILMAN, JOHN VON SZELISKI, LEONARD BERKMAN, AND JOHN RODERICK

Robert Heilman and John von Szeliski explore the nature of tragic drama from two very different angles, the first considering the tragic choice(s) made by the protagonist, the second, the overriding world view of the playwright. In his 1973 study, Heilman adopts a traditional generic perspective. If melodrama presents a simplistic dichotomy between good and evil, with the former vindicated and the latter punished so order can be restored, tragedy posits a more ambiguous conflict between equally good imperatives, so that either choice will be imperfect, leading to disorder and 'catastrophe.' Turning to *Streetcar*, Heilman positions it as approaching, yet not quite reaching tragedy. Because of the 'paradoxical attraction' of both Blanche and Stanley, it moves beyond simply a clear-cut duality between a virtuous victim and a vicious victimizer. And because Blanche shares in the blame for her husband's suicide, Heilman detects the requisite 'complicity, or tragic guilt, in the heroine.'[26] Nevertheless, he questions the depth of her self-knowledge, since the sounds of the Varsouviana that haunt Blanche's memory are handled only as 'lyric' moments rather than dramatic markers indicating her gradual arrival at awareness; moreover, what precipitates the madness that leads to her punishment in the asylum is more 'self-pity' than tragic acceptance of guilt, demonstrating the 'seductive appeal [of] sinking luxuriously into illness as an aesthetic experience.'[27]

Although *Cat on a Hot Tin Roof* seems at first to evoke the trappings of melodrama, finally, Heilman believes, it can be seen as tragic. Initially, Brick is mired in blaming others, especially Maggie whom he tries to punish by withholding sex, rather than accept his own responsibility in Skipper's death. And Heilman worries whether Williams will find a way for Brick to transcend sinking under the painful loss of some 'idyllic Eden' through alcohol. Although Williams's original Act Three was assuredly a better embodiment of the playwright's disbelief in a character's too-sudden change, Heilman credits the revised version with presenting a Brick who breaks free of the pattern of blame to admit guilt, actively arriving at 'sentience' and accepting, if not exactly readily embracing, recompense for past failures. So Williams moves beyond a 'pathetic' narrative of a young man's physical collapse:

■ Williams catches Brick at a less irremediable stage of collapse than he does Blanche in *Streetcar*, he almost eliminates the element of victim that is a bona fide part of Blanche, [and] he gives more authority to the protagonist's crucial rejection of another.[28] □

The title of Williams's *Streetcar* is accorded visual prominence on both the dust jacket and endpapers of John von Szeliski's 1971 book, in which he judges the work one of the three 'greatest' American dramas (along with *Glass Menagerie* and *Death of a Salesman*) though none of them deserves the honorific 'tragedy,' concluding they are, at best, 'near-tragedies.' The tragic vision presupposes a well-articulated worldview that must, he argues, be optimistic, since tragedy and pessimism are mutually exclusive. If a character 'negates life' by professing to believe that existence is meaningless and the world is worthless and so well lost, that leaves no reason for struggle; the emotional or spiritual destruction he or she suffers can evoke only a 'useless pity,' and the fear generated will be far from the Aristotelian awe in the face of the universe. Even more injurious to the creation of tragedy is the playwright's conveying 'dread' over existence, which von Szeliski sees evidenced in Williams's 'simplistic' belief that only the weak can be truly human in an inhuman world and inevitably encounter 'brutal suppression,' a situation that reveals itself in the 'violence' and 'hysteria' in the writing. Consequently, Williams pens, at best, tragedies of 'sensitivity,' in which the malad-justed individual—oftentimes the neurotic artist figure—must attempt to escape the coarseness of the 'majority' by assuming a succession of roles and retreating into an illusory world, only to find him- or herself being destroyed and brought down to the level of the enemy.

In his comments on *Streetcar*, von Szeliski makes the case that both Blanche and Stanley are 'too weak' to be classified as tragic. This is psychically true of Blanche because her goal of restoring herself to health through finding some kind of love is not 'large enough' and her sensitivity is not an adequate compensation for her lack of self-knowledge. Meanwhile, Stanley's weakness resides in his moral obtuseness; he belittles Blanche's pretensions that she is superior to him, all the while not recognizing that he acts evilly in his insensitivity toward her. Williams's treatment of Blanche's neurotic sensibility recalls for von Szeliski a 'case history' in its commonness, and overall the play strikes him as too predictable, whereas the greatest tragedies have an element of the 'incredible' and 'remote' about them. Although Williams's mastery of a dark poetic symbolism helps raise the play above melodrama, the impression that the sensitive are already 'doomed' to a hopeless cycle of meaninglessness, even one assuaged by physical sexuality and escape into illusion, severely limits its reach:

■ Although he can show us how *not* to live, his pessimism does not equip him for displaying or suggesting a program for the ideal, for positive life, which is a product of tragic enlightenment. ... Seeing the world's corruption, Williams's rather fearful and pessimistic reaction is to show, not what might have been, but what *is* happening to the weak and unusual people for whom he is able to have feeling. ... But their stories are not the matter for tragedy: the tragic loser must have the potential which pessimism is unable to grant him and he must have been, at some time, a supreme winner.[29] □

Many of the first reviewers unhesitatingly affixed the label 'tragic' to *Streetcar*. One of the earlier scholars to do so, and from a quite original perspective, was Leonard Berkman, who, in a 1967 essay, found Williams atypical among post-World War II American dramatists by going against the prevailing opinion of the tragic hero(ine) as a morally little common man already doomed to defeat and so 'futilely' struggling with no possibility of victory. Berkman not only agrees with Williams that victory must be within the potentially tragic protagonist's 'grasp,' but recognizes that Williams is virtually alone among his contemporaries in proposing that the final end of that struggle is an intimate, one-on-one love relationship that is *'paramount among life's pursuits.'*[30] Even if the end is defeat, the fight against the forces that would deny that goal is itself defining:

■ Not only is Blanche's struggle to achieve intimacy central to the tensions of the play, but the very difficult, classically noble means which she must exert to achieve it—the admitting of humiliating truths, the giving of compassion in the face of shock, the learning to moderate her life so that her continued individuality is compatible with the individuality of others—stand in testament to a by no means peculiarly mid-twentieth century view of heroism.[31] □

Berkman argues that it is a disservice to look upon Blanche as the 'fragile,' 'rejected,' self-pitying artist figure, or as somehow symbolic of the wider civilization under attack by the forces of savagery (especially since the War brought about a destruction far worse than that of the sensitive in its extermination of the Jews). Rather, Blanche has repeatedly been thwarted in her search for intimacy, forced to acknowledge its 'limits': in a family eating itself away morally and financially; in a marriage to Allan that was never a real marriage because it was not based on honesty and 'trust'; and in the household of Stanley and Stella whose 'sexual intimacy' mocks the lack of it in her own life. When she refuses to exonerate herself from 'responsibility' in Allan's death, the possibility that she will no longer be excluded from human communion arrives in the form of Mitch, who would offer 'sex with compassion' and 'restore Blanche to grace.'[32] Yet, ironically, being truthful with him about her past turns her in his eyes into the 'whore-image' she sought to elude. Stanley's rape of Blanche is the ultimate denial of intimacy, resulting in 'a guilty lie' and his own 'pathetic use of sex to obliterate the conscience' that would have led to the 'forgiveness' both he and Stella now crave. Recognizing the 'irrevocable impossibility' of achieving any intimacy other than the 'kindness' proffered by the Doctor, Blanche achieves her heroism, however, in the knowledge that she is cut off forever from the mutual intimacy with another human being that her creator values above all else.

John Roderick, in a 1977 essay, writes in response to those spectators and critics who look upon *Streetcar* as tragic, but then find themselves faced with a conundrum: the difficulty of deciding whether their sympathies lie with Stanley or Blanche as hero(ine). Roderick answers by saying such indecision might not signal a dramaturgical flaw. In fact, it would not be unusual for audiences simultaneously to admire and upbraid a character who appears in a mixed mode of 'brilliant tragicomedy,' akin to the 'problem plays' of Shakespeare's late period. Polarities and 'irreconcilables' will abound throughout a work like *Streetcar*, Williams's 'inclusion of the comic with the tragic' being only one of them:

■ But Williams's comic reversals are far too systematic and numerous to be relegated solely to the function of release. The comic elements play their role in aggressive self-preservation just as the tragic possibilities invite the antithetical notion of self-destruction.[33] □

To support this contention, Roderick approaches the play from three angles: as a work that exists on a social as well as a psychological level; as a work in which Stanley and Blanche each display both Dionysian and Apollonian characteristics; and as a work whose thematic allows both characters to be read as morally victorious to a certain degree.

In the first instance, reading the action of *Streetcar* on a social level renders Blanche the heroine, a Chekhovian person of sensibility and last vestige of an old order with all its culture and beauty not just dying out but actually being destroyed at the hands of Stanley, who is responsible for bringing an entire class to its knees. The play, however, demands equally to be read on a psychological level, in which case Stanley would be the hero, warding off a sexually promiscuous intruder who threatens his 'normal,' healthy marriage—whose positive nature is indicated by the raucous yet joyous sexuality of Eunice and Steve in the subplot. As a 'profanation of Stanley's sacred, if crude, marriage,'[34] Roderick sees Blanche as sharing in the 'blame' for her rape by Stanley, whose domain she has threatened.

A similar doubleness in audience response results when the play is considered along the Dionysian/Apollonian dyad. Initially, Stanley is the play's Dionysus, flaunting his procreative power, while Blanche, disdaining her sister's marriage, assumes the mask of the Apollonian. But Roderick regards her attempt at control 'false' and 'tainted,' since it represses expression of her truer emotions. Stanley, however, is also Apollonian in trying to uphold his authority by discrediting Blanche, the Dionysian 'disrupter.' So once again ambiguity prevails. As a foil to the Blanche–Stanley conflict, the Blanche–Mitch relationship functions contrapuntally—and Roderick would say comically—as part of Williams's strategy to discredit Stanley. Mitch in physique and affectations might appear ludicrous and obtuse next to Stanley, yet Stanley's own tirades oftentimes come across as comic. Both Mitch and Stanley, however, will serve as agents of Blanche's destruction, as she earlier had of Allan's.

Roderick's third angle of attack is grounded in the audience's moral response to Williams's dual protagonists. Blanche must enter on a purgatorial journey for her part in Allan's death, as evident in incessant baths to remove guilt; yet she suffers as well from witnessing so many deaths at Belle Reve, which she tried to escape through desire. Williams is sympathetic toward her, not only because of the aesthetic values attached to her class, but also because he understands the necessity of her flight into an imaginative ideal, given the fragility of her hold on reality. And so, though she may be guilty of indiscretions, she 'has earned' her Madonna-like costume. Her elevation is underscored by the pealing of cathedral bells, by the courtesy of the poker-playing buddies standing as she exits, and by her own elevated language. Likewise, Stanley as a 'vital' force of life has secured his own home and future within a community of likeminded participants. Yet Williams takes care not to make either moment too saccharine, tainting Blanche's exit with Stanley and Mitch's 'intrusive violence' and what it augurs in the asylum. As final evidence of Williams's tragicomic vision, Stella's absorption in the child and passivity toward Stanley's advances situate their continued union 'a long way from the best of all possible worlds.' Given the centrality of women characters in Williams's work, attention to them figures prominently in critical analyses. Some scholars, however, ground their approaches more substantively in theorizing about gender and sexuality, as will be seen in the next chapter on feminist studies of the playwright.

CHAPTER SIX

Feminist Perspectives

THE WOMAN'S PLACE/SPACE: JACQUELINE O'CONNOR, ANDREA DWORKIN, AND PHILIP KOLIN

Much of the first two decades of serious academic criticism about Williams was dominated by discussion of his enormous understanding in drawing women characters and his unusual sympathy for their predicament. In 1997, in a useful overview of those studies, Jacqueline O'Connor took this criticism to task for its tendency to conflate characters with one another and thus reduce salient differences and complexities by categorizing them as variations on the Southern gentlewoman, whose desire to perpetuate the values of a genteel aristocratic past results in sexual frustration and maladjustment evidenced in promiscuity, hysteria, and even insanity.[1] Even given the centrality of women in his works, this is not to say that Williams would ever have thought of himself as a (proto-) feminist—just as the artist Degas, concentrating on the female figure of young women in the ballet or older women in the bath would not have either. At the same time, however, feminist critics can find Williams deconstructing categories of masculine and feminine identity, subverting patriarchal discourse, normalizing transgressive behavior, and otherwise critiquing the oppression, powerlessness, economic dependency, and sexual objectification of women.

Although O'Connor ranges widely in her consideration of Williams's women, beginning with Lucretia Collins from *Portrait of a Madonna* (her sensitive treatment of this forerunner of *Streetcar* is as thorough as anyone's), she gives special prominence to Blanche, whose 'mental decline and fall are dramatized most completely.'[2] To situate her argument as well as differentiate it from others, O'Connor provides overviews of two bodies of literature: modern discourses on madness (by theorists such as R. D. Laing and Michel Foucault); and recent treatises about hysteria in women (by such writers as Elaine Showalter and Phyllis Chesler). O'Connor's own approach will look at female dementia from essentially two angles: as a societal construct of a brutalizing society that confirms its own sanity by designating the Other as mad; and, most especially, as a patriarchal response to rein in what it sees as a disruption of the social order by committing the madwomen in its midst to asylums. What is transgressive must be silenced. That transgression may reside simply in the very presence of the mad among us, or it may be bodied forth in actions that societal mores deem abnormal and have difficulty accommodating. According to O'Connor, Williams demonstrates how:

> ■ society, threatened by madness, reacts by suppressing behavior that appears menacing; his plays suggest that individual freedom and originality are sacrificed to maintain the community's illusions about its normalcy. ... Williams's dramas distinctively portray his mad characters with a combination of brutal honesty and tenderness. Perhaps more than any other modern playwright, he creates these characters with sympathy. ... Although their sensibilities may be finer, and more highly developed, they are deeply troubled by their emotional problems and fare worse than their coarser counterparts.[3] □

No matter the source of the perceived transgression, the largely male-dominated society does the censoring and exorcising, something particularly easy to accomplish when the woman is dependent upon the man, either economically for sustenance or emotionally for satisfaction of desire. In the instance of *Streetcar*, if Stanley represents what is sane, then that sane is brutish, and his rape of Blanche foreshadows and parallels what will happen to her when she is institutionalized.

O'Connor is particularly astute about the way that the visual picture Williams creates intensifies his thematics. The stage space that Blanche can safely occupy becomes ever more constricted. When she enters, she has no place she owns—Belle Reve having been lost—or can call her own; the trunk holding all her possessions symbolizes her transitoriness. For privacy, she must retreat into the offstage bathroom, a confined space that foreshadows her room in the asylum. Since society has successfully repelled the threat her sexual promiscuity posed to its veneer of normality, she is an absent presence in the final stage image, having forfeited any claim on being believed because of her earlier embroidery of the facts. If, as O'Connor proposes, the rape is to be seen as 'punishment' for Blanche's violation of society's sexual standards as they apply to women, then her only escape is to go mad. The reduction in her physical space is accompanied, O'Connor notes, by a restriction in her language, which becomes progressively hesitant and fractured until she is reduced to silence, disciplined by the status quo she threatened to upset. For if language is seen as a tool of reason, then, of course, the deranged will falter. But if Blanche is made emblematic of the Other, the play's final impact comes from the audience's realization of her sameness to them: 'through her, we see how close the edge is, how quickly our sanity can be brought into question.'[4]

In her somewhat inaptly named treatise, *Intercourse* (1987)—which has led at least one library to shelve it with sex-instruction manuals—Andrea Dworkin sees Blanche's madness as a punishment for her failed attempt to find not only a physical place but an emotional space where sexual desire and love are not dichotomous. She reads Stanley's violation of Blanche as an act of 'revenge' against a woman whose rarified sensibilities he can neither understand nor ever attain. Stanley is mindless animal sensation, devoid of interior struggle and unconcerned with repercussions, and so at home in a world where wives like Stella and Eunice see roughhousing as a normal part of making love. Blanche, on the other hand, is imbued with an artistic sensibility that renders her different in a way prized by Williams: what Dworkin terms her 'stigma,' an indelible sign that marks her as vulnerable, is not only sexual desire but even more her ability to 'feel,' and yet 'the question is, how does a person with a sensibility survive being driven by the excesses and demands of that very sensibility into sex?'[5] Unlike Stanley, she has an ability to love, but that capacity has been in conflict with her sexual needs, leaving her ever more desperate and lonely and remorseful. She refuses to buy into the masculinist code of the woman at the mercy of the aggressive male uncaring of any higher imperatives of the mind and heart:

■ Blanche pays the price for having a human sexuality and a human consciousness. She has been raped; she knows it. There is nothing in the text of the play, despite the way it is sometimes staged, to suggest that she wanted it all along. In fact, there is a pronounced and emotionally vivid history of her wanting its opposite—a sexuality of tenderness and sensitivity.[6] □

Her punishment for wanting what a world ruled by men like Stanley fails to acknowledge, sex infused with kindness, is madness. And Stella, in refusing to admit the truth of Blanche's rape, is complicit, so that the male agenda of untrammeled sexuality devoid of deep feeling can reign.

Philip Kolin, in a 1993 essay, also focuses on how the nature of love as embodied in the female is qualitatively different from that expressed by the male, as Dworkin had suggested, is true of Blanche's insistence that 'tenderness' be a component of sex. Starting from the premise that (largely) male critical strategies have marginalized Eunice by seeing the comic Hubbell subplot of fight/separate/make up as a parodic reflection of the Kowalskis' tense relationship, Kolin re-centers Eunice's role as a 'focal point' for embodying Williams's thematic motifs of 'tenderness of heart, solicitude for others, and a sense of community.'[7] To accomplish this, he considers Eunice not in her connection to Stella but, rather, as she is played off against Blanche who, unlike the upstairs neighbor, is unable to achieve sexual fulfillment—a point Kolin can make only by reading Eunice and Steve's lusty reconciliations after ferocious arguments as more positively satisfying for Eunice than most critics have.

Kolin, like O'Connor, makes trenchant observations about the spatial dynamics of Williams's set description. If Stanley commandeers the domestic space of the Kowalski flat for largely masculine pursuits, he would like to relegate the women whom he wants to be submissive to the 'upstairs.' Yet that upstairs space, Kolin argues, should be seen as emblematic of hearth and home. It assumes the aura of a 'sanctuary' or safe house, a 'benevolent location' over which Eunice rules as a well-nigh god-like protector—unlike the bedroom downstairs where women are open to victimization. Eunice thus becomes a maternal caregiver, a provider of sustenance, and a proponent of female sisterhood/friendship (Kolin alludes to Shakespeare's romantic comedies, among other literary antecedents), which stands in sharp contrast to the boisterous one-upmanship of the male at play. Not only is Eunice especially hospitable to Blanche upon her arrival, but she serves as a kind lady-in-waiting at her leave-taking, in contrast to the Matron who is 'an anti-Eunice, a masculinized woman.'[8] Rather than viewing Eunice as a party to Blanche's final expulsion through the advice she gives to Stella, Kolin says she is 'appalled' by it and can be forgiven for recognizing the pragmatics of survival:

■ Whether all feminists agree with her or not, we see the compassion, the counsel, and the caring Eunice offers her friend, a new mother who needs reassurance to go on with her life with Stanley. Ironically, Eunice represents the Realpolitik of the (male-dominated) nuclear family and expresses what's needed ('Don't look') to survive and move forward in this particular moral economy.[9] □

As a counter to her trivialization by other male critics, Kolin hopes to recuperate Eunice and elevate her to her rightful place as an embodiment of the feminine qualities that Williams offers as essential counterweights to the brutality of a patriarchal society.

TEXTUAL BODIES: SUSAN BORDO AND ANCA VLASOPOLOS

Traditional feminist criticism of classic American films explores what has come to be called the 'male gaze' and how it objectifies the women up on the screen. In *The Male Body* (2002), Bordo turns her attention to the 'female gaze,' examining why, other than for reasons of the sheer beauty of Brando's body on stage and perhaps especially on film, women are fatally attracted to Stanley. Not that they don't know better, for they understand, particularly at the end, that despite his 'sexual magnetism' Stella deservedly must desert him. Calling *Streetcar* a 'psychosexual portrait' of why male brutality does not immediately send woman audience members fleeing but might actually increase their compulsive attraction, Bordo concludes that it is not Stanley's viciousness which excites them but rather 'the intensity of his passion':

> ■ The rape scene is Stanley at his least sexually appealing, because it reveals how compassionless and cruel he really is. The Stanley whom women thrilled to was not the man who selfishly shattered other people's bodies and dreams, but the man whose sexual vitality [is] unhobbled.[10] □

Bordo sees Blanche as a woman whose complete history (in the words of the original film trailer) 'was written by men.'[11] Yet Stanley, too, is vulnerable and insecure: dependent on Stella, almost as a child is attached to its mother; and exhausted by the false bravado demanded of men if they are to fulfill society's cartoonlike expectations. Coexisting, therefore, with the feminist import of the play, is a perhaps cynical cautionary critique of 'macho and its discontents.'[12]

What receives just fleeting mention by Bordo—Blanche as a text that men have written—is given full-blown treatment in a 1986 essay by Anca Vlasopolos, probably the most significant feminist voice on Williams's *Streetcar*, who argues that Stanley's discourse of patriarchy challenges Blanche's interpretive authority. Vlasopolos's starting point is that a generic approach to Williams's drama as a 'problem play' that attempts to 'domesticate' the violent action does not adequately account for the audience's response to its characters. Blanche embodies not only delicate sensibility but disordered sexuality as well, and so audiences find themselves, however uncomfortably, implicated in the violence against her and siding with her destroyer. Vlasopolos's goal is to provide a more satisfactory explanation for the audience's 'pragmatic shrug' at Blanche's final 'gender-determined' displacement from Stanley's domain.

The audience response 'oscillat[es]' as they embrace either Blanche's or Stanley's interpretation of people and events, while the play's aural and visual stylistic techniques problematize how they understand the competing narratives the two characters compose as each attempts to write a definitive history. As the play opens, Blanche, displaced from Belle Reve, short on financial and emotional resources, and ill-at-ease socially in the unrefined class system of the Quarter, finds herself in a weaker position than Stanley, whose pure physicality and violent treatment of objects precious to her prefigures the climactic rape. Yet on the level of verbal discourse, Blanche appears to have the upper hand: Stanley is vulgar and crude, mired in present fact, whereas she is genteel and poetic, harnessed to the past. Her attempts to impose her reading of reality, including a history predating Stanley, are met with his reading of her history as 'criminal' in its flaunting of sexual mores. She, in turn, counters his accusations with a reading of him as apelike, a threat to culture and civilization's advance. Both are vying for the support of the onstage interpretive community, particularly Stella and Mitch, whose acquiescence to their interpretation of history is needed if they hope to prevail. Although Stanley sees himself as vulnerable to being supplanted by Blanche in their eyes, what he can fall back upon is the language of patriarchy to 'inscribe' her future:

> ■ Blanche's fall from authority, her subjection, is masterfully captured by Williams in her being turned over to the supreme authority in charge of language, in charge of interpreting the past and predicting the future in the twentieth century: psychiatry, the scientific judgment of the soundness of the soul.[13] □

Stanley's rape of Blanche is a private act, 'his ultimate reduction of her to the whore of his history who provokes and enjoys yet another encounter.'[14] Blanche's 'expulsion' to the asylum—ironically providing the home she has been seeking throughout her wandering—is, on the other hand, a public punishment, making her the mythic sacrificial victim. Her reading of history is erased as her words of truth are discredited, termed a lie by Stella and Eunice who pragmatically value the status quo with Stanley; any intimation of rape must be erased so his inscription as 'normal' and unthreatening to the 'social fabric' of this patriarchally ruled community can be perpetuated. Moreover, the private violation of the rape is figured forth in the publicly sanctioned attack by the Matron. Although the theatre audience, unlike the one onstage, does not doubt the truth of Blanche's rape narrative, they remain implicated in the historiography of violence insofar as they consider Blanche's exile from society 'inevitable.' Thus Williams makes his point that no one is 'safe as long as the measure of insanity depends on the powerlessness of the individual.'[15]

Vlasopolos is, like O'Connor and Kolin, particularly insightful about how Williams's visual system in *Streetcar* undergirds her notion of conflicting narratives. The Kowalski flat is divided between the public, masculine space that is the scene of the poker game and the private inner space of the bedroom that Blanche artfully tries to feminize and make into an environment protective of her fragility. Yet even before first Stanley and later the Matron invade that space, the old

tattered gown she pulls from the trunk indicates the hopelessness of
her situation. In a patriarchal world that always judges female sexual
desire as somehow transgressive, Stanley and his story will always
trump Blanche and her story.

IS THERE A MISOGYNIST IN THE HOUSE? SANDRA GILBERT AND SUSAN GUBAR, KATHLEEN LANT, JOHN KUNDERT-GIBBS, AND GULSHAN RAI KATARIA

In the first volume of their epoch-making study, *No Man's Land: The
Place of the Woman Writer in the Twentieth Century* (1988), Sandra Gilbert
and Susan Gubar consider *Streetcar* within the context of the domestic
scene just before and after World War II. Whereas the Depression years
served to undermine the economic stability of men, questioning their
ability to provide for their families, the war years placed them in actual
physical peril. While soldiers away at war tended to objectify women
as pin-ups, the women left at home needed to fulfill many of what
were once men's roles. Although by the 1950s the ideal of domesticity
reached its heyday, it was only in the home that men ceded authority
to women, since increasing numbers remained in the workforce. Yet on
the sexual front, men desired women to be 'obediently serviceable' and
compliant. Into this world comes the wife batterer Stanley. At first, Gilbert and Gubar associate Williams with other misogynist writers who, in
their 'new campaign against women ... reconstitute the penis as a pistol
with which to shoot women into submission.'[16] They eventually, however, back off from that position, critiquing Stanley's stud-like actions
and even his voluptuousness with Stella at the play's end. At the same
time, they do not feel Williams exonerates Blanche for her retreat into
a 'fantasy world,' judging it for being as destructive as Stanley's 'sexual
violence' and presenting her rape as a justifiable punishment:

> ■ Because she has seduced and betrayed, used and abused men whose
> own marginality in the heterosexual world made them especially vulner-
> able to her fakery—sensitive men, students, and most especially her
> homosexual husband—she has had a 'date ... from the beginning' with
> the masculinist Stanley, who represents in his brutishness the phallic
> origin of the male species.[17] □

Because Blanche, however, as the sexually desiring female ultimately
suffers 'obliteration' in madness, Gilbert and Gubar conclude that Williams
reserves his harshest critique for 'compulsory heterosexuality' as normative
in a society that reads gender and sexuality through a distorting lens.

In a 1991 essay, Kathleen Lant responds directly to Gilbert and Gubar, arguing that reading *Streetcar* largely within a 'feminist context' means they ignore the hostility toward women that Williams has imbedded in his play. Accusing Williams of a double standard, she sees him as applauding, even reveling in, Stanley's extraordinary sexuality, the very same thing for which the playwright not only condemns Blanche but punishes her by rape, since apparently only for a male can sexuality be 'pure' rather than 'debased.' Even though Stanley destroys Blanche, confirming her anonymity in a masculine world, he yet reigns ascendant at play's end because she exists literally and metaphorically as 'a repository for all the mistaken notions our culture harbors about rape.'[18] Williams has, in short, made Blanche the embodiment of all the predictable stereotypes—including the past sexual history, the flirtatious games, the flaunting of desire, the virtual prostitution of herself—that render the victim guilty for causing the crime.

From Lant's perspective, the roots of *Streetcar's* misogyny run even deeper; found in the premise that 'male privilege' is not to be challenged. Although Williams is not unaware that society is sexist and that women are dependent and vulnerable, he adopts society's prejudices by characterizing Stella's relationship with Stanley, in spite of its being abusive and degrading, as 'life-giving.' She willfully blinds herself to the reality of her situation to ensure her security. Blanche, however, implicitly challenging the institution of marriage and man's supposedly unquestioned power within it, thinks herself 'too noble' to acquiesce and so has no future but 'maddened hysteria.' Moreover, Blanche incurs guilt in Williams's eyes for 'abusing and using "sensitive men"'[19] seen from his 'sexist attitude,' Blanche neglects her duty to place the man first:

> ■ He defines her in sexual terms (since she is no longer a virgin, she must be a degenerating whore), and he condemns her for failing to provide the self-sacrificing, womanly support her husband, Allan, needed. Williams's unacknowledged, unconscious misogyny weakens his development of Blanche as a strong, exciting character, and Blanche is damned no matter how she behaves.[20] □

John Kundert-Gibbs, in a 1998 essay, uncovers a similar 'subtle' misogyny in *Cat on a Hot Tin Roof*, locating it in the castrating female and the woman denied fulfillment of her maternal instincts. He situates Maggie among those women characters whose 'aggressive' pursuit of sexual satisfaction and attempt to cast herself as the desiring subject are aptitudes ordinarily assigned as appropriate for the male rather than the female. This assumption of masculine strength and power, seen in Maggie's assertive language and avarice for property as well as her need to 'fetishize herself' in a 'semipornographic' manner so that she might once again be sexually attractive to her husband, has the unwanted effect of castrating Brick and turning him into a 'feminized' object. (Given Williams's obviously admiring physical descriptions of Brick, Maggie might even be a surrogate expressing the playwright's own attraction.) That so much of *Cat* seems to be conveyed through a predominantly feminine perspective 'indicates that, at a deep level, the traditional link between masculinity and sexual desire and agency has been flipped on its head.'[21]

The triad of Maggie/Brick/Skipper, in which she acts in a destructive manner toward Skipper that alienates her even further from Brick and results in his withholding sex from her, makes her 'the commodified link in the misogynist exchange of women between men.'[22] The only thing that would validate Maggie's position as woman is fulfillment of her maternal instinct, which provides the strongest evidence of the misogynistic attitude at the heart of Williams's play. Maggie however, can only achieve motherhood by forcefully reducing Brick to a less-than-willing progenitor, by denying him both his liquor and his crutch, which in Kundert-Gibbs's view confirms the play as a statement about 'the impossibility of a female subject':

■ Maggie and Brick switch denoted genders, Maggie becoming the man in the relationship while Brick becomes the woman returning at last to the complementarity of heterosexuality. Though this may seem an empowering move on Maggie's part, and in fact might feasibly result in a child by them, the fact that she must essentially become the stereotype of a man (with the associated violence) reduces this to a pyrrhic victory.[23] □

In a 1982 essay, Gulshan Rai Kataria poses a direct challenge to such a misogynist reading of Maggie as a castrating female, employing as her framework Toni Wolff's redaction of C. G. Jung's discussion of the Archetypal Feminine. Whereas Jung categorized his types on the basis of personages from myth, Wolff bases hers on the personal function the woman serves; and so the Helen (or 'companion woman') of Jung becomes the Hetaira in Kataria's system, the priestess who finds her 'psychic fulfillment' in love for a man that will complete him, regardless of whether he fathers a child through their union. Yet Maggie faces a detached and alienated husband who appears neither to love her nor to want to be loved by her, which only makes her more sexually passionate; this, in turn, requires that she use all her feminine wiles to rearouse Brick's sexual desire. He tries to write her out of existence, but she persists until she prevails, which justifies those qualities that might otherwise be viewed negatively—her aggressiveness and assertion of control, her guilefulness and vindictiveness—that turn her into a 'dangerous Hetaira' who shares much of Big Daddy's zest and energy as she fights to achieve her ends.

Through her relations with Skipper, who appeared to threaten her marriage, Maggie was intent on jarring Brick out of his adolescent belief in some 'idyllic romance,' but she misjudged the traumatic effect revealing Skipper's impotence would have on her husband. Given Brick's own unconscious anxiety over being homosexual, she ended up 'trifl[ing] with the shadow side of his personality'[24] and increasing his performance anxiety. Everything she does to break through his mask of composure is intended, however, not primarily to gain a hold on Big Daddy's property but rather to defend Brick's dignity and self-esteem:

> ■ She wants to extricate him from the whirlpool of detachment and withdrawal. She wants him not to give in to defeat and passivity. Rather, she wants him to fight his way out of the labyrinth of despair and non-involvement. She enthuses and provokes him to grapple with life.[25] □

An apt gloss on Kataria's reading of Maggie's determined and persevering love would be Shakespeare's Sonnet 116 ('Love is not love which alters when it alteration finds'). Essentially altruistic, Maggie makes a conscious choice to become less so that Brick might be 'rejuvenate[d]' and become more. Williams thus presents a Maggie who is empowered, able to fulfill herself as a woman, but in a manner that challenges any simplistic preconception. His is a perspective, then, that resists easy compartmentalization, whether it be by feminist critics or others, of the appropriate nature of female sexual desire. The focus in the next chapter turns to same-sex relationships and the eroticized male body as both desiring subject and object as we examine queer theoretical approaches that reveal Williams to be even more subversive than the feminist studies would indicate.

CHAPTER SEVEN

Queer Theory as Lens

WRITING FROM/ABOUT THE CLOSET: JOHN CLUM, DAVID SAVRAN, AND MICHAEL PALLER

Tennessee Williams famously outed himself, publicly admitting to cruising 'the waterfront,' during a television interview with David Frost in 1970, and wrote even more openly about being gay in his *Memoirs* published a half-dozen years later. But long before that, his homosexuality was widely known, as he did nothing to keep it particularly secret among acquaintances, fellow workers, and those who wrote about theatre. Among commentators, it has become a critical commonplace that he was able to be more candid about sexuality in his fiction and poetry meant for private consumption, something he was prevented from doing in his dramas intended for the commercial theatre during the moderately repressive era of the 1940s and 1950s. In the journals that he kept, mostly during the years between 1936 and 1958 (and now available with commendably thorough annotations by Margaret Thornton), it is possible to trace details that fill in both the biographical and creative picture of his development as gay man and artist: from his first treatment of homosexuality as subject in a one-act play 'Escape'—alternatively titled 'Summer at the Lake'—in 1937; through his first consummated homosexual affair in 1939 with a man named Doug in Laguna Beach; to his reading of William Baxter's 1951 novel, *Look Down in Mercy*, that appears to have inspired the Brick–Skipper relationship in *Cat*.[1] Even more to the point, as Anne Fleche has written in a philosophic inquiry into the nature of Williams's stylistic technique, the notion of the stage as a 'queer space' must be added to that of the stage as a 'subjective/mental' and 'feminine space.' Performing his own sexuality would necessitate escaping the closet, which the theatre resembles since it includes what cannot be seen because it lays hidden outside its boundary: 'Williams was experimenting with permeable fourth walls, translucent scenery, and the theatre's obsessive need to establish and transgress borders. Themes of sexuality, madness and memory interweave in his oeuvre, questioning, over and over, how to get out of the inside... .'[2] Theatre, then, because from Fleche's point of view it visually stages both what is 'out' (openly revealed) and what is 'in' (secret and closeted) offers a peculiarly apt medium to the gay author.

When John Clum, in 1989, surveys Williams's work, beginning with the early short stories through the later plays, from the vantage point of their treatment of gay characters, he finds in them a 'constant attitude toward homosexual acts' as 'perversions of longing.'[3] He attributes this to Williams's attempt to dissociate his own homosexual nature, which he admitted in private, from any public acknowledgement until his increasingly autobiographical and didactic dramas late in his career. This tension within the playwright himself resulted either in an indirect handling of homosexuality of a coarse and brutal nature that could be read as 'subversive' yet 'sympathetic,' or, more often, in a 'judgmental' decidedly 'homophobic discourse.' Clum singles out *Streetcar* as 'the quintessential closeted gay play, and Blanche DuBois [as] in many ways the quintessential gay character in American closet drama,'[4] since she must resort to performativity as a protection in a world that countenances only what it considers as normal and nontransgressive expressions of sexual desire and activity—much the same way that gay men are restricted and oppressed. Although Clum refrains from calling Blanche a man in drag as some less judicious critics have, he does speak of her as a 'transvestite replacement' and a 'crypto-gay character'[5] because of the way that some of her own dialogue and that about her ('turn the trick,' 'straight,' 'queen') might be coded as homosexual. Clum sees Allan Grey as driven to self-destruction after exposure of his hidden sexuality, and the stud Stanley as feeling excitement at being turned into the object of desire that makes him 'dangerously attractive to the gay men'[6] in the audience.

Clum's considerably more extensive treatment of *Cat* finds Williams at best evasive and at worst homophobic. Granted, the play's bedroom setting was the locale for the love of Straw and Ochello, whose patrimony, certainly monetary and perhaps even sexual, has descended down through Big Daddy; but the tender nature of that homosexual relationship is, Clum repeatedly and somewhat mistakenly protests, mentioned only in a stage direction but left otherwise unspoken in the play's dialogue, evidencing Williams's 'inability' or 'disinclination' to privilege it openly:

■ The bed ... represents an unstated ideal relationship that seems unattainable for the heterosexual marriages in Williams' play. In positing this ideal, the play is subversive for its time, yet the love of Straw and Ochello never seems a possibility for homosexuals either. It is more of a figure of speech ..., since the only positive words used to describe the relationship are silent hints in the stage directions. The only operative terminology for homosexuals the play allows is Brick's homophobic discourse.[7] □

Brick, whose idealized friendship with Skipper has thwarted his ability to enter into any truly mature relationship, is, like Allan before him, obsessed with being labeled unmanly, let alone gay and so 'fear[s] exposure.' Thus, when Big Daddy offers understanding and reassurance Brick can only echo conventional society's 'heterosexist ranting,' thereby revealing that 'Homophobia is at the core of his sexual and emotional malaise.'[8] Clum's inclusion of Big Daddy (along with Brick) among those who cannot countenance same-sex love is not borne out by the text itself, where Big Daddy does openly credit seeing that love as the source of his tolerance. Williams's 'positive discourse' about gay sexuality is, therefore, not as 'unrealized' as Clum would have his readers believe. Clum does, nevertheless, credit Williams with an 'uncanny ability' to push the boundaries of what a Broadway audience found acceptable without resorting to gay stereotypes, even if the play does end with a 'compromised version' of marriage and parenthood that perpetuates a heterosexual economy.

David Savran, in *Communists, Cowboys, and Queers* (1992), devotes just enough space to *Streetcar* to argue against those like Clum who might consider Blanche as a man in drag, since this 'makes nonsense of Blanche's panic at discovering the homosexuality of her late husband, of Stanley's brutally normative masculinity and of the carefully gendered specificity of sexual violence.'[9] Situating Williams in the context of the Cold War period that demanded secrecy rather than openness, Savran judges him—despite the dearth of openly gay characters in the major plays—as decidedly the 'most progressive and radical in his figuration of homosexuality,' offering an 'astonishingly bold rejoinder'[10] to homophobic discourse and social practice. In an age where spying and surveillance were key determinants, and most popular playwrights appropriated the traditional language of shame and remorse where homosexual acts were concerned, Williams is almost alone in writing positively of the homosexual desire that—as the Kinsey report had validated—already always inheres inside the male. Granted, however:

■ Williams wrote (to borrow [Thomas] Yingling's phrase) 'under a number of screens and covers' that would allow him to represent 'his homosexuality in other guises: as a valorization of eroticism generally and extramarital desire, in particular; as an endorsement of transgressive liaisons that cut across lines of social class, ethnicity, and race, and violate midcentury social prescriptions; and as a deep sympathy for the outsider and the disenfranchised, for 'the fugitive kind.'[11] □

Cat's set design puts onstage the closet space almost always relegated to an offstage position, a room that is simultaneously 'private erotic chamber' but also one whose privacy is 'monitored' and thus 'violated.'[12] Inhabiting this room are three 'fragmented' characters: Big Daddy, both macho and 'carrier' of gay sensibility, is a mix of desire and disgust, of misogyny and antihomophobia; Brick, alcoholic yet firm of body, broken yet godlike, is both the fetishized and castrated male; Maggie is greedy and determined, yet altruistic and honest. Her liaison with Skipper, while ritually castrating him, reawakens her erotic attractiveness to the previously nondesiring husband, for now 'Brick fetishizes her body as the symbolic repository of Skipper's own sexuality whose phallus becomes reinscribed in her body and so allows her to be produced as an object of desire.'[13] Her lie that she is carrying Brick's child does not, according to Savran, privilege heterosexuality; rather, since even the dead Skipper will always remain a part of the triangle, it perpetuates the homosexual economy of the Straw and Ochello/Pollitt plantation: even if the lie is made true, Brick's sexual identity will not be unambiguously resolved. Yet despite such oblique discourse and displacement of the male homosexual subject, as demanded by the commercial theatre of his day, Williams, by absenting Skipper and drawing attention to that absence, actually achieved his distinctive voice.

In 'A Room Which Isn't Empty ... ' (2003), Michael Paller repudiates even more strongly than had Savran the inherent homophobia whose disturbing presence Clum believed he detected in Williams's major dramas. Arguing for the centrality within *Streetcar* of the absent Allan Grey—on the surface 'rendered invisible' and seemingly 'marginal to the action'[14]—for what happens to Blanche, Paller traces his erasure back to the first-night reviewers, that was later reinforced by queer critics during the 1990s. From Paller's perspective, Williams's use of the stereotypical description of Allan as the effeminate and effete poet was a strategy the playwright felt compelled to adopt in order to make Allan's homosexuality clear to the audience given the time the drama was written, and therefore should not be taken as evidence of homophobia or self-denigration. Furthermore, Allan commits suicide not out of any shame or 'panic and fear' of his own (homo)sexual nature that society rejects as abnormal; instead, what the play charts is Blanche's 'shame and guilt'[15] over her 'deliberate cruelty' that drove Allan to suicide. Rather than being silenced, Allan functions as an avenging fury who keeps the past from becoming lost; he is heard commandingly through the Varsouviana polka and gunshot that haunt Blanche, with her guilt resolved in the punishment of madness. Along with ignoring Allan's pivotal position, the early critics, according to Paller, also attempted to 'normalize' heterosexual actions by romanticizing and exculpating Blanche from responsibility, as well as (won over by Brando's performance) by setting Stanley up as an object for identification.

Paller, instead, throws into question whether there is any 'affirming view of straightness in the play,' arguing that it might better be seen as an example of 'heterophobic discourse'[16] rather than of homophobia. In approaching *Cat*, Paller links Williams's own dilemma as a gay dramatist writing for a closeted Broadway theatre in the 1950s to the struggle of Brick, who is paralyzed by fear of exposure and by the need to disavow or keep secret what the straight world would deem justification for ostracizing him. The guilt and self-loathing, then, are not over the fear of possibly being homosexual, but over the 'shame at denying it,'[17] when some part of him might actually have wanted to tell the truth; this leads to the moral 'paralysis' that Williams delineates as central to Brick's problem. On the vexed question of whether Brick is gay or not, Paller concludes that Brick's 'regard for Skipper was not just that of the average heterosexual male;' he 'did indeed love Skipper, but could not admit it to him or to himself.'[18] The fear resides, therefore, in naming himself as gay or being perceived by a merciless world as gay. Finally, Paller—writing from the inside as a theatre practitioner rather than just from the outside as a scholar/critic—is acutely aware of the actor's need to arrive at choices on the basis of the text before he can fully inhabit the character, to understand that opposing desires create inner conflict. So, rather than 'adopt Williams's own uncertainty' about his character's sexual nature:

■ the actor playing Brick may have to hold in his head two opposing objectives. ... The one would be to tell the truth about his feelings for Skipper (as he does when it comes to other subjects); and the other to protect the position he has attained in life. It is the clash of these two opposed desires that produces his paralysis.[19] □

In the case of *Streetcar*, Paller uses his understanding of the choices an actor/director must make to challenge the position of Clum and others that Blanche is a man in drag. Responding to Clum's notion that resorting to the theatricalization of experience makes the closet bearable, Paller argues that 'If [Blanche] is always acting, then she is never sincere. ... [but] simply a campy drag act' which would obfuscate any sense of 'coping with a desperate situation'[20] brought about by her cruel rejection of the gay Other.

THE GAY MALE GAZE: DEAN SHACKELFORD, ROGER GROSS, AND MARK WINCHELL

In a series of articles (1998–2001) that look at Williams's dramatic output from the one-act plays of the early 1940s through the major works of the mid-1950s, Dean Shackelford asserts that by means of the plays' 'stereotypes and symbols signifying a gay subtext, Williams encodes his own same-sex desire, as well as his voice as a gay subject.'[21] The dramatist, therefore, is not only 'outing' himself but also 'outing' the widespread existence of homosexuality within an American society that for too long denied and punished it as unnatural. After defining the 'closet' in the context of the theoretical writings of Eve Kosofsky Sedgwick and Judith Butler as a liminal physical and psychological space that holds in tension the inclinations to conceal and reveal, Shackelford maps out three avenues of inquiry into Streetcar: first, Allan Grey's 'destruction' by a 'repressive society'; second, Blanche DuBois's function as a projection of Williams's gay identity; and third, Stanley's role as the object of the gaze in undermining heteronormativity. Perhaps overstating the case as Paller also does, Shackelford calls Allan the 'central character' in the play, since it is his exposure by Blanche, through her pulling off from him the mask of heterosexuality, that causes his suicide and drives the subsequent action. It is true (as Paller points out as well), that the absent Allan is hardly silent, made present literally through the polka and gunshot that Blanche hears in her mind and that propel her to assuage her guilt, initially by seducing other young men to save them from homosexuality—something she failed to do for her young husband. By outing Allan, Shackelford argues that the once-genteel Blanche is herself forced into the closet to hide the fact that she is the promiscuous fallen woman. Since she is made 'Other' in this way, she becomes, in the critic's words, a 'proto-gay character' and, as such, a projection of Williams's own gay subjectivity, the dramatist's alter ego. Thus she is not only 'villain' but 'tragic heroine' as well.

This surrogate role becomes particularly clear when Blanche, by looking with desire at Stanley's physical body, does just what Williams and the gay members of the audience seek as well, but that the mores of the time tried to forbid. To turn the heterosexist Stanley into the primary object of the gay male gaze and fetishize his body is 'a subversive move that destabilizes traditional masculinity,'[22] one that potentially creates anxiety among straight males in the audience and may even lead to doubts about their own heterosexuality. Since his body has now been rendered attractive to gay men, Stanley must reassert his masculine power and prove to himself his own normativity by continued abuse of his wife Stella and by punishing Blanche through rape. Because, however, the aggressively sexual female is 'a counterpart of the gay other,' her rape parallels destructive acts against gays, making it the conventional American male response 'to the threat of otherness'[23] and a means to reestablish heterosexual hegemony.

When Shackelford turns to Cat on a Hot Tin Roof, he continues his consideration of Williams's deployment of the gay male gaze, with

Maggie's frequent references to the attractiveness of Brick's body creating the effect of eroticizing it for members of the audience— whether female or male, homosexual or heterosexual. After remarking that traditional feminist theories of the gaze (popularized by such film critics as Laura Mulvey) 'skirt the issue of male sexual objectification,'[24] Shackelford posits that Williams as a gay dramatist is projecting his own desire for Brick onto Maggie, so that her gaze becomes his own gaze and that of the gay audience. But—and this is Williams's most subversive move—not just of the gay audience but of the heterosexual male audience as well, who identify with Brick as 'the quintessential male ideal in American culture'[25] and are thus made to question their own secure sexual identity. It is unsettling for them to see that sex and gender categories are fluid, or that the heterosexual male might be attracted to the gay male, and vice versa. And this is where Shackelford's contextualizing of *Cat* within the sociohistorical framework of the 1950s comes into play. The period of the play's composition, which equated homosexuality with other un-American or treasonable activities, made Williams's treatment of homosexual desire, as potentially tender and loving, courageous, with his representation of the gay subjects, Skipper, Straw, and Ochello, as 'out' as the times would allow. But this was also a period that perpetuated an ideal image of the hypermasculine American man: good at sports, maybe heroically so; cool and detached and emotionally controlled; bonded by a camaraderie, often fused by alcohol, that they would hesitate even to refer to as homosocial, let alone admit to being possibly homoerotic; and quick to castigate as sissies or degenerate those who do not uphold the stereotypical image of manhood. So to have Brick, representative of 'the quintessential male ideal in American culture,' acknowledge that his male-to-male intimacy with Skipper may indeed have included sexual desires is a 'radical' move:

■ Not only does Williams call into question American views of masculinity and homosexuality, he hints strongly that heterosexual men may be attractive to gay men, that gay men may be both erotically appealing and masculine, and that masculinity / femininity, heterosexuality / homosexuality may merely be constructed norms—not realities.[26] □

When Shackelford discusses the stage space in *Cat*, he suggests that the bedroom which was the closet for Straw and Ochello is at the very center of Brick's lack of desire for and sexual problems with Maggie, his impotence linked to the gay-marriage bed. It is the 'compulsory heterosexuality' of America in the 1950s that oppresses the antihero Brick, and that Williams castigates in a play that stands out from all others of its time in its positive image of gay male love as enshrined in the 'pro-gay' Big Daddy's memory of Straw and Ochello and what their relationship taught him about tolerance for the varieties of love that the human heart can feel and the human body express. Although Shackelford denies finding any evidence that Straw or Ochello ever exploited or sexually abused Big Daddy, he does conclude that Big Daddy is 'bisexual.' Yet he resists, as other critics have not, regarding his cancer (a subject as 'taboo' as homosexuality was at the time) as in any way a punishment. Because of Big Daddy's position as surrogate son to Straw and Ochello, the inheritor of their patrimony both economic and ethical, Shackelford posits that Williams's play may provide 'the first representation of the gay family in American drama.'[27]

In 'The Pleasures of Brick ... ' (1997), Roger Gross develops further the notion of how the gay spectator responds to the desire enacted on stage, positing that it calls up a complicated mix of the hysteria and melancholia that *Cat* induces; as a consequence, his explanation of how the gay male gaze works is more deeply psychological than Shackelford's. The spectacle of the silk pajama-clad physique of Brick, who refuses to be the desiring subject and so remains passive and thus feminized, is always on display, eroticized by Maggie's gaze, and therefore made the object of the spectator's desire as well. Precisely because Brick refuses to reciprocate the desire focused upon him, the gay spectator experiences 'hysterical fantasies' over the 'impossible object,' which meld with the more generalized hysteria of a theatrical space already invaded by the grotesque 'no-neck monsters' and the thunderstorm raging outside. Gross claims that the impression Brick creates of an 'untouchable' makes him appear a death-like figure, so that 'his onstage lack of desire is treated as more scandalous than any imputation of past homosexuality.'[28] Brick's character traits, his remoteness and lack of interest in others, his sense of dejection and reduced self-esteem, render him the traditional melancholic. He yearns for the lost idyllic time with Skipper, an innocent state before women came on the scene that, for Gross and others, finds its nearest literary parallel in the relationship between Leontes and Polixenes when boys in Shakespeare's *Winter's Tale*. Herein Williams constructs the 'male homo-imaginary before awareness of difference in sexual orientation,'[29] created as an alternative to the Lacanian imaginary of the mother and child before the intrusion of the nay-saying father.

The bedroom stage setting, locus of Straw and Ochello's undeniably tender conjugal relationship, is designed to evoke the boys' adventure novels of Robert Louis Stevenson, which only adds to Brick's nostalgia for an 'irretrievable past' and contributes further to the melancholia and loss. Maggie, however, by questioning the innocence of the homoimaginary and making male bonding a thing of guilt, 'problematizes' such relationships and creates a crisis over male identity. In the eyes of the gay spectator, then, this not only makes Brick even more desirable, but casts a stigma upon Maggie as the agent of compulsory heterosexuality, thus engendering feelings of misogyny at woman's destruction of the male homoimaginary. Melancholia, Gross believes, thus takes on an erotic dimension for the gay spectator. The masterful way that Williams conceives and manipulates the overwhelming presence of Brick's body, Gross concludes, is able to contain:

■ the discrepancy between a feminized, hysteric desire toward Brick that subverts sexist and heterosexist norms, and a masculinized, melancholic impulse toward Brick that reinforces misogyny and the myth of the male homo-imaginary.[30] □

Elaborating further on notions broached by Shackelford, Mark Winchell, in his 1995 essay, examines *Cat*—which he calls 'scandalous,' 'subversive'—in the context of Leslie Fiedler's tracing of the pattern of ideal male friendship of the nonlustful, innocent variety in the American literary tradition, where homoeroticism, 'the love that dare not *know* its name'[31] is always lurking just below the surface as a reality that cannot be admitted. Although Winchell finds Williams finally 'ambivalent' about the exact nature of the relationship between Brick and Skipper, he offers several different perspectives on it. These range from Gooper and Mae's reading of Brick's 'arrested development' and sexual deviancy through Maggie and Big Daddy's tolerance, even normalizing, of the relationship in the face of widespread social opprobrium. Although male relationships have always had the potential of verging over into the homoerotic, Brick is particularly on the defensive, not only because of his unrealistic adolescent desire to remain innocent and his prejudice against any sexual activity that violates convention, but mostly because to 'be the *object* of lust raises questions of gender identity.'[32]

Winchell spends much of his time talking about Girardian triangulation, the triad of two men and a woman: the homophobic Skipper's attempted liaison with Maggie is evidence of his repressed lust for Brick; and Brick's acceding to Maggie's sexual demands at the end may be his way of 'vicariously' establishing a bond with the dead Skipper. So the play's ending is not necessarily one of 'heterosexual normalcy.' In fact, the explicitly homosexual relationship between Straw and Ochello, marked by their fidelity to one another as well as by their once providing a home for Big Daddy, evinces an ideal of home and family not found in the play's other relationships, thus supporting the notion that society must be open to the many forms in which love—unbounded by 'sexual orientation'—can evidence itself. As Shackelford intimates as well, the play's radical contribution may be that:

■ Straw and Ochello did not run away from home, or try to escape petticoat government, but lived totally within the confines of civilization. ... In [them],

Williams subverts the American myth of male companionship, not just by making its homoeroticism explicit but by domesticating it.[33] □

QUEERING THE AMERICAN SOUTH: GEORGES-MICHEL SAROTTE AND MICHAEL BIBLER

One of the very earliest critics to comment substantively on Williams's treatment of homosexuality in his plays is the French academic, Georges-Michel Sarotte, who approaches the works through psycho-biography in *Like a Brother, Like a Lover* (1978). He uncovers in the early life of the playwright the 'classic psychoanalytical case history,' along with hypothesizing, furthermore, that 'Williams never treats heterosexuality without embodying himself in the heroine.'[34] So, in a guarded way, the dramatist projects onto Blanche both his sensitive side and his sexual voraciousness, her luring of young men paralleling the playwright's cruising for lovers. And if Stanley is, from one perspective, a stand-in for the unaccepting father whom Williams 'hated,' he is also, in his muscular physical appeal, the 'Other' that Williams wished himself to be. When Sarotte returns to *Streetcar* again two decades later in a 1995 essay, he does so with awareness of the cultural pluralism of the postwar South, noting the multiethnicity of Stanley's working-class buddies; his friendship, however, does not extend to Blacks or other marginalized groups, such as artists and liberated women, let alone homosexuals. From this vantage point, the Kowalski flat in the Elysian Fields section of New Orleans becomes 'a microcosm of the U.S. in the 40s and 50s.'[35] Although Stanley, by marrying Stella, may have been trying to effect a 'social integration' of Southern aristocracy and Northern industrialism that would be cemented by their child's birth, he still must crush Blanche who, in the absence of Allan, represents 'difference' in all its many manifestations, sexual and otherwise. The Frenchman Sarotte, in fact, ingeniously reads the color coding at the end of *Streetcar* to find in it evidence for Williams's sociopolitical critique of a 'repressive' society:

■ In this last scene, Blanche (i.e., 'the white one') is dressed in red and blue, and she would like her dead body to be dropped into the blue sea. It is fitting that in *Streetcar* Blanche's colors should be white, red, and blue, the colors of the American flag.[36] □

In *Cat*, the four homosexuals with whom Williams identifies—Sarotte is virtually the only critic to give notice to the gay fraternity brother whom Brick reports was run off campus—are again absent, a sure sign of society's intolerance of gays. Since Skipper embodies 'Otherness,' he cannot be admitted into the 'theatrical space,' with the ghostly yet palpable presence of Straw and Ochello's love relegated mostly to stage directions. Although the connection is oftentimes drawn between Blanche's rejection of Allan and Brick's of Skipper, Sarotte considers Maggie as the chief death-bringer. This does not, however, remove responsibility from Brick, whom Sarotte sees as a terribly conflicted character: embodiment of America's idolization of attractive physique, wealth, education, and athletic prowess; part victim of a nostalgic adolescent ideal of friendship that he was afraid to leave behind for a mature understanding of love; and part 'prisoner of the image of virility imposed by society'[37] that does not countenance homosexuality or permit him to accept the right(ness) of men loving one another. In short, Brick is guilt-ridden and 'terrorized' at the very thought of 'transgression,' and *Cat*, like *Streetcar* before it, forms a 'plea' for acceptance rather than rejection of the feminine within the masculine, and of a less discriminatory and hypocritical and 'more androgynous Society.'[38]

In *Cotton's Queer Relations* (2009), Michael Bibler, from a New Historicist perspective, considers Tennessee Williams in the context of a larger, groundbreaking project about same-sex relationships in Southern settings as they appear in works by several twentieth-century American writers—with a Faulkner novel such as *Absalom! Absalom!* (1936) providing the closest counterpart to Williams's plays. Adopting Leo Bersani's term 'homo-ness' to describe these relationships, Bibler hopes to demonstrate that, for a writer like Williams, an accepting attitude toward homosexuality implies a humane and liberally progressive stance to other issues of social equality in race, class, and gender in the periods of the New Deal, World War II, and the Civil Rights Movement. Unlike vertical hierarchical relationships based on exerting power over the other, homosocial and homosexual relationships are more horizontal and egalitarian in nature; moreover, when the queer couple are White males (as they are in Williams), their intimacy can be tolerated within the paternalistic meta-plantation system because it appears to leave other systemic inequities unchallenged. Yet an author like Williams intends, and his viewers understand, the implicit criticism of racial prejudice and gender bias, and so these works, by exposing the dark underbelly of the meta-plantation, actually go toward 'destabilizing' it and hinting at an alternative social order.

When Bibler turns specifically to *Cat*, he remarks that the otherwise exalted homo-ness seen in a committed relationship of tenderness like Straw and Ochello's actually poses a threat to the plantation system, not only because it is not regenerative but because it depends for its continuance on the 'enduring oppression' of women and, in the 1950s when mechanization of farming was not yet complete, of Blacks. This means that Williams, 'through his sympathetic depictions of the play's Black characters and of Maggie,' will end up 'critiquing networks of oppression that protect and enable the homo-ness that he celebrates.'[39] Bibler makes several points about the relationship between Williams's queer couple: only the homophobic Brick, whose own repression and denial are coded as abhorrent, remembers it in an intolerant way; their love has assumed the status of myth because it is unseen and occurred in the past; and its positive characteristics underline the defects of all the other relationships in the play. Furthermore, the onstage bed that symbolizes and encapsulates it stands in contrast with the intrusion of the unsympathetic, prejudicial outside world, represented by the 'monstrosity' of the entertainment system with liquor cabinet. Since, however, it is the owning of property that is the main proof of male superiority on the meta-plantation, Brick could live and be accepted as homosexual in that liberated space, were it not for his own panic over how the outside world would judge him.

Focusing much less on details about Brick and Skipper than other queer theorists do, Bibler spends more time exploring Big Daddy and Maggie. He judges Big Daddy's tolerance of homosexuality 'inadequate'; zeroing in on the word 'overseer,' he reminds audiences that Big Daddy's position has depended upon exploitation of Black workers, even proposing that this (rather than any 'willingness to sleep with his gay employers'[40]) may be the 'cause' of his cancer and evidence of his own mendacity. It is precisely the social inequality upon which the system depends that Williams criticizes—and which leads to a kind of textual indeterminacy that the playwright, Bibler believes, can never quite avoid. Big Daddy makes it very clear that he wants to leave his patrimony to one of his 'kind,' to someone who is like him; and this legacy, as Bibler notes, involves more than simply the land:

> ■ The meta-plantation's pattern of patrilineal inheritance privileges the notion of sameness that also supports homo-ness between elite white men. Even though patrilineal inheritance depends on heterosexual relations and procreation (though not entirely, as evidenced by Big Daddy's adoption), this pattern of kinship is deeply joined with homosexuality. Indeed, if we look simply at the names involved, the legacy of homosexuality is quite explicit in the fact that one can't make Brick without Straw.[41] □

If Big Daddy's notorious elephant joke was intended to underscore a heterosexual union leading to a child, then its omission would indicate that love for a woman is somehow less intense than that of man for man. But that would preclude procreation, and so 'sexist logic,' whether one agrees with it or not, must govern the way that femininity is constructed within a masculine economy if the blood line is to be maintained.

Herein lies another of the inequities of the meta-plantation: women are dependent upon men for any kind of financial security, thus reducing their independence. Therefore, Maggie is forced to 'negotiate a limited deployment of her own sexuality,' constructing an identity which is 'fluid' and even 'androgynous' in her relationship with Skipper that is coded as 'symbolically homosexual.'[42] Her 'fantasy of pregnancy' underscores the power such fluidity makes available to her. In Brick's decision to sleep with Maggie, heterosexuality and homosexuality overlap, and the 'categories of gender and sexuality become permanently blurred,' leading to the sense that 'more equitable relations'[43] are possible. Bibler reads this as evidence of Williams's agenda in *Cat* to put forth an alternative social structure: one in which 'homo-ness' might liberate society from the White male hierarchies of paternalism and patriarchalism into a social organization more open and accepting of differences in race, class, and gender.

Although the queer and feminist theoretical approaches that have been surveyed in this chapter and the preceding one are only two of the many hermeneutic strategies that have found favor among contemporary critics, they have been the most consistently productive in analyzing Williams's works. Among its other distinctions (albeit a lesser one), *Streetcar* is virtually the only modern American play that has been subjected to a wide variety of other poststructuralist and deconstructive critical practices, and it is that phenomenon which provides the subject of the next chapter.

CHAPTER EIGHT

Contemporary Critical Theory and *Streetcar*

SIGNS AND READERS: KATHLEEN HULLEY AND JOHN BAK

In the same way that the academy was hesitant at first to accept dramatic texts as a legitimate subject for exegesis as literature, so, too, were scholars much slower in applying contemporary critical theory to drama than they had been to narrative fiction. In the particular case of Williams, Michael Paller has suggested that the playwright's distinctive emphasis on 'the behavior of individual humans' may itself have made his works more recalcitrant to heavily theoretical inquiry:

■ This dedication to human action, and his skill at portraying it, makes Williams's plays especially resistant to poststructuralist and postmodern criticism, more interested as it is in constructions and theories than in human beings behaving in concrete circumstances for specific reasons.[1] □

Generally speaking, feminist/gender studies and queer theory have been the most fruitful among recent approaches to drama, almost certainly having to do with its nature as performance. And this has been apparent in scholarly treatments of Williams's plays with their emphasis on sexualized/textualized bodies, as has been seen in the previous two chapters. Williams's decided belief in symbolism as foremost among the strategies in the playwright's arsenal—as, indeed, an essential element in the 'language' of drama—also implies that a semiotic approach based on how the reader/audience responds to the linguistic and visual signs the playwright has provided will be a particularly useful interpretive tool.

In a 1982 essay, Kathleen Hulley offers a succinct discussion of what a semiotic approach to the theatre entails from the perspective of the audience, more so than from that of the critic. Since a dramatic text is intended for performance, she argues that theatre cannot exist without an audience, and one that is always cognizant that what happens

101

upon the stage is make-believe, not reality but only its imitation or 'simulacrum.' Everything on the stage, therefore, has not only an existence in itself, but simultaneously refers to something else, so that 'the stage is a semiotic space par excellence' and theatre is 'a system of signs'[2] that can only be read through a shared understanding of codes and conventions, such as allusions and intertexts from mythology or the literary tradition. The audience as a discourse community, then, must construct the meaning, which necessarily will be subject to shifting and alteration; all theatre thus 'deconstructs the process by which meaning is produced.'[3] In this, Hulley likens theatre to desire itself, which is always directed toward something absent, just as the dramatic artifact is a 'trace' marking an absence of an event that will only come to exist through the agency of the audience. Meaning always lies, therefore, just beyond what is present on stage. The fact that 'the audience fills with significance the emptiness opened by the sign'[4] problematizes the viewer's response, which in its subjectivity risks 'unlimited meaning' while in its studied conventionality borders on 'tyrannizing meaning.'

Hulley begins her treatment of *Streetcar* by looking at the play's epigraph—something extradramatic that readers of the text first take in but that theatergoers may well not know—equating Hart Crane's 'broken world' with the theatre space itself as a locus of shadows rather than ideal forms. What the audience initially experiences resembles a montage, fragments of sights and sounds of the French Quarter whose 'symbolic register' is almost immediately apparent, followed by the set-within-the-set of the Kowalski flat that gradually and yet inevitably must become more expressionistic and even surrealistic. For it comes to represent the interior world of Blanche's mind, which is 'too multivalent' ever to be adequately captured by a conventionally realistic stage setting. Blanche's histrionic role-playing, adopting and then throwing off mask after mask as she pursues her multifarious desires, is symptomatic of her hysteria and offers a cautionary tale for the audience: although untrammeled desire might seem like freedom, it can result in a failure to find a solid identity, just as the audience in its role flirts with the dangers inherent in interpreting multivalent, nondiscursive symbols.

In Hulley's reading, each of the play's central characters modulates among different roles as actor, producer, and audience in a series of 'stagings.' If Blanche begins as an actor whose performance as a sexually desiring subject commands the attention of others, she loses that position when Stanley shifts from being the audience at her play to a producer of his own, in which he will define what is sexually permissible according to social codes. Williams, however, does not necessarily side with Stanley's legalism, limited as it is by being antimetaphoric, lacking in both art and imagination and in any belief in the transcendent value of love. Stanley distrusts the 'symbolic function' of language; his is a 'sterile world where meaning has become merely a function of social use.'[5] Hulley suggests that elements of the play's visual and aural style, emblematic of Blanche's subjectivity as she is violently raped, might also point to Stanley's 'disintegration,' since the transgressive rape introduces an element of disorder into the world, violating as it does all bounds of societally sanctioned desire.

It is left to Stella as the play's chief choral figure—a role analogous to that which the audience comes to assume—to see the conflict between Blanche and Stanley in ritualized and mythicized terms. Stella cannot maintain the safety of a neutral observer, but must now produce her own play, either excluding Blanche's 'boundless desire' or rejecting the 'security' Stanley offers. The 'happy marriage' may be as much mask as reality; but then it is the nature of an audience surrogate to allow a sign to point in different directions at one and the same time. Hulley argues that if *Streetcar* were stylistically a totally realistic play, then it would be about the triumph of Stanley's and Stella's passion; however, for Williams to create an 'unreal space' is an act of capitulation to the suppression of desire in order that 'social order' can reign—an ending which had been signaled from the very beginning by the streetcar destination named 'Cemeteries.' Just as crucial to Hulley's purpose in delineating a comprehensive reading of the symbol systems at play in *Streetcar* is her goal to establish a larger perspective on Williams's achievement that can be appreciated more fully when a semiotic approach is employed:

■ The problem Williams presents is that to limit the productive power of the symbol is repressive, while to allow the symbol unlimited power is chaos. By representing the either/or categories of contextual control through the death of desire, Williams surpasses the issues of 'sane' or 'insane', 'truth' or 'illusion' to expose the ambivalent social law which makes those terms significant.[6] □

Like Hulley, John Bak, in a 2009 essay, embeds a cogent exegesis of semiotic theory within his analysis of *Streetcar*, although he is particularly interested in the way that audience response in assigning 'fixed signification' to the theatrical (or 'performed') text might actually limit, or even discount, the 'multiple meanings' expressed by the playwright in the dramatic (or 'written') text. As the founding theorists of the Prague School of the late 1930s and 1940s postulated, 'every object or action is a sign,'[7] and so in the case of theatre it is the spectators who authorize the meaning of a given sign—which meaning may run counter to authorial intent. Referencing Kier Elam's standard work from 1980, *The Semiotics of Drama and Theatre*, Bak underscores that this disjunction, wherein the 'performance semiotic' modifies the 'textual' one, is precisely what occurs in the case of Stanley's violence against

Blanche in *Streetcar* when the spectators limit the signification of rape to violation—despite the fact that Williams 'attempt[s] to control the collectivist understanding of "rape" by interweaving several iconic and symbolic equivalents of the rape throughout the fabric of the play.'[8] What occurs with each individual production, however, is that the mimesis is taken for the only possible reality and an 'artificial' rather than an authorial signification arises. This is further complicated in the case of certain actions such as rape, when the playwright is constrained by what can be represented upon the stage, where the actor is called upon to 'materialize discourse.'

Because Bak understands that Williams is, by nature, a 'symbolist,' elements of his works that audiences insist on interpreting solely on the realistic level may have a figurative or metaphoric import that is actually primary for the dramatist himself. (Furthermore, a tendency to interpret that rape solely as brutal has perhaps been hardened in the minds of audiences by their prior acquaintance with Kazan's film of *Streetcar* and its images of the sharp edges of the broken bottle and the forcefully spurting firehose.) Bak further proposes that for Williams personally, as a homosexual cruising for trade, sex is never purely a matter of tenderness, although at the same time he is at pains 'to reconcile his own compulsions for rough sex with those of his inculcated spirituality.'[9] Only in this way is Williams able to satisfy those sexual desires and longings that a puritanical upbringing had forbidden, turning what had been considered sinful into something sacramental. Bak traces this pattern of violent sex eventuating in 'spiritual truth' through a number of rapes appearing in Williams's works, culminating in Stanley's violation of Blanche. Because, in the Williams encomium, physical sexuality is a necessary component for being completely human, even rape—whose signification Bak argues must not be limited to just 'violent sexism,' degrading and dehumanizing—may somehow bring about a morally beneficial result: 'Williams thus employs rape neither to demean women nor to abase masculine desire [but] to excoriate religious dogma for having appropriated human sexuality and sequestered it from various worldly appetites.'[10]

Bak goes to great lengths to argue that for Blanche specifically the rape provides a much needed path to retribution and 'spiritual reckoning,' as the *'Dies Irae'* [Day of Wrath] of his article's title implies:

■ (Stanley's) potent sexuality will destroy a desire for the flesh that has completely consumed her life (and those of her ancestors) and placed her on a one-way, nonstop streetcar toward death. ... if she can use Stanley to help her derail the streetcar of desire, she might have a chance to continue existing, if only in her imagination, in that now-moribund Old South.[11] □

In order to support this position, Bak must read the birth of the Kowalskis' baby as signifying that Blanche's violation has had a 'salubrious' effect, somehow an ending devoutly to be wished for. And likewise for its audience, Bak argues that her rape is the only 'possible' point of closure at which *Streetcar* could logically arrive.[12]

AT PLAY IN THE FIELD OF TEXTS: NICHOLAS PAGAN AND PHILIP KOLIN

In his 1993 'postmodern' critical biography of Williams, Nicholas Pagan writes against the grain of traditional literary biography, which he sees as fatally flawed in its assumption that the life of the biographical subject can ever be objectively known and recreated. While traditional biography posits the knowability of the subject, the new form that he will attempt under the aegis of the theoretical writings of Roland Barthes and Jacques Derrida—neither of whom, Pagan asserts, argues for the nonexistence of the author—will acknowledge the essential inaccessibility of some ur-Williams. Furthermore, Pagan will not subject the texts to thematization that would hope to find in them meanings, ethical or otherwise; nor will he impute authorial intentions to them, as that cuts off and constrains rather than opening up and ramifying. Instead, he proposes employing a more playful method, one that will engage the reader's active role in the process of 'signification' that had once been considered the domain of the author alone; for once the author's life is seen as the fiction that it is, then it, too, can be approached and read as just another text. What Pagan ignores in the process, of course, is that Williams himself regularly thematized his play *Streetcar* in his extra-dramatic pronouncements, particularly in his oft-repeated remarks about the destruction of beauty by barbarity.

Pagan will be content, instead, to explore what he calls Williams's 'stylistic signature' from a number of different perspectives. First, he will toy around with the opening letters of key names and words in the play, specifically the 'bl' of both 'Blanche' and 'Blues' and the 'st' of 'Stanley' and 'streetcar.' If the Blues exist on the margin, so, too, does Blanche in both her gender and sexuality. Exploring her name from a Barthesian angle with 'to blanch' meaning 'to gloss over,' Pagan notes the way in which she focuses on 'whiteness' and her astrological sign, Virgo, while Stanley refers to her as 'queen' and questions whether she is 'straight.' This produces a confusion in gender identity, suggesting that Blanche, while 'obviously female,' might also be denominated as male; furthermore, the substitution of 'De Boyes' for 'DuBois' could be a tactic implying that she, as a lover of boys, might be a stand-in for the playwright himself. Williams could be seen, in fact, as having modeled his life on hers: if Blanche uses her incessant role-playing in an effort to cover over the truth of her sexuality, so also might Williams be attempting to hide by inscribing himself in her.

■ Once again it is through a woman's discourse that a space is opened up to accommodate homosexuality. Once again the homosexual is only present through words. The name appears but not the person.[13] □

Shifting to a Derridian stance on signification, Pagan goes on to pursue the supposed opposition between Stanley, an embodiment of the male power structure who expropriates Blanche by objectifying her through the male gaze, and Blanche, who seemingly refuses to play by men's rules while at the same time being a desiring subject. A lover of young boys, Blanche is as sexually voracious as Stanley and just as much an expropriator; as such, she 'occupies' not only a feminine but a masculine 'space' as well. Although Stanley succeeds in expropriating Stella (there's the 'st' again), he fails to do so with Blanche, just as the audience itself must because of her fluid identity.

Second, Pagan plays around with the several occurrences of the stud poker game within *Streetcar*, exploring how it might apply to Blanche, to Williams himself, and to the reader. Because of her continual role-playing and dissimulation that makes her real self elusive, Blanche is seen as the 'wild card,' though Pagan muses that perhaps the heart—wherein Blanche claims never to have lied—is a 'place outside' make-believe and not containable within it. Williams himself, as author, is a player as well, dealing cards with significations he may not be fully aware of. And active readers, by their 'appropriations of the text,' also enter into the game-playing too, with the result that, because of a multiplicity of readers, 'the signature is always deferred.'[14] The text, consequently, can never be hemmed in by the critic's seeking to determine the play's meaning(s) or the author's intention(s), as traditional exercises in literary biography always are.

While Pagan focuses on names and their significations, Philip Kolin, in a 1997 essay, looks at paper and its significations to arrive at one of the most original and ingenious readings available of *Streetcar*. With brief nods to theorists as various as Jacques Lacan and Luce Irigary, Michel Foucault and Jacques Derrida, he argues for the ubiquity of paper in all its myriad forms, both literal and metaphoric—including as character signification and as a material object ready for authorial inscription:

■ Some of the papers are legal documents, visible and objective; others are invisible, yet no less empirical, evidentiary and binding; and still others are occluded, imprisoned within the play. Almost every major signifier in *Streetcar* is (de)constructed out of paper—mortgages, foreclosures, directions, letters, poems, telegrams, newspapers, appraisals, songs, even moons.[15] □

Taking it as a given that Williams was repeatedly sexualizing and textualizing himself through his oeuvre, Kolin proposes not only that the characters here should be seen as writers and/or performers who are scripting/fictionalizing their identities for the audience to read, but equally as personages whose alternating power is determined through the paper(s) they deploy. Kolin's strategy is to illustrate the ebb and flow of power by paralleling and contrasting Blanche's and Stanley's associations with paper. Whereas Blanche's rootlessness and disconnection are bodied forth by the slip of paper bearing directions to her sister's home, Stanley's commanding presence is embodied in the bloodstained meat wrapper that he wields. If the worthless deeds and other documents in the 'feminine space' of Blanche's trunk chronicle a history of loss and a past come to waste, Stanley will employ putative legal opinions and appraisals in order to write a revised and renewed history. And if the poems of a dead lover and the literary texts Blanche taught assert the truth value of art, the only economy Stanley will abide is the one evidenced by unambiguous fact; not Hawthorne and Poe, but only Napoleon and Huey Long will function for him.

Kolin is particularly astute in his explication of the Kleenex on which Blanche pens her note to the illusory Shep Huntleigh and the Chinese lantern with which she covers the naked lightbulb. Like her 'blanched' complexion, the Kleenex is soft and fragile (as is the nearly invisible moth that serves as metaphor for her), rendering the Kleenex 'the objective correlative of Blanche's desire—insubstantial, vulnerable and visionary.'[16] It announces dependence upon a fantasy future, unlike the legalistic validity that Stanley would demand. While the photograph of Stanley in his army uniform testifies to his obsession with the 'evidentiary,' the lantern allows Blanche to fashion/falsify her image and mute the male gaze, thus deflecting Stanley's desire. Paper, for a person of Stanley's mindset, if it is to contain and advance one's power, must be unambiguous and dependably interpretable; because the lantern falsifies and fosters indeterminacy 'it challenges his inscribed authority as king'[17] and so must be destroyed.

Kolin concludes by reminding his readers that the drive to disclose is always paralleled by the imperative to conceal, and so *Streetcar's* 'text can only be fully realized, therefore, through a process of emancipating [the] suppressed papers.'[18] Chief among these, perhaps, are those about Williams's own sexual identity that he was forced to occlude because of the repressive time in which the play was written. Just as Blanche wants to hide the papers of her promiscuous past, so, too, do Stanley and Stella want to conceal the papers committing Blanche to the asylum.

And yet, paradoxically, the legal maneuvering of that absent document indicts him—along with the audience as witness—in the same type of maneuver that he had earlier tried by using the papers in Blanche's trunk to incriminate her.

DEEPER INTO THEORY: WILLIAM KLEB, PHILIP KOLIN, AND NICHOLAS PAGAN

In the critical works discussed in the preceding section, Pagan and Kolin allude, mainly in passing and without much framework, to a number of theorists whose terminology they assume the majority of their readers have assimilated. In this section, William Kleb, together once again with Kolin and Pagan, makes a more concerted use of the theoretical concepts of, respectively, Foucault on surveillance of the sexually Other and Barthes on physical bodies as texts. Kleb posits that, because of a shared focus on sexuality and madness, Williams might almost be considered as an 'imaginative prefiguration' of Foucault. Furthermore, one of the theorist's central contentions, that 'The individualizing mechanisms of modern civilization are focused on figures situated at the margins of society,'[19] adumbrates Williams's thinking as well. In his 1993 essay, Kleb begins his critical exegesis by indicating how the French philosopher arrived at his notions of the Same and the Other, which he will then employ to explicate *Streetcar*. In his *History of Sexuality* (1976–84), Foucault rejects the 'repressive hypothesis' which claimed that a period of laxity in societal mores during the seventeenth century was followed by enclosing the sphere of sex and the reproductive function within the confines of the home, leaving only the brothel and the asylum as sites for unwholesome expressions of sexual desire. Rather, he sees as a characteristic of modernity a 'proliferation' of discourses about sexuality that attempted to normalize what had once been treated as peripheral or abnormal, most particularly (insofar as Williams is concerned) the hysterical woman and the homosexual. Thus, to speak openly of sexuality becomes a rebellion against repression and a 'transgressive move,' part of a revolt evidenced by such things as the Kinsey Reports, whose publication was roughly coterminous with the appearance of Williams's drama. Kleb then proceeds to read *Streetcar* as just one of many possible discourses on sexuality, showing that behavior which was widely considered as abnormal was, in fact, 'common, lodged in the average home and the normal heart.'[20]

In the eyes of society, Blanche's Otherness resides in her maladjusted sexuality and her madness (or Unreason), which make her a threat to the moral order of things, and so, in Foucault's terms, society must protect itself by excluding or confining her. The chief institutions devised for this disciplinary purpose are the clinic, the prison, and the asylum. As a threat to the Same, Blanche's power has been undermined, and so her tactic must be to 'reconstitute her otherness (or difference) as sameness.'[21] In order to accomplish this, she needs to drive a wedge between Stella and Stanley and between Mitch and Stanley, which she attempts to do by calling upon those things in her sister and putative lover/savior that make them akin to Blanche in her difference: Stella's shared psychological legacy of improvidence and decline from Belle Reve, and Mitch's sensitivity and aesthetic sensibility that keep him from being just one of the guys. In both instances, however, Blanche fails to make them the Same as her: Stella reaffirms marriage to Stanley over kinship with her sister, and Mitch, allowing Stanley to save him from her clutches, rejects Blanche. The pattern of the play, as Kleb sees it, is one of interrogations and confessions, and Stanley employs this strategy to weaken Blanche; all the while, she, in turn, is trying to take over and transform the space of normal, conjugal love that he has heretofore ruled. She thus 'creates an expanding symbolist shadow—the primordial feminine Other'[22]—that is most entrancing and threatening, that he can only expunge through the rape that will reestablish his political power as king of his realm, however circumscribed it might be.

Paradoxically, however, Blanche might be seen as wresting control from Stanley in two ways. The first, as seen through the prism of Foucault, accords her 'the final move':

■ By the late eighteenth century, [Foucault] argues, modes of punishment founded on spectacle and physical pain were gradually being replaced by the reformist penal institutions characteristic of modern society—institutions based on continuous surveillance (discipline in the original sense of the word), sites for the observation, analysis, and instruction of confined individuals. The object of the punishment, therefore, shifted from the body of the condemned to the personhood, the soul, [constituting a] humanization of the penal system. ...[23] □

Admittedly, on one level this simply substitutes one type of subjugation for another, leaving Stella in league with Stanley as 'guardians' of the sameness or the status quo. Stella, however, gives indications that her resurrected relationship with Stanley has been 'fundamentally redefined' to undermine his absolute control. Additionally—and this is the second way in which Blanche might be seen as asserting power—when she raises doubts in Stella and Mitch about Stanley as sexually deviant she transfers her 'Otherness' onto him. As a result, Stella 'reads Stanley differently now—in terms of Blanche. This is Williams's project, as it is Kinsey's and Foucault's—to relocate the Other within man's nature, whitening the same.'[24]

Finally, Kleb equates the asylum to which Blanche is exiled to the theatre in which Williams practices: both are sites for analysis, where those behaviors that society considers marginal are subjected to a critical eye. The audience, however, will not see them as disciplinary places where 'sexual abnormality' and 'mental disorder' are conflated, but as sites where Blanche and Williams can be released to live where they are most at home—on the margins.

In a determinedly theory-based essay of 1999, Philip Kolin distinguishes between Stanley as a text of desire ('*plaisir*') and Blanche as a text of desire eventuating in bliss ('*jouissance*'). Seeing an affinity between Barthes' 1973 *The Pleasure of the Text* and Williams's play of twenty-five years earlier, Kolin first calls upon the French thinker's analogy between the literary text and the human body; this turns the written work, like flesh waiting to be explored, into an erotic object to be desired by the reader that provides pleasure akin to the sexual. Because Williams oftentimes equated writing with the sex act—the blank paper being the flesh upon which he inscribed his sexual desires—the text of a play like *Streetcar* becomes the dramatist's 'fetishized body' in search of an 'erotic encounter' with the reader/audience. For Kolin via Barthes, however, it is not only the text but the bodies of the characters as well that become 'erotic sites.'

Evidence for this intervention can be found on the dust jackets and covers of various printed versions of the play (Blanche in her nearly transparent slip in Thomas Hart Benton's famous illustration; a photo from the original film version of the bare-chested Brando as Stanley) that initiate the seduction of the reader, just as the onstage bodies of the T-shirted Stanley, the pregnant Stella, and the newsboy with the alluring lips do so in the theatre. Kolin goes on, then, to apply the Barthesian characteristics of '*plaisir*' and '*jouissance*' in order to demarcate the two central figures. Stanley is, in his clothing and animal imagery, the commanding phallic male, rough in action, crude if legalistic in word, lower class in the way that the French Quarter's populace-at-large is mired in pleasure. Blanche, on the other hand, is an exile from the genteel past of Belle Reve, eloquent in language about art and poetry and music, aware that 'purity' of heart raises her above simply base hedonism. Existing outside conventionality, in some sense a creature of the dark, Blanche is also indeterminate, without a 'fixed center,' to which Kolin attributes the difficulty critics have had in pinning down her multifarious personality:

■ As *Streetcar* criticism over the last fifty years has cogently demonstrated, Blanche is an 'impossible text' within the void of bliss, diverse, impenetrable, unknowable. She has been classified through a host of

> wildly opposing signifiers including the Mater Dolorosa, Cleopatra, a
> fallen aristocrat, Southern belle, the 'Mona Lisa of dread' (Bedient), even
> the Cumaean Sybil, and yet she is all and none of these. ... Blanche,
> the White One, has affinities with the blinding negative light of Albert
> Camus's *L'Etranger*, the frightening enigma of *Moby Dick*, the bliss and
> trepidation of suspended existential time.[25] □

Finally, however, Kolin is at pains to remind his readers that, for Barthes,
'plaisir' and *'jouissance'* are not absolutely dichotomous but bleed over
into each other, so that Stanley does not lack a 'feminine side' nor is
Blanche exempt from 'scandalous pleasure.'

In another article, this one dating from 1993 and once again drawing
heavily upon Barthes, Pagan looks for traces of Williams's presence as
author not only in *Streetcar* but in *Cat* as well. While acknowledging the
attraction for critics of the Artaudian notion that the essence of theatre
lies not in language but in physical spectacle that appeals more immediately to the senses, Pagan is more sympathetic to the Derridean position
that representation is a *sine qua non* of theatre which 'is forever trapped
within language, and within that language it frequently represents itself
as body'[26]—in Williams's particular case, the homosexual body. At the
same time that he admits the existence of the author about whom we
can know certain biographical facts, independent of the text, Pagan is
more taken with the Barthesian notion of the author as a construct of
the reader that emerges during interpretive activity, so that Williams is
'a product of our reading,'[27] and not simply of individual works but of the
literary corpus as a whole. On this basis, Pagan proposes that Williams
is engaging in a kind of 'cruising' in which he offers his theatre-as-body
to the audience, trying to attract them and gain their acceptance of him,
just as when he approached other gay men seeking sexual satisfaction.
(Pagan even goes so far as to posit an analogy between the aging homosexual body losing its attractiveness over time and the decline in the
appeal of Williams's drama for audiences and critics at later points in his
career, making him vulnerable to rejection.)

As regards *Streetcar*, Pagan reminds his readers that it is nothing new
to hypothesize that Williams is employing Proust's 'Albertine strategy'
that would justify reading Blanche as a gay male in disguise; however,
he is more intent upon Blanche's repeated efforts to engage the attention of men by offering herself as the object of the male gaze, especially
since she fears that her sexual attractiveness may be fading, leading
her to obsess nostalgically about her past successes. In *Cat*, something
similar occurs with Brick, whose physical attractiveness seems to have
peaked, prompting a remembrance of past glory. In both plays, the
openly homosexual characters are absent from the stage, constrained
by what the commercial theatre of the time would allow, and yet both

texts imply a 'subversion' of society's sexual mores. The 'thing' that must be left unspoken is the homosexual body and the practices in which it engages; and the 'strangers' that Blanche extols and relies upon are both sexual suitors and the audience itself. Williams's plays are his love act, in which he gives his 'heart' to the spectators and readers; and 'the way that Williams's theatre veils and unveils the homosexual body'[28] is one of the tricks that he employs to seduce them. Pagan argues, in fact, that the homosexual by his absence actually gives works like *Streetcar* and *Cat* a more intense erotic charge than if he were present onstage, since 'as soon as this body is subjected to the glare of the stage lights, Williams might be seen as attempting to represent the unrepresentable source of much of his theatre's power.'[29]

THEORY IN A NEW KEY: LAURA MORROW AND EDWARD MORROW

One of the signs of postmodernity is the application of critical methodologies across disciplines, and so Chaos Theory, originally the province of scientists and mathematicians, has entered into the hermeneutic arsenal of literary and cultural commentators. In applying Chaos/Antichaos Theory to Williams's *Streetcar* in their 1993 essay, Laura and Edward Morrow embrace a larger agenda of demonstrating how this paradigm can function as 'a reintegrative nexus for the arts and sciences.'[30] The specific conclusions they arrive at concerning *Streetcar* and its characters, particularly having to do with questions of determinism and free will, are not, finally, all that different from the conclusions reached by others; what they have provided, instead, is simply another basis for confirming what must always remain tentative, since that is the nature of all interpretive readings. Their critical strategy, however, must necessarily involve a good deal of arcane terminology—things like 'basins of attraction' and 'canalization' which they elucidate—beginning with the point that the word 'chaos' itself as used here has a completely opposite denotation from the usual understanding of it as an unformed, topsy-turvy world in the throes of upheaval. In essence, Chaos Theory studies how minute changes in systems of behavior can produce complex outcomes (in the same way that the interactions between and among dramatic characters can generate complex works of art). Antichaos Theory, on the other hand, looks for evidence of a potentially high degree of order within apparently disorderly systems, suggesting that what may appear as random might in fact be determined. Approaching the central characters as complex systems connected by a network of desire, the Morrows see Stanley as exemplifying Chaos in the way that his following of simple rules, things like the legal and moral right to property or the belief that words model an already-existing reality, leads to complex behavior; these proscriptions, nonetheless, are fatally flawed because such 'absolutism' and 'logocentrism' are too uncritical about the assumptions they make and cannot accurately reflect any 'fuller truth.' Blanche, in contradistinction, is deployed as a representative of Antichaos, an apparently disorderly yet complexly organized system that 'crystallizes' into an orderly one. Her environment has not foreordained her fate, but it has determined her 'attractors,' which are 'illusion' and 'seduction.' These, in turn, together form her 'basin of attraction': 'she seduces men with her body and herself with her dreams,' and because 'History is iterative, Blanche will always seduce whomever she can'[31]— though the Morrows regard her as actually trying to 'rewrite' her history by using her sexuality (and a series of men as objects) in a 'right' fashion to make amends for the failure of her very first relationship with Allan.

One of the hallmarks of Blanche's 'disorderly behavior' that firmly sets her apart from Stanley and Stella is found in her deployment of language. Stanley, whose 'basin of attraction' is 'power,' uses words pragmatically: a creature of facticity, language for him must convey with precision the material object at hand. Blanche, on the other hand, desires to use words in order to enhance the world of reality, to raise it to the level of art, even if this poetic tendency finally distorts things. So the world of the French Quarter that Stanley and Stella have inured themselves in is a 'closed system' that Blanche's arrival threatens to break open or 'reprogram' as she tries to impose her gentility on their boisterous lives. She is introducing a disruptive element into their already-established 'network,' marked by such things as Stella's finding of security within domesticity (alien to Blanche's past), or Stanley's fostering of homosocial bonds. But each individual is also a 'network,' composed of a variety of behaviors that can become 'canalized' or frozen depending on a person's natural proclivities. In that sense, Blanche 'is "frozen" into a system of indiscriminating, compulsive, self-destructive seduction,' just as Stanley's behavior within marriage is frozen into a pattern of 'battles for dominance in which he commits violent excess, is punished by [Stella] and/or the law, and is, ultimately, forgiven by Stella.'[32] Given their 'canalized' behavior, a conflict between Blanche and Stanley—played out in her flirtatiousness towards him and his violation of her—for dominance over Stella is tragically inevitable. (Stella, meanwhile, since she is not frozen in a pattern of canalization, remains more adaptable because more random in her responses.) And yet, while Stanley seems to prove the survival of the fittest, an understanding from the perspective of Antichaos theory would problematize his victory: 'Natural selection results in survival, but do not equate selection with an ability to adapt.'[33]

The Morrows read the image of the streetcar itself in a novel way to undergird how employing Chaos Theory helps readers think about issues of determinism and choice in the play:

■ The route of a streetcar is predestined, fixed, a 'canalized function,' as it were. Once on board the streetcar, one may see where it is headed; but howsoever evident may be the terminus of the network of track, one cannot change the direction of its course. It is, we believe, significant that Blanche is of Huguenot ancestry; as Protestants in a Catholic-dominated country, they, too, disrupted the accepted order (albeit for altruistic reasons) and thereby brought suffering on themselves.[34] □

The Morrows continue on to suggest that Blanche in her old environment could never have changed; when, however, she entered a different basin of attraction—for instance, by visiting Stella's flat or being courted by Mitch—change would have been more possible, were it not for the fact that her system of psychic behavior was frozen. So, finally, they conclude that Williams in *Streetcar* has written a work approaching tragedy in the Euripidean mode, in which it is not fate that predestines the characters, but rather a mix of their psychology and personal values. The outcome may be inexorable, as with the Greeks, but here it is not one imposed by the gods.

The Morrows' essay, like others examined in this chapter, focuses exclusively on only one of the two plays that have been the subject of this study. By turning to assessments of film and television adaptations of Williams in the section that follows, we can once again fittingly—in that it is the final chapter—engage both *Streetcar* and *Cat*.

CHAPTER NINE

Film and Television Adaptations

SEXUALITY AND CENSORSHIP: MAURICE YACOWAR, GENE PHILLIPS, AND NANCY TISCHLER

It seems safe to wager that most people's first introduction to Tennessee Williams comes not through reading one of his plays or seeing one onstage, but rather through watching a cinematic version, either on the movie screen or television. The commercial film industry has been particularly drawn to his works as source material for fifteen major movies, seven of them appearing in the period between 1950 and 1968; and another half-dozen were produced for showing on television between 1975 and the end of the century. Included among them are notable adaptations of *Streetcar* and *Cat* intended for one or other media. Williams, of course, had a longstanding connection with the movies, going back to his brief time as an usher in a theatre and his days as a Hollywood screenwriter before his first success as a dramatist; in fact, as has been shown, an awareness of filmic techniques probably helped account for such elements of his playwriting as the episodic structure of *Streetcar* and the spotlighting of characters to simulate close-ups during the monologues in *Cat*.[1] Yet the influence was apparently reciprocal, benefitting both: for while Williams's plays—albeit usually with altered endings—reached numbers of viewers far in excess of what they ever could have on stage, their Hollywood adaptations answered the demands of more sophisticated viewers just at the time when the new medium of television was cutting into the moviegoing audience; in fact, a case can be made that because of their mature subject matter, the films of Williams's works became precursors of whatever art theatre movement American cinema can ever boast of having, while at the same time they eventually helped to bring about a loosening of Production Code restrictions on the content and explicitness of entertainment meant for adults.

After outlining the reconceptualization necessary to accommodate a playscript to the greater reality, subjectivity, and popularity (albeit with some loss in acceptable subject matter) of the film medium, Maurice Yacowar, in *Tennessee Williams and Film* (1977), establishes his criteria for a successful adaptation: finding 'visual equivalents' for the verbal content and, insofar as thematic content is concerned, 'serv[ing] the thrust and intent of the original.'[2] He then proceeds to read the film versions of Williams's dramas as visual texts, much in the same way one would a piece of literature. In discussing *Streetcar Named Desire* (1951), which he finds a 'sensitive, faithful adaptation,'[3] Yacowar notices the heat, noise, and jostling by others that irritate Blanche, and the added outdoor scenes that Kazan designs as 'projections' of the heroine's mind. He reads Kazan's shooting of the rape scene—such a horrible violation that it must be seen in reflection rather than head-on—symbolically, with Stanley represented by the 'solid bottle' and Blanche by the 'fragile mirror'; the aftermath, with the phallic fire hose cleansing the street, suggests that she 'needs to be washed away like trash,'[4] although whether, as Yacowar proposes, this should also be seen as indicating 'new life' coming after the 'past is washed away' seems less certain. Finally, in considering how the adaptation responds to the censors' demands that Stanley be punished through Stella's rejection, Yacowar detects an ambiguity: the apparent reversal in the film from how the play had concluded, with Stanley 'abandoned' and Blanche 'triumphant,' may be, he feels, an uncritical response to what appears on the 'surface' rather than a recognition of what happens in reality. At the same time, linking the film to Kazan's own biography as someone who named names during the House Committee on Un-American Activities hearings, Yacowar sees the director as valorizing 'the truth-teller as heroic.'[5]

Although Yacowar considers Richard Brooks's 1958 film of *Cat on a Hot Tin Roof* 'a creative, faithful performance of the text,'[6] he argues just as strongly that the director has, by rearranging events, skewed Williams's meaning; the film—with its visual echoes of Welles's *Citizen Kane* in the shots of a basement full of goods bought on a European trip and of the 'Rosebud' sled in Big Daddy's valise—digresses from the focus of its original source:

■ The new scene works dramatically ... [b]ut the scene violates the thematic proportions of the play. ... in the film the men move from the more serious topics to this one [mindless acquisition]. The effect is to suggest that materialism is a more serious concern than mendacity and its obverse, the courage to face life and death directly.[7] □

And yet, reading Brick as wounded by lack of a father's love without ever addressing the son's individuation and maturation, Yacowar himself skirts around, even elides the issue of homosexuality, claiming that what Brick exhibits, through the visual symbol of the crutch, is 'a sexual disability rather than a deviance.'[8] This does not prevent Yacowar, however, from making incisive comments about the way that suspicion by others can create doubt and destroy self-confidence, or from reading visual imagery in an enlightening manner, such as seeing the car wheels stuck in the mud as a metaphor for 'moral paralysis.' Nothing that Yacowar points out about the film, however, would seem to justify his judgment that it is 'remarkably frank'—especially given that all references to Straw and Ochello's homosexual love have been excised.

Gene Phillips is interested throughout his 1980 book, *The Films of Tennessee Williams*, in two issues: first, in theorizing how the literary and cinematic media relate to one another, especially the extent to which a film adaptation 'has preserved the intent and spirit of the Williams play';[9] and, second, the effect of censorship upon the movies, again, specifically, whether the treatment of questionable subject matter is inimical to serious expression of 'moral purpose.' Downplaying somewhat the importance of the visual images in drama, Phillips believes that cinema is actually closer to narrative fiction than to theatre, which depends to a greater extent upon dialogue. While providing sensible readings of Williams's dramatic texts, he oftentimes depends heavily upon Kazan's notes as a director. The film version of *Streetcar* can remain largely faithful to the 'heightened realism' of Williams's original by eschewing much of the 'opening out' typical of adaptations and using the shifting point of view of the camera and walls literally closing in to suggest confinement, precisely because the playwright himself had employed cinematic techniques in the structuring. When the film does move outside the Kowalski flat— in the beginning sequence, to intimate Blanche's desperate journey beyond cemeteries to a paradise that can exist only in her imagination, or by staging her courting of Mitch in front of a dance casino that recalls the site of Allan's suicide, or by showing Stanley's betrayal of Blanche's past to Mitch in a factory with noisy machinery—the imagery is often portentous, Phillips finds.

Although Phillips believes that a mature audience would still understand the nature of Allan's sexuality, the film, because of the Breen office, has 'obscured,' even 'obliterated,' any evidence of homosexuality, as well as acceded to the censors' demand that Blanche's rape by Stanley must be 'entirely eliminated' unless he is somehow punished. If Phillips feels as well that there is ample reason to find Blanche 'subtly encourage[ing]' Stanley's actions, he does point out that seeing her reflection in the mirror at the end (the same mirror through which the rape was filmed) 'repairs her illusion [of being] the immaculate Southern belle once again,'[10] He also, however, discerns 'ample reason' for believing in the reclamation of Stella and Stanley's marriage, despite the emphatic lines to the contrary added to the film at the censor's insistence. The Legion of Decency demanded twelve cuts, amounting to about four minutes of running time, especially to reduce the premeditation of Stanley's violation of Blanche.[11] Phillips, however, still judges that the ultimate result is an adult film in the best sense of the word:

■ *Streetcar* marked the first time that the censor's office was confronted with a Hollywood film that was definitely not family entertainment. ... [But] Williams's fine play and Kazan's skillful direction proved that any subject could be proper material for the screen if treated with the kind of discretion and artistry that this movie exhibited.[12] □

Even though, without marshalling much supporting evidence, Phillips follows William Faulkner's lead and calls Big Daddy the 'central character' of *Cat on a Hot Tin Roof*, he provides a convincing reading to account for Brick's character in a film that largely excises the homosexuality central to the play. James Poe, in writing the original screen treatment, had attempted to handle Skipper and the gay subtext through flashbacks; Richard Brooks, the final scriptwriter and director, needed to find some substitute for the homosexual implications. He accomplishes this by presenting Brick as an immature adolescent fixated on the athletic glory of a romanticized past who '[has refused] to grow up and meet the responsibilities of adult life,'[13] which accounts for his distant relationship and rebuffing of Maggie's advances, his dependence on alcohol, and his shying away from fathering a child.

Almost by way of postscript, Nancy Tischler's two essays of 1997 and 2002 on the film of *Streetcar*, by drawing upon materials examined while she coedited (along with Albert Devlin) Williams's letters, provide an example of how newly unearthed primary materials can shed light on topics long of interest to scholars. She frames her 1997 essay by referring to two letters Williams wrote to his literary agent, Audrey Wood, twenty-five years apart: the first speculates on possible endings for the play, including Blanche's suicide; the second asserts the intimate connection he always felt with Blanche, 'assailed' by the Stanleys of this world. In Tischler's biographical reading, Williams's need to express a violent side within himself leads her to suggest that 'Blanche is maybe asking Stanley to rape her so that she can expiate her sins against Allan.'[14] Such a focus on Blanche as 'tarnished' prostitute could not, however, be permitted on film at that time; so Tischler discovers from archival material that the producer Irene Meyer Selznik involved Lillian Hellman in writing an acceptable treatment for a film version. Although Hellman promised not to distort the play, she saw Allan's homosexuality (which Williams had adamantly refused allowing the British stage censors to remove) as dispensable, explained away as a figment of Blanche's imagination, and so she suggested other possible explanations for Allan's suicide, including impotence.

Tischler's second article, after remarking on how Vivien Leigh as Scarlett in *Gone with the Wind* resonates in Blanche's desire for both the gritty and the romantic, turns to Hellman's proposed handling of the other aspect of the play that censors found objectionable: the rape— which, as the culmination of Blanche's attraction to Stanley's threat, Tischler (again from a biographical perspective) reads as analogous to Williams's own propensity toward rough trade. As possible ways of treating the rape, Hellman suggests that Stanley might refuse Blanche's advances, so that the rape becomes her '"delusion,"' and that she might even run from the house in a kind of mad scene; or that some unspecified outside force might prevent the rape—though Stanley would still be guilty as symbolic of the brutality bent on destroying gentility. In any event, in charting Blanche's 'inevitable fall,' the rape would be rendered unnecessary since the pattern of decline was set into motion years before. After quoting from Williams's letter to Charles Feldman beseeching that the Legion's demands for additional cuts not be acceded to, Tischler concludes that the film of *Streetcar*, as it finally exists, is still 'a completed work of art' and 'screen masterpiece.'[15]

FILM THEORY AND GENRE: CHRISTINE GERAGHTY, AND BARTON PALMER AND ROBERT BRAY

Although the title of her 2008 book, *Now a Major Motion Picture: Film Adaptations of Literature and Drama*, may sound unpromising from an academic perspective, Christine Geraghty's is the only scholarly analysis of the film version of *Streetcar Named Desire* to employ classical film theory in a systematic way. Geraghty concedes the standard reasons why plays are more easily adapted than novels (compressed time span, fewer characters and plot lines, intended for performance in a communal space), although she eschews the predictable focus on how a completed film differs from its dramatic source. Instead, she situates her analysis in the essays of André Bazin, the French film theorist working contemporaneously with Williams's most productive period. While the more traditional view sought to establish the hierarchy of theatre over film—a more active audience engaged with a work of art versus largely passive observers of popular culture—Bazin 'shifted the ground'[16] of the discussion to emphasize the different ways that space is organized in the two media and to insist that any adaptation respect that distinction: the theatre space is bounded by the stage itself, whereas space in cinema, and thus the life being represented, continues outside the frame of the screen. Consequently, the successful adaptation must 'exploit the resources of cinema to acknowledge its source in theatre,' whose text is inherently more dependent on words and whose 'essence' is the 'exploration of internal dilemmas.'[17]

Turning specifically to the film of *Streetcar*, Geraghty notes its heavy indebtedness to theatrical style and form: in its stage-like set composed of small rooms; in its infrequent movement to out-of-doors (and then usually to serve as markers between scenes); in its camera angles and editing that privilege the spectator's point of view as the observer over the classic Hollywood shot-reverse-shot technique; and in its dependence upon long speeches without close-ups. Using Bazin's terms, Geraghty judges that Kazan's handling of space is not as cinematic as it might have been, still bearing more the mark of the theatre. While acceding to the notion that Brando's performance evinces complex elements of 'bisexuality' as well as of 'homoeroticism,' she contests the judgment that eroticizing Brando's body by making it the object of both the female and the male gaze has 'strip[ped] him of his masculinity'[18] as some commentators have claimed.

Considering *Cat on a Hot Tin Roof* as an example of the family melodrama wherein the woman is 'brought under male control,'[19] Geraghty underscores Williams's favored status as a purveyor of 'controversial themes' and 'theatrical respectability' in a Hollywood responding to the challenge of television with adult movies in widescreen and color. Brooks's *Cat* largely respects its source as a stage play, most often filming the action from the observer's perspective so that the camera is the eye of the spectator. This means, however, that 'Maggie's desire for Brick is denied the visual expression'[20] that would have arisen from a more subjective use of camera angles. Instead, the film's handling of the gaze is more traditional, with both Newman's and Taylor's bodies on 'sexual display' for the audience. Rather than latent homosexuality, Brick's central problem is a 'repressed relationship' with his father that must first be resolved before there can be any restitution of the fractured marital union. Although Geraghty identifies certain issues the film raises, such as the slave economy on which the wealth of the Pollitt plantation is built, she feels things like conspicuous consumption can only be mildly criticized if the ending of this movie is to strike a mainly positive note. But her discussion and analysis of the specifics of the film is really too foreshortened, and here is a place where falling back on Bazin's criteria of 'use of space and the actor's body in performance as a source of pleasure'[21] for the viewer rather than mere faithfulness to the dramatic source fails to account for just how substantially different in content Brooks's film is from Williams's play.

The subtitle of *Hollywood's Tennessee* (2008) by R. Barton Palmer and Robert Bray indicates that it is intended as a social and cultural history of 'Postwar America' along with being the most extensive consideration to date of the films adapted from Williams's dramas. Although Kazan's screen version of *Streetcar* needed to acquiesce to the Production Code's insistence that there be no mention of either Allan's homosexuality or Blanche's promiscuity and that the rape not be explicitly shown—which necessarily entailed a loss of artistic freedom and control for director and playwright—the resultant film leaves the play 'relatively intact' and is still, to the minds of Palmer and Bray, 'remarkable' and 'groundbreaking' in that it treats openly topics and themes that were 'once proscribed.' They appear to make this judgment mainly on two bases: first, that the characters resist any easy or conventional moral judgment; and, second, that the film still presents sexual desire in an open and unadulterated fashion, particularly in the steamily erotic scenes between Stanley and Stella which are no less blatant in their sensuality than the play had been. If there is a loss, it comes in the slightly more muted and toned down presentation of the two central figures, such that 'The film hardly offers anything like the disturbing yet compelling mix of misogynistic violence and forbidden eroticism that gives Stanley's contentious relationship with Blanche its dramatic and cultural power.'[22]

In their discussion of *Cat* on screen, Palmer and Bray echo Phillips's analysis of Brick as an athletics-obsessed adolescent who needs to reject an idealized version of a vanished youth and replace it with a more mature outlook that embraces the responsibilities of an adult male ready to assume the role of father; but they extend their analysis to speculate on what this embrace of fatherhood will really mean for his position within the domestic realm. As Geraghty does, too, they situate their discussion of *Cat* within the context of the film genre of the family melodrama during the postwar and Eisenhower years as theorized by Thomas Elsaesser, among others.[23] Melodrama, which is generally defined as expecting of its audience an emotional response of pathos in excess of what the characters warrant by their actions, became a profitable staple of adult-themed Hollywood films complete with, at least on the surface, happy endings. Yet a fissure exists between the characters' apparent acceptance of the conservative roles society expects them to embrace, particularly as pertains to sex and gender, and their deep-seated desires for an authenticity that would challenge those roles; therefore, what is laid bare is a 'contradiction of mid-century American culture: its exaltation yet proscription of untrammeled individuality.'[24]

Cat in its Broadway production, deliberately adjusted by Kazan to appeal to a middlebrow audience, had narrowed physical desire to equate with the procreative impulse, 'celebrating the social importance of heterosexual coupling.'[25] That 'imperative' is, however, called into question in Brooks's decidedly 'radical alteration,' where Williams's deliberate ambiguities give way to a more socially conservative posture, where homosexuality and even adultery are swept away, and where heteronormativity reigns as the only legally and religiously sanctioned choice for adult life. Brick's intense friendship with Skipper is now rendered as a 'misdirected symptom of his immaturity,' so that the screen version, in short, now 'powerfully instills one of the key elements of 1950s ideology—the recuperative power of family solidarity.'[26]

Palmer and Bray masterfully address the film's handling of the movement around the plantation: 'The Pollitt mansion, inside and out, becomes a more plastic playing space, with the characters' restless movement through it indexing their turmoil and transformation.'[27] They identify the basement, where the emphasis on excessive materialism as antithetical to love (à la *Death of a Salesman*) and the reconciliation of father and son occur, as a masculine or patriarchal space, with the floors above it becoming a domestic space that is still largely matriarchal, despite the temporary rebellion of Gooper against the tactics of Mae. Nevertheless, if at first glance it appears that the movement toward melodrama is complete—with Brick asserting his desire for Maggie and Big Daddy snatching the leadership of the family back from Big Mama—Palmer and Bray would argue that Brick's capitulation is 'hollow,' and that what the film instead presents is a study in the crisis men faced at the time, when any homosexual desire or even homosocial inclination had to be denied in order to conform to the ideal of home and family and propinquity. So man must leave the basement space and be domesticated into fatherhood (and the passing on of property to an heir by birth), condemned to a kind of feminizing conformity. Yet this is part and parcel of the genre that *Cat* so well exemplifies; the film:

■ endorse[s] a contradiction at the heart of melodrama: to believe both that the individual finds himself only within the family, and also that individuality exists only in a space beyond the conventional demands of domestic life. Despite a very conventional ending, Brooks's version follows Williams's closely in presenting Brick as a character who cannot break his attachment to what society defines as the only acceptable set of roles and responsibilities for a mature man, but who also cannot easily abandon his urge toward self-fashioning.[28] □

RESPONDING TO THE SMALL SCREEN: PAMELA HANKS AND JUNE SCHLUETER

In her 1986 essay, Pamela Anne Hanks grounds her ideas about John Erman's 1984 television adaptation of *Streetcar* in reader response theory as articulated by Wolfgang Iser, among others—which holds that meaning, rather than inhering exclusively within a text, is produced by interaction with the reader and so subject to continual change over time.

As she puts it into practice, however, this theory is mediated by gender and feminist studies, and the resultant essay, because it focuses upon Blanche's rape, forms an interesting companion piece to Bak's semiotic study considered in the previous chapter. Hanks begins by attempting to understand her reaction to a discomforting still photo from the TV production used as the cover of a paperback reprint of the play; the illustration positions the viewer so that she is looking over Stanley's naked back and shoulder at the face of Blanche as she is being violently raped. Being forced to see Blanche's expression prompts Hanks to think about herself as a voyeuristic spectator who is rendered 'guilty' for participating in the degradation of a vulnerable woman eroticized by the camera's eye. Even more disturbing is Hanks's uneasy sense that she, as a female observer, night 'derive pleasure from her own victimization,' even though, in this case, 'desire ... leads to madness, to a willed annihilation of selfhood.'[29] Hanks believes that this response contrasts sharply with what she imagines the common reaction would have been looking at the still photo of a bare-chested Stanley from the original film version that appeared on an earlier paperback cover, which embodied the somewhat sympathetic approach to him of audiences at the time. What has intervened between the two covers is the woman's movement that destabilized the traditional construction of female sexuality, so that now the drama's center could be 'given back to Blanche,'[30] where it rightfully belonged all along.

Now that society's attitude toward the expression of female sexuality was less repressive, women were not as inclined to accept unquestioningly Hollywood's stereotypical coding of the 'submissive woman.' Women's once-sanguine attitude toward Stanley as 'ignorant ... sensitive, misunderstood' and their 'sentimental satisfaction from the beautiful tragedy' of Blanche while watching the 1951 film version have been shattered by the conviction that Stanley is 'a brutal animal ... a misogynist' and their horror at Blanche's 'victimization at the hands of a social order that will punish her brutally should she violate its codes.'[31] Consequently, the camerawork near the end of the television version sends a 'more threatening' message: 'From the floor, where the viewer is positioned with Blanche, the iconography is clear: Submit or be violently destroyed.'[32] The new implication is that for a viewer to justify Stanley's action for any reason—sudden lust, temporary lack of sexual gratification from a pregnant wife, even Blanche's flirtatiousness—is tantamount to expunging 'woman's selfhood.' Whereas Kazan had visualized the rape as if it were the 'figures' of Beauty and the Beast 'enacting an archetypal embrace in a mirror,'[33] under Erman's direction a now unsubmissive Ann-Margret (whom Williams 'insisted' take on the role of Blanche for television) refuses to remain in the restricted space the patriarchy has assigned to her, 'objectifies' male bodies by eroticizing them, knows how to appropriate the gaze so that she becomes the subject, and aggressively 'fights back' during the rape against Stanley's 'gratuitous cruelty.' As if to make Stanley's 'sexual rage' less offensive to the male viewer, Erman gradually pulls the camera back to hide the scene behind nylon curtains, but he cannot, finally, blunt the horror of the attack for female spectators:

■ Although [Stanley's] back is to the camera as we look over his shoulder into the terror in her face, we know what his face looks like, without seeing it, just as we know what he is thinking; for the shot is a companion piece to the one in which he threw Stella on the bed, rage in his voice. ...[34] □

Depending on the spectator, the rape may be not just a singular act but rather 'symbolic' of something larger: to the extent that male viewers regard the rape as a response to women's urge for 'power to transgress gender-differentiated roles,' then they are implicated in a 'gang-rape,'[35] while for females in the audience, this Blanche, unlike Vivien Leigh's, seems even more 'silenced' and 'doomed' in her fight to assert the ultimate value of 'compassion' in a repressive society. In either case, Hanks's larger agenda is to make readers aware of the gendered 'interpretive strategies' that Williams intended that they all along would apply to his drama.

The most thorough text-centered analysis of Erman's television adaptation, which is altogether more naturalistic and less expressionistic in its cinematic approach than the Kazan film, is provided in a 1985 essay by June Schlueter who, given the iconic status—'inevitable, indelible, inimitable'[36]—of the original movie, asks whether the new version should have been made at all. At the very least, Erman restores those elements that the Production Code forced Kazan to jettison: mention of Allan's homosexuality; explicit representation of Blanche's rape; and Stella's failure to repudiate Stanley for it. But beyond this, Schlueter's detailed comparison/contrast demonstrates that Erman presents a much more physically sensual and tigerish Blanche in Ann-Margret, whose 'shameless flirtation' and 'blatantly sexual overture'[37] make her a subject exerting control; a cruder and more orally fixated Stanley (Treat Williams); and a more performative cat-and-mouse game involving Mitch, with whom Blanche admits her past without mitigating it, rendering her, in Schlueter's estimation, less vulnerable and less sympathetic. In filming the rape more directly, and thus emphasizing the cruelty and violence of Stanley's animality, Erman is:

■ not restoring censored material ... but giving visual form to the implications of the text. ... In choosing to be explicit, Erman may well have been yielding to the tastes of a popular audience and to the convention of television violence; but it is more likely that he saw in this moment not only the triumph of [Stanley[over the vestal virgin of Belle Reve, but the consummation of the earlier scenes between these two sexual beings. In Erman, the moment of rape visually joins the 'deliberate cruelty' that Blanche deplores ... and the sexuality that has been seething for months.[38] □

And yet, what Schlueter sees as the problematic nature of Williams's text, in which Stanley appears to win exoneration as 'the final physical manifestation of power,'[39] would seem not to be corrected by Erman's revisioning, since Stella, rather than rejecting Stanley, goes arm-in-arm with him past the poker players into their bedroom. (Perhaps, however, Schlueter has missed Williams's subtle textual hints in the original play of a relationship changed and fractured, with Stella less narcotized by Stanley's touch and the child supplanting Stanley in her life.) As Schlueter notes, nevertheless, Erman 'embellishes' Williams's ending, making more explicit, through the scene of a car going toward the cathedral on its way to the sanitarium and the sound of bells (along with the earlier secular sacramentals of candles and purificatory baths and rain) the elevation of Blanche as a kind of violated Madonna, a motif that goes back to *Streetcar's* early source in the one-act *Portrait of a Madonna*. Schlueter, recognizing the slight move toward sentimentality, still judges it 'an effective—and needed—final moment of redemption' used to conclude a version that has a justifiable claim to being considered 'an artifact of value not as a reproduction, but as an original.'[40]

Gene Phillips pays disappointingly brief attention—although his comments are as extensive as anyone's have so far been—to the 1976 telecast of *Cat*, directed by Robert Moore and starring Laurence Olivier as Big Daddy. Based on the 1974 revision of the play that Williams apparently considered definitive, the teleplay, as Philips says, is notable for restoring 'all of the homosexual implications,'[41] reinserting the material on Skipper and Straw and Ochello that had been omitted from Brooks's film. To add to what Phillips notes, the action moves freely around the Pollitt manse, beginning in the bathroom where Brick is soaking his injured leg, though not into the basement where Brooks had taken it, so that a glass chandelier in the hallway must stand as evidence of the futility of putting material possessions over love and thinking immortality can be bought. In general, the grotesquerie of the minor characters is diminished, and the handling of the Black servants is more muted and respectful. Robert Wagner's Brick is less angry and more detached to the very end than Newman was, and Natalie Wood's Maggie conveys more subtle power and determination than Taylor had. But Olivier's Big Daddy, somewhat resembling Mark Twain in his wavy hair and white suit, shows little of Ives's vital lust for life; and the crucial confrontation between him and Brick is lacking in emotional intensity and impact—giving indisputable support to Phillips's conclusion that the TV version does not 'probe the complex relationships as well'[42] as the earlier movie had. Maggie's announcement of new life coming is met not by Big Daddy's affirmation but simply by instructions to call in his lawyer. The visual image of his wearing the birthday robe is left to carry the resonance of Brick and Maggie's child as a counterweight to Big Daddy's approaching death, while Brick's passive submission to Maggie's necessary greater strength, and his quizzical skepticism over her declaration of love, capture the tonality that Williams initially intended for *Cat's* ending.

CONCLUSION

It is no small measure of Williams's achievement as a dramatist that, in the variety and depth of his characters and the range and largeness of his themes, he can be spoken of in the same breath as Shakespeare. *A Streetcar Named Desire* seems as close to *Hamlet* as any American playwright is likely to come, just as *Cat on a Hot Tin Roof* does to *King Lear*. More than one critic has compared Blanche to the Danish Prince, and not just in the difficulty the role presents for the actor; it is true as well of her psychological complexity and the moral and ethical dilemma she faces. And what else is her paean to 'poetry and music' and 'tenderer feelings,' coupled with her *'don't hang back with the brutes!'* warning against the possibility of humankind's backsliding if not Williams's 'What a piece of work is man' speech?[1] *Cat*, too, is *Lear*-like, not only in the magnitude of Big Daddy's passion as he divides his kingdom and relinquishes power preparatory to facing death, but also in the breaking and restitution of bonds between parent and child.[2]

Yet Williams's sensibility and artistic style are clearly modernist, in his emphasis on the fragmentation of personality, in the search for order and meaning that can be found only in human communion and an embrace of shared values in a disorderly and seemingly unwieldy cosmos, as well as in his formal experimentation with techniques for dramatizing human subjectivity and consciousness. Perhaps because the twentieth century and beyond has been so traumatized by war and other apocalyptic events, one of the most persistent motifs among modernist (and postmodernist) artists has been their almost obsessive concern with time and memory, encapsulated visually in Salvador Dali's famous painting *The Persistence of Memory* (1931) and seen in novels from Marcel Proust's *Remembrance of Things Past* (1913–27) to Julian Barnes's *The Sense of an Ending* (2011) and in the theatre from the plays of J B. Priestley to Samuel Beckett's *Krapp's Last Tape* (1958), Harold Pinter's *Landscape* (1969) and *Old Times* (1971), and Edward Albee's *Three Tall Women* (1991). In his extra-dramatic writings, Williams has addressed both of these topics: the first, in an essay where he bemoans 'the corrupting rush of time' itself, which is 'life's destroyer';[3] and the second in the Production Notes to his first major success, where he suggests that developing strategies for dramatizing memory presents one of the great challenges, while simultaneously offering possibilities for bold technical innovation. Regretting the passing of a lost, idyllic time certainly weighs on both Blanche and Brick, as does the inevitability of a future circumscribed by madness and loss of desire/desirability for Blanche and mortality for Big Daddy—whereas Maggie by seizing the present day can open up the future for Brick, and even posthumously for Big Daddy. Although Blanche and Brick are both haunted by guilty memories, there is nothing in the dramaturgy of either work *per se* (unlike the case with *Glass Menagerie*) that would denote them specifically as memory plays. At the same time, however, some of the lengthy monologues in *Cat* that were spotlighted and delivered directly to the audience in the initial Broadway production, might conceivably be thought of as memory sequences; and the expressionistic handling of Blanche's psyche also opens up that possibility. In fact, one recent production of *Streetcar* actually interpolated a young Allan and Blanche who materialized in dim lighting upstage to replay the crucial scene from the past when she rejected him.[4] Since at least one critic, as mentioned in an earlier chapter, considers Brick as the central consciousness of *Cat*, might not Brick's recollection of Skipper and himself chastely clasping hands from their separate beds legitimately be staged in a similar manner? Indeed, it is just such re-imaginings of the plays for production (as has happened with Shakespearean re-interpretations) that might open up new modes of inquiry for academic scholars and critics.

A second avenue that has received little attention is the pedagogical one: how might the insights afforded by scholarly criticism be used to inform school and university classroom instruction of *Streetcar* and *Cat*? To take just one example, could what is known about the shaping of the dramatic text into a theatre text in the production and performance process—including the way that description of stage setting and character movement assume textual authority in printed editions intended for solitary readers as well as actors/directors—provide a basis for practical pedagogy in teaching the plays 'visually' within an instructional setting?[5] And, finally, while much has been made by the critics about supposed influences upon Williams, especially Chekhov and Lawrence, little has been done to probe Williams's influence on later playwrights— beyond Miller's well-known admission that *Streetcar* influenced the style and staging of *Salesman*, which was designed and directed by the same Mielziner/Kazan team that had brought Williams's play to the stage.[6]

Williams's coming to prominence as a major dramatist converged fortuitously with the beginnings of academic acceptance of the dramatic text as an appropriate subject for serious literary study; consequently, by examining the secondary material about Williams one is really able (as has been seen throughout this monograph) to trace the history and development of criticism and critical theory from the 1950s onward: from appreciative biographies and New Critical close reading and explication; through psychoanalytic and Marxist and semiotic approaches;

on to feminist/gender and queer theory; arriving at New Historicist and poststructuralist interpretive strategies, the latter indebted largely to the French intellectuals. Although many topics have been more than adequately covered, some areas of potentially fruitful investigation remain. The issues of race and ethnicity and assimilation into the working class community of the postwar South in the New Orleans of *Streetcar* have been attended to; but an equally thorough examination of racial (the Black servants) and class (the 'upstart' Maggie) tensions within the patriarachal structure of the society in *Cat*, complete with its representatives of the church and the legal system, remains to be undertaken. And while Blanche and Brick have been much compared, less has been undertaken to see Blanche and Maggie in light of one another: not only are each of them sexually desiring female subjects, but both are also Other, outsiders because of their past social status, attempting to find their place within an alien power structure unwelcoming to them. Who holds the power (whether sexual or economic, on the domestic scene or in matters of feeling and the heart), how one negotiates that power, and how that power is used and enforced so that people might not just co-exist humanely but achieve full humanity are issues to which both *Streetcar* and *Cat* speak. These works attest as well to the dramatist's mastery in the handling of physical space—onstage and off, public and private, revealed or closeted—to indicate who wields literal power and control as well as to dramatize, oftentimes through symbol and metaphor, the interiority of the character's psyche.

Finally, with the exception of spotty comments that indicate links between Williams's view of the South and Faulkner's, there has been little consideration of the position plays like *Streetcar* and *Cat* hold within the larger landscape of canonical American literature, particularly the important fiction of the late 1940s and 1950s, and of how Williams may be representative of the larger culture, and of what in a lasting and original way he contributed—and continues to contribute—to it. In short, is there anything about Williams's central emphases that might be said to make him a peculiarly American writer, over and above such culturally specific topics as, for example, the precarious fate of the returning veteran or the excessive adulation for the sports hero? Certainly one of his chief concerns has always been with the tension that arises when the individual attempts to forge an identity true to himself within an oftentimes narrow and repressive society that tries to thwart the free expression of what it sees as different, if not abnormal. So the playwright's focus has always been on the marginalized outsider, particularly the sexual Other, whom the society wants to contain or neutralize—make Same—to reduce any threat to the status quo. Any and every perceived minority, defined by its sexuality, race, or ethnicity, or simply made vulnerable to misunderstanding by its fragile psyche or artistic sensibility, receives Williams's special regard and sympathy. Some of the more recent scholarly attention and reconsideration has been focused on his position among gay writers and artists, yet Williams is not only of the margins but deservedly at the very center of culture, high and low, academic and popular, scholarly and common—as the inclusion of his works in school and university curricula and their frequent revival on stages around the world attest. Although the continued scholarly and critical fascination with *Streetcar* and *Cat* may reside in different sources—including in the case of the first, the audience's complex attitudes toward Stanley and Blanche and the range of issues about modern civilization the play raises and, in the case of the second, the ambiguities about Brick's sexuality and the existence of multiple textual variations—what John Bak has written about *Streetcar* could just as easily apply to *Cat*: 'For all its attention, *Streetcar* remains a riddle no closer to being solved today than it was a half-century ago.'[7]

Notes

INTRODUCTION

1 Tennessee Williams, 'Poem for Paul,' in Lyle Leverich, *Tom: The Unknown Tennessee Williams* (New York: Crown, 1995), p. 419.

2 Tennessee Williams, 'Tennessee Williams Presents His POV,' in *Where I Live: Selected Essays*, ed. Christine R. Day and Bob Woods (New York: New Directions, 1978), pp. 116–17.

3 Tennessee Williams, *The Glass Menagerie* (New York: New Directions, 1970), p. 7.

4 Williams, *Menagerie* (1970), p. 23.

5 Williams, 'Forward to *Camino Real*,' *Essays* (1978), p. 66.

6 Tennessee Williams, quoted in Don Ross, 'Williams on a Hot Tin Roof,' in *Conversations with Tennessee Williams*, ed. Albert J. Devlin (Jackson: University Press of Mississippi, 1986), p. 52.

7 Tennessee Williams, *Cat on a Hot Tin Roof* (New York: New Directions, 2004), p. 117.

8 For full texts, see: 'Portrait of a Madonna,' in *27 Wagons Full of Cotton and Other One-Act Plays* (New York: New Directions, 1945), pp. 87–104; 'Interior Panic,' in *The Tennessee Williams Annual Review*, 9 (2007), pp. 6–24; and *Collected Stories* (New York: Ballantine Books, 1985), pp. 319–43.

9 Tennessee Williams, *The Night of the Iguana* (New York: New Directions, 2009), p. 124.

10 Tennessee Williams, *Memoirs* (Garden City, NY: Doubleday, 1975), p. 252.

11 Brooks Atkinson, '"Streetcar" Tragedy—Mr. Williams' Report on Life in New Orleans,' in *Twentieth Century Interpretations of 'A Streetcar Named Desire,'* ed. Jordan Y. Miller (Englewood Cliffs, NJ: Prentice-Hall, 1971), pp. 32–3. Along with Atkinson's, Miller reprints ten other early reviews (pp. 27–52). Philip C. Kolin reproduces and comments upon eleven newspaper notices from the play's pre-Broadway runs in New Haven, Boston, and Philadelphia in 'The First Critical Assessments of *A Streetcar Named Desire*: The *Streetcar* Tryouts and the Reviewers,' *Journal of Dramatic Theory and Criticism*, 6.1 (1991), pp. 45–67. S. Alan Chesler, although focusing on scholarly commentaries, surveys some reviews as well in '*A Streetcar Named Desire*: Twenty-Five Years of Criticism,' *Notes on Mississippi Writers*. 7 (1974), pp. 44–53.

12 Brooks Atkinson, 'Theatre: Tennessee Williams' *Cat*: Writer Depicts Some Restless Delta Folk,' *New York Times*, March 25, 1955, p. 18.

13 Eric Bentley, *In Search of Theatre* (New York: Vintage Books, 1959), pp. 85–6.

14 Eric Bentley, *What is Theatre? Incorporating 'The Dramatic Event' and Other Reviews, 1944–1967* (New York: Atheneum, 1968), p. 231.

15 Bentley, *What Is?* (1968), p. 225.

16 Harold Clurman, *The Divine Pastime: Theatre Essays* (New York: Macmillan, 1974), p. 14.

17 Clurman, *Pastime* (1954), p. 16.

18 Walter Kerr, 'A Secret is Half-Told in Fountains of Words,' reprinted in *The Critical Response to Tennessee Williams*, ed. George W. Crandell (Westport, CT: Greenwood Press, 1996), p. 119. Crandell includes two later reviews of *Cat* as well (pp. 120–5). Also, S. Alan Chesler gives brief mention to some of the periodical criticism in his material about *Cat* in 'Tennessee Williams: Reassessment and Assessment,' in *Tennessee Williams: A Tribute*, ed. Jac Tharpe (Jackson: University Press of Mississippi, 1977), pp. 861–6.

19 Kerr, 'Secret' (1996), p. 120.

20 Williams, *Essays* (1978), p. 71.

21 Williams, *Essays* (1978), pp. 71–2. Williams's article appears in a somewhat altered form in *Five O'Clock Angel: Letters of Tennessee Williams to Maria St. Just, 1948–52* (New York: Knopf, 1990), pp. 108–10, with a different concluding paragraph linking his argument 'That "Truth" has a protean nature, that its face changes in the eye of each beholder' to a 'point' made recurrently by Luigi Pirandello.

22 Walter Kerr, *Journey to the Centre of the Theatre* (New York: Knopf, 1970), p. 102.

23 Williams, *Essays* (1978), p. 19. The essay is reprinted under a new title, 'The Catastrophe of Success,' as the introduction to *Glass Menagerie* (1970), pp. 11–17.

24 Mary McCarthy, 'Theatre Chronicle: Oh, Sweet Mystery of Life,' *Partisan Review*, 15.3 (1948), p. 360.

25 William Becker, 'Reflections on Three New Plays,' *The Hudson Review*, 8.2 (1955), p. 268.

26 Tennessee Williams, *A Streetcar Named Desire* (New York: New Directions, 1980), p. 178.

27 For reviews that assume the form of mini-essays about two other productions of *Streetcar* in the first decade of the new century see Maria Margaronis, 'Blues for the True at Heart,' *Times Literary Supplement*, October 18, 2002, pp. 20–1, and Daniel Mendelsohn, 'Victims on Broadway II,' *The New York Review of Books*, June 9, 2005, pp. 31–3.

CHAPTER ONE

1 Quoted in Lewis Funke and John E. Booth, 'Williams on Williams,' in *Conversations with Tennessee Williams*, ed. Albert J. Devlin (Jackson: University Press of Mississippi, 1986), p. 100; and quoted in Studs Terkel, 'Studs Terkel Talks with Tennessee Williams,' in *Conversations* (1986), p. 88.

2 Tennessee Williams, *Memoirs* (Garden City, NY: Doubleday, 1975), p. 102.

3 Elia Kazan, 'Notebook for *A Streetcar Named Desire*,' in *Directors on Directing: A Source Book of the Modern Theater*, ed. Toby Cole and Helen Krich Chinoy (Indianapolis, IN: Bobbs-Merrill, 1963), p. 365.

4 Tennessee Williams, quoted in Charles Higham, *Brando: The Unauthorized Biography* (New York: New American Library, 1987), p. 58.

5 Kazan, 'Notebook' (1963), p. 364.

6 Kazan, 'Notebook' (1963), p. 265.

7 Kazan, 'Notebook' (1963), pp. 366, 272, 374, 378.

8 Kazan, 'Notebook' (1963), p. 370.

9 Kazan, 'Notebook' (1963), p. 370.

10 Kazan, 'Notebook' (1963), p. 376.

11 Kazan, 'Notebook' (1963), p. 377.

12 Kazan, 'Notebook' (1963), p. 378.

13 Elia Kazan, *A Life* (New York: Knopf, 1988), p. 542.

14 Kazan, *Life* (1988), p. 541.

15 Kazan, *Life* (1988), p. 543.

16 Kazan, *Life* (1988), p. 544.

17 David Richard Jones, *Great Directors at Work: Stanislavsky, Brecht, Kazan, Brook* (Berkeley: University of California Press, 1986), p. 187.

18 Jones, *Directors* (1986), p. 195.

19 Jones, *Directors* (1986), p. 189.

20 Brenda Murphy, *Tennessee Williams and Elia Kazan: A Collaboration in the Theatre* (Cambridge: Cambridge University Press, 1992), p. 25.

21 Tennessee Williams, *Cat on a Hot Tin Roof* (New York: New Directions, 2004), p. 15.

22 Williams, *Cat* (2004), p. 16.

23 Marian Price, '*Cat on a Hot Tin Roof*: The Uneasy Marriage of Success and Idealism,' *Modern Drama*, 38 (1995), p. 324.

24 Price, 'Marriage' (1995), p. 327.

25 Tennessee Williams, *The Rose Tattoo* (New York: New Directions, 2010), p. 1.

26 Price, 'Marriage' (1995), p. 333.

27 Price, 'Marriage' (1995), p. 329.

28 William Sacksteder, 'The Three Cats: A Study in Dramatic Structure,' *Drama Survey*, 53 (1966–67), p. 256.

29 Sacksteder, 'Three' (1966–67), p. 257.

30 Brian Parker, 'Bringing Back Big Daddy,' *The Tennessee Williams Annual Review*, 3 (2000), pp. 91–9. On the process of composition, production, and publication, see George W Crandell, *Tennessee Williams: A Descriptive Bibliography* (Pittsburgh, PA: University of Pittsburgh Press, 1995), pp. 127–43.

31 Parker, 'Back' (2000), p. 98.

32 Parker, 'Back' (2000), p. 98.

33 Philip C. Kolin, *Williams: 'A Streetcar Named Desire'* (Cambridge: Cambridge University Press, 2000), pp. 156–7. Were Kolin to update his production history, he would certainly give some attention to the 2010 performance at the *Comédie-Française*, as well as to Ivo van Hove's 1999 production that stripped bare both actors and stage furnishings to make an onstage bathtub the play's focal point, and to the highly acclaimed revival starring Cate Blanchett; for a review of the last named, see Ben Brantley, 'A Fragile Flower Rooted to the Cruel Earth,' *The New York Times*, December 3, 2009, pp. C1, C6.

34 Kolin, *Williams* (2000), p. xvi.

35 For the complete text of *Belle Reprieve*, consult *The Harcourt Brace Anthology of Drama*, 2nd edn., ed. W. B. Worthen (New York: Harcourt Brace, 1996), pp. 1232–42.

36 Carolyn Clay, 'Islands in the Storm,' (rev. of *Pussy on the House*), *The Boston Phoenix*, March 4, 2011, p. 24.

37 Clay, 'Islands' (2011), p. 24.

38 George W. Crandell, '*Cat on a Hot Tin Roof,*' in *Tennessee Williams: A Guide to Research and Performance*, ed. Philip C. Kolin (Westport, CT: Greenwood Press, 1998), p. 119.

39 Hilton Als, 'The Theatre: Love and Disaster,' *The New Yorker*, March 17, 2008, p. 89. Another reviewer (Jeremy McCarter, 'Upper Broadway,' *New York Magazine*, March 28, 2008, p. 67) chose to not even mention that this was an all-Black production.

CHAPTER TWO

1 Esther Merle Jackson, *The Broken World of Tennessee Williams* (Madison: University of Wisconsin Press, 1965), p. 46.

2 Kenneth Holditch and Richard Freeman Leavitt, *Tennessee Williams and the South* (Jackson: University Press of Mississippi, 2002), p. x.

3 For a discussion of the Clarksdale, Mississippi, residents upon whom Williams may have modeled characters of *Streetcar*, consult Panny Mayfield, 'Mississippi's Tennessee,' *Mississippi*, 9.5 (May/June 1991), pp. 38–44. See Charles S. Watson, 'The Cultural Imagination of Tennessee Williams,' in *The History of Southern Drama* (Lexington: University Press of Kentucky, 1997), p. 179 for specifics about real-life models for Big Daddy, including the playwright's own father. Allean Hale, a leading expert on Williams's early years, proposes that Brick might be a composite of three classmates from his brief time at the University of Missouri in 'How a Tiger Became the Cat,' *Tennessee Williams Literary Journal*, 2.1 (1990–91), pp. 33–6.

4 W. Kenneth Holditch, 'The Last Frontier of Bohemia: Tennessee Williams in New Orleans,' *The Southern Quarterly*, 23.2 (Winter 1985), p. 18. Holditch's essay appears in somewhat altered form as 'South Toward Freedom: Tennessee Williams,' in *Literary New Orleans*, ed. Richard S. Kennedy (Baton Rouge: Louisiana State University Press, 1992), pp. 61–75.

5 Kimball King, 'Tennessee Williams: A Southern Writer,' *The Mississippi Quarterly*, 48 (1995), p. 627.

6 Jacob H. Adler, 'The Rose and the Fox: Notes on the Southern Drama,' in *South: Modern Southern Literature in its Cultural Setting*, ed. Louis D. Rubin, Jr. and Robert D. Jacobs (Garden City, NY: Doubleday, 1961), pp. 358–9.

7 J. H. Adler, 'Rose' (1961), p. 363.

8 J. H. Adler, 'Rose' (1961), p. 369.

9 Thomas E. Porter, *Myth and Modern America Drama* (Detroit, MI: Wayne State University Press, 1969), p. 163.

10 Porter, *Myth* (1969), p. 169.

11 Porter, *Myth* (1969), pp. 172–3.

12 Robert Bray, '*A Streetcar Named Desire*: The Political and Historical Subtext,' in *Confronting Tennessee Williams's 'A Streetcar Named Desire': Essays in Critical Pluralism*, ed. Philip C. Kolin (Westport, CT: Greenwood Press, 1993), p. 189.

13 Bray, 'Subtext' (1993), p. 190.

14 Bray, 'Subtext' (1993). p. 191.

15 Leonard Quirino, 'The Cards Indicate a Voyage on *A Streetcar Named Desire*,' in *Tennessee Williams: 13 Essays*, ed. Jac Tharpe (Jackson: University Press of Mississippi, 1980), p. 41.

16 Quirino, 'Cards' (1980), pp. 33–4.

17 Quirino, 'Cards' (1980), p. 35.

18 Quirino, 'Cards' (1980), p. 40.

19 Quirino, 'Cards' (1980), p. 46.

20 George W. Crandell, '"Echo Spring": Reflecting the Gaze of Narcissus in Tennessee Williams's *Cat on a Hot Tin Roof*,' *Modern Drama*, 42 (1999), p. 428.

21 Judith J. Thompson, *Tennessee Williams' Plays: Memory, Myth, and Symbol*—University of Kansas Humanities Studies, vol. 54 (New York: Peter Lang, 1987), p. 48.

22 Thompson, *Memory* (1987), p. 51.

23 Thompson might have done more with the possible religious iconography behind several sculptural character configurations in the play, not only Big Daddy's laying on of hands as a kind of blessing of Maggie and the reconsummation of her marriage to Brick, but also of possible allusions to Michelangelo's art in Act Two: a 'Pietà,' albeit of father and son, or perhaps even an echo of the 'Creation' from the Sistine Chapel ceiling, with the Father (Big Daddy) stretching out his arm to bring the Son/Adam (Brick) to life.

24 Thompson, *Memory* (1987), p. 77.

25 Thompson, *Memory* (1987), p. 78.

CHAPTER THREE

1 Tennessee Williams, *Where I Live: Selected Essays*, ed. Christine B. Day and Bob Woods (New York: New Directions, 1978), p. 60.

2 See Thomas P. Adler, 'Culture, Power, and the (En)gendering of Community: Tennessee Williams and Politics,' *The Mississippi Quarterly*, 48.4 (1995), pp. 649–55.

3 Robert J. Corber, *Homosexuality in Cold War America: Resistance and the Crisis of Masculinity* (Durham, NC: Duke University Press, 1997), pp. 1–43.

4 Paul J. Hurley, 'Tennessee Williams: The Playwright as Social Critic,' reprinted in *The Critical Response to Tennessee Williams*, ed. George W. Crandell (Westport, CT: Greenwood Press, 1996), p. 126.

5 Hurley, 'Social' (1996), p. 127.

6 Arthur Miller, 'The Shadow of the Gods,' in *Theater Essays*, ed. Robert A. Martin (New York: Penguin, 1978), p. 191.

7 Hurley, 'Social' (1996), p. 135.

8 Hurley, 'Social' (1996), p. 133.

9 Tennessee Williams, *Cat on a Hot Tin Roof* (New York: New Directions, 2004), p. 173.

10 Hurley, 'Social' (1996), p. 137.

11 Larry T. Blades, 'The Returning Vet's Experience in *A Streetcar Named Desire*: Stanley as the Decommissioned Warrior under Stress,' *The Tennessee Williams Annual Review*, 10 (2009), p. 18.

12 Blades, 'Returning' (2009), p. 28.

13 Lionel Kelly, 'The White Goddess, Ethnicity, and the Politics of Desire,' in *Confronting Tennessee Williams's 'A Streetcar Named Desire': Essays in Critical Pluralism*, ed. Philip C. Kolin (Westport, CT: Greenwood Press, 1992), p. 125.

14 Kelly, 'Goddess' (1993), p. 128.

15 Kelly, 'Goddess' (1993), p. 131.

16 Kelly, 'Goddess' (1993), p. 130.

17 Curiously, although the presence of the Black woman in *Streetcar's* opening scene has been frequently remarked upon, critics have given virtually no notice to the Black servants of the Pollitt family (the female Sookey and the male Lacey) or to the intersection of race and class in *Cat*.

18 George W. Crandell, 'Misrepresentation and Miscegenation: Reading the Racialized Discourse of Tennessee Williams's *A Streetcar Named Desire*,' *Modern Drama*, 40 (1997), p. 339.

19 Crandell, 'Miscegenation' (1997), pp. 344–5.

20 Mary F. Brewer, *Staging Whiteness* (Middletown, CT: Wesleyan University Press, 2005), p. 72.

21 Brewer, *Whiteness* (2005), p. 72.

22 Brewer, *Whiteness* (2005), p. 74.

23 Brewer, *Whiteness* (2005), p. 76.

24 Brewer, *Whiteness* (2005), p. 77.

25 Tennessee Williams, *Essays* (1978), pp. 8, 13.

26 Williams, *Essays* (1978), pp. 12–13.

27 Michael Paller, 'A Playwright with a Social Conscience,' *The Tennessee Williams Annual Review*, 10 (2009), p. 107.

28 Brenda Murphy, *Congressional Theatre: Dramatizing McCarthyism on Stage, Film, and Television* (Cambridge: Cambridge University Press, 1999), p. 3.

29 Bruce McConachie, '*Cat* and the Grotesque in the Cold War,' *Tennessee Williams Literary Journal*, (1998), p. 49.

30 McConachie, 'Grotesque' (1998), p. 47.

31 McConachie, 'Grotesque' (1998), p. 49.

32 McConachie, 'Grotesque' (1998), p. 57.

33 McConachie, 'Grotesque' (1998), p. 58.

34 John S. Bak, '"sneakin' and spyin'" from Broadway to the Beltway: Cold War Masculinity, Brick, and Homosexual Existentialism,' *Theatre Journal*, 56.2 (2004), p. 249.

35 Bak, 'Existentialism' (2004), p. 240.

36 Bak, 'Existentialism' (2004), pp. 244–5.

37 Bak, 'Existentialism' (2004), p. 234.

38 Bak, 'Existentialism' (2004), p. 245.

39 Bak, 'Existentialism' (2004), p. 249.

40 Rita Colanzi, 'Caged Birds: Bad Faith in Tennessee Williams's Drama,' *Modern Drama*, 35 (1992), p. 452.

41 Colanzi, 'Faith' (1992), p. 461.

42 Colanzi, 'Faith' (1882), p. 463.

CHAPTER FOUR

1 Susan Harris Smith, 'Generic Hegemony: American Drama and the Canon,' *American Quarterly*, 41 (March 1989), p. 12.

2 C. W. E. Bigsby, *Modern American Drama: 1945–1990* (Cambridge: Cambridge University Press, 1992), p. 1.

3 Smith, 'Hegemony' (1989), p. 17.

4 Nancy Anne Cluck, 'Showing or Telling: Narrators in the Drama of Tennessee Williams,' *American Literature*, 51.1 (March 1979), p. 84.

5 Cluck, 'Narrators' (1979), p. 92.

6 T. E. Kalem, 'The Laureate of the Outcast,' *Time*, March 7, 1983, p. 88.

7 The first issue of *Modern Drama*, the premiere scholarly journal in its field, did not appear until 1958.

8 Nancy M. Tischler, *Tennessee Williams: Rebellious Puritan* (New York: Citadel Press, 1961), p. 15.

9 Tischler, *Puritan* (1961), p. 143.

10 Tischler, *Puritan* (1961), p. 143.

11 Tischler, *Puritan* (1961), p. 214.

12 Tischler, *Puritan* (1961), p. 215.

13 Arthur Ganz, 'The Desperate Morality of the Plays of Tennessee Williams,' *The American Scholar*, 31.2 (Spring 1962), p. 282. For notes on Williams's connection with, and adherence to, organized religion, see Thomas P. Adler, 'Religion,' in *The Tennessee Williams Encyclopedia*, ed. Philip C. Kolin (Westport, CT: Greenwood Press, 2004), pp. 211–15; Kenneth Holditch, 'Acts of Grace,' Afterword to Tennessee Williams, *The Night of the Iguana* (New York: New Directions, 2009), pp. 139–47; and Gene D. Phillips, 'Tennessee Williams and The Jesuits,' *America*, 136.25, June 25, 1977, pp. 564–5.

14 Ganz, 'Morality' (1962), pp. 282, 280.

15 Ganz, 'Morality' (1962), p. 294.

16 Ganz, 'Morality' (1962), p. 294.

17 Ganz, 'Morality' (1952), p. 288.

18 Ganz, 'Morality' (1962). p. 294.

19 Benjamin Nelson, *Tennessee Williams: The Man and His Work* (New York: Ivan Obolensky, 1961), p. 212.

20 Nelson, *Williams* (1961), p. 149.

21 Nelson, *Williams* (1961), p. 152.

22 Nelson, *Williams* (1961), p. 218.

23 C. W. E. Bigsby, *A Critical Introduction to Twentieth-Century American Drama, Volume Two* (Cambridge: Cambridge University Press, 1984), pp. 19, 15.

24 Bigsby, *Modern* (1992), p. 51.

25 Bigsby, *Modern* (1992), p. 46.

26 Bigsby, *Introduction* (1984), p. 64.

27 Bigsby, *Modern* (1992), p. 49.

28 Bigsby, *Introduction* (1984), p. 67.

29 Bigsby, *Introduction* (1984), p. 93.

30 Bigsby, *Introduction* (1984), p. 92.

31 Thomas P. Adler, *'A Streetcar Named Desire': The Moth and the Lantern* (New York: Twayne, 1990), p. 20.

32 Adler, *Moth* (1990), p. 65.

33 Tennessee Williams, *A Streetcar Named Desire* (New York: New Directions, 1980), p. 169. Williams may have been making specific reference here to an often reproduced painting, *The Madonna of the Grapes* (1640), by the French artist Pierre Mignard (1612–95), now in the Louvre.

34 Adler, *Moth* (1990), p. 46.

35 Thomas P. Adler, *Mirror on the Stage: The Pulitzer Plays as an Approach to American Drama* (West Lafayette, IN: Purdue University Press, 1987), p. 20.

36 Thomas P. Adler. *American Drama 1940–1960: A Critical History* New York: Twayne, 1994), p. 151.

37 Thomas P. Adler, 'Culture, Power and the (En)gendering of Community: Tennessee Williams and Politics,' *The Mississippi Quarterly*, 48.4 (1995), p. 660.

38 Adler, 'Politics' (1995), p. 659.

39 Felicia Hardison Londre, 'A Streetcar Running Fifty Years,' in *The Cambridge Companion to Tennessee Williams*, ed. Matthew C. Roudane (Cambridge: Cambridge University Press, 1997), p. 47. This same volume of essays includes Albert J. Devlin's similarly wide-ranging overview of *Cat*, '"A place of stone": *Cat on a Hot Tin Roof*,' pp. 95–113.

40 Londre, 'Running' (1994), p. 47.
41 Felicia Hardison Londre, *Tennessee Williams* (New York: Frederick Ungar, 1979), p. 122.
42 Londre, 'Running' (1997), p. 58.
43 Londre, 'Running' (1997), p. 48.
44 Londre, 'Running' (1997), p. 57.
45 Londre, 'Running' (1997), p. 55.
46 Londre, 'Running' (1997), p. 60.
47 Londre, 'Running' (1997), p. 61.
48 Marc Robinson, *The Other American Drama* (Cambridge: Cambridge University Press, 1994), p. 58.
49 Robinson, *Other* (1994), p. 32.
50 Robinson, *Other* (1994), p. 38.
51 Robinson, *Other* (1994), p. 42.
52 Robinson, *Other* (1994), p. 40.
53 Robinson, *Other* (1994), p. 42.
54 Robinson, *Other* (1994), p. 47.

CHAPTER FIVE

1 Jo Mielziner, *Designing for the Theatre: A Memoir and a Portfolio* (New York: Bramhall, 1965), p. 124.
2 See Thomas P. Adler, 'Tennessee Williams's "Lyricism": Towards an Androgynous Form,' in *Realism and the American Dramatic Tradition*, ed. William W. Demastes (Tuscaloosa: University of Alabama Press, 1996), pp. 152–77.
3 Esther Merle Jackson, *The Broken World of Tennessee Williams* (Madison: University of Wisconsin Press, 1965), p. vii.
4 Jackson, *World* (1965), p. 89.
5 Jackson, *World* (1965), p. 87.
6 Mary Ann Corrigan, 'Realism and Theatricalism in *A Streetcar Named Desire*.' *Modern Drama*, 19.4 (1976), p. 389.
7 Corrigan, 'Theatricalism' (1976), p. 389.
8 Corrigan, 'Theatricalism' (1976), p. 395.
9 Although Fleche's work could have been discussed in the later chapter on Contemporary Theoretical Approaches, it seemed more appropriate to handle it here in connection with Corrigan's, since both are considering how what Williams called 'personal lyricism' veers away from strict realism.
10 Anne Fleche, *Mimetic Disillusion: Eugene O'Neill, Tennessee Williams, and U. S. Dramatic Realism* (Tuscaloosa: University of Alabama Press, 1997), p. 8.
11 Fleche, *Mimetic* (1997), p. 107.
12 Fleche, *Mimetic* (1997), p. 16.
13 Fleche, *Mimetic* (1997), p. 93.
14 Fleche, *Mimetic* (1997), p. 103.
15 Fleche, *Mimetic* (1997), p. 107.
16 To cite examples of other bases for such patterns, two critics suggest, in brief notes, how characters themselves or their names can be symbolic. Bert Cardullo proposes that the blind Mexican flower peddler symbolizes death, both past and to come, as well as an outsider who has lost her sexual allure ('The Blind Mexican Woman in Williams's *A Streetcar Named Desire*,' *Notes on Modern American Literature*, 7.2 [1983], item 14), and that the unnamed child represents the physical barrier that has come between Stanley and Stella, while also symbolizing Stella's new opportunity for 'self-fulfillment' ('The Role of the Baby in *A Streetcar Named Desire*,' *Notes on Contemporary Literature*, 14.2 [1984], pp. 4–5). Philip Kolin argues that Skipper's name in *Cat* not only references gay males cruising after 'lusty sailors,' but underscores the disabled Brick's hobbling around as well as his friend's

need to 'skip' Maggie sexually ('Williams's *Cat on a Hot Tin Roof*,' *The Explicator*, 60.4 [2002], pp. 215–16).

17 Henry I. Schvey, 'Madonna at the Poker Night: Pictorial Elements in Tennessee Williams's *A Streetcar Named Desire*,' in *From Cooper to Philip Roth: Essays in American Literature*, ed. J. Bakker and D. R. M. Wilkinson (Amsterdam: Rodopi, 1980), p. 72.

18 Schvey, 'Madonna' (1980), p. 73.

19 Joseph N. Riddell, '*A Streetcar Named Desire*—Nietzsche Descending,' reprinted in *Twentieth Century Interpretations of 'A Streetcar Named Desire*,' ed. Jordan Y. Miller (Englewood Cliffs, NJ: Prentice-Hall, 1971), p. 80.

20 Riddell, 'Nietzsche' (1971), p. 89.

21 Riddell, 'Nietzsche' (1971), p. 82.

22 Riddell, 'Nietzsche' (1971), p. 86.

23 Riddell, 'Nietzsche' (1971), p. 87.

24 Richard B. Vowles, 'Tennessee Williams: The World of His Imagery,' *Tulane Drama Review*, 3.2 (1958), p. 54.

25 Vowles, 'Imagery' (1958), p. 56.

26 Robert B. Heilman, *The Iceman, the Arsonist, and the Troubled Agent: Tragedy and Melodrama on the Modern Stage* (Seattle: University of Washington Press, 1973), p. 117.

27 Heilman, *Tragedy* (1973), p. 118.

28 Heilman, *Tragedy* (1973), p. 126.

29 John von Szeliski, *Tragedy and Fear: Why Modern Tragic Drama Fails* (Chapel Hill: University of North Carolina Press, 1971), pp. 173–4.

30 Leonard Berkman, 'The Tragic Downfall of Blanche Du Bois,' *Modern Drama*, 10.3 (1967), p. 232.

31 Berkman, 'Downfall' (1967), p. 252.

32 Berkman, 'Downfall' (1967), p. 254.

33 John M. Roderick, 'From "Tarantula Arms" to "Della Robbia Blue": The Tennessee Williams Tragicomic Transit Authority,' in *Tennessee Williams: A Tribute*, ed. Jac Tharpe (Jackson: University Press of Mississippi, 1977), p. 122.

34 Roderick, 'Tragicomic' (1977), p. 119.

CHAPTER SIX

1 Jacqueline O'Connor, *Dramatizing Dementia: Madness in the Plays of Tennessee Williams* (Bowling Green, OH: Bowling Green State University Press, 1997), pp. 29–32.

2 O'Connor, *Dementia* (1997), p. 35.

3 O'Connor, *Dementia* (1997), pp. 101–2.

4 O'Connor, *Dementia* (1997), p. 103.

5 Andrea Dworkin, *Intercourse* (New York: The Free Press, 1973), p. 41.

6 Dworkin, *Intercourse* (1973), p. 44.

7 Philip C. Kolin, 'Eunice Hubbell and the Feminist Thematics of *A Streetcar Named Desire*,' in *Confronting Tennessee Williams's 'A Streetcar Named Desire': Essays in Critical Pluralism*, ed. Philip C. Kolin (Westport, CT: Greenwood Press, 1993), p. 106.

8 Kolin, 'Eunice' (1993), p. 117.

9 Kolin, 'Eunice' (1993), p. 118.

10 Susan Bordo, *The Male Body: A New Look at Men in Public and in Private* (New York: Farrar, Straus, and Giroux, 1999), p. 140.

11 Bordo, *Body* (1999), p. 38.

12 Bordo, *Body* (1999), p. 142.

13 Anca Vlasopolos, 'Authorizing History: Victimization in *A Streetcar Named Desire*,' *Theatre Journal*, 38 (October 1986), p. 325.

14 Vlasopolos, 'History' (1986), p. 333.

15 Vlasopolos, 'History' (1986), p. 336.

16 Sandra M. Gilbert and Susan Gubar, *No Man's Land: The Place of the Woman Writer in the Twentieth Century, Volume 1: The War of the Words* (New Haven, CT: Yale University Press, 1988), p. 46.

17 Gilbert and Gubar, *No Man's* (1988), p. 51.

18 Kathleen Margaret Lant, 'A Streetcar Named Misogyny,' in *Violence in Drama*, ed. James Redmond (Cambridge: Cambridge University Press, 1991), p. 226.

19 Lant, 'Misogyny' (1991), p. 227.

20 Lant, 'Misogyny' (1991), p. 233.

21 John Kundert-Gibbs, 'Barren Ground: Female Strength and Male Impotence in *Who's Afraid of Virginia Woolf?* and *Cat on a Hot Tin Roof*,' in *Staging the Rage: The Web of Misogyny in Modern Drama*, ed. Katherine M. Burkman and Judith Roof (Cranbury, NJ: Fairleigh Dickinson University Press, 1998), p. 236.

22 Kundert-Gibbs, 'Barren' (1998), p. 240.

23 Kundert-Gibbs, 'Barren' (1998), pp. 245–6.

24 Gulshan Rai Kataria, 'A Hetaira of Tennessee Williams: Maggie,' *Indian Journal of American Studies*, 7.1 (1982), p. 50.

25 Kataria, 'Hetaira' (1982), pp. 52–3.

CHAPTER SEVEN

1 The affair with Doug inspired a previously unpublished poem, beginning with the lines 'Your passion is arranged in decimals/I counted 200 blond hairs on your forearm,' that is reproduced in facsimile in Williams's *Notebooks*, ed. Margaret Bradham Thornton (New Haven, CT: Yale University Press, 2006), p. 152. In a later entry from 1954 that would be echoed by critics praising Williams's ability to understand a gender and sexuality different from his own, he comments admiringly about Hemingway's 'remarkable interest in and understanding of homosexuality, for a man who wasn't a homosexual. ... The final line in *Islands in the Stream* is one man saying I love you to another' (p. 648).

2 Anne Fleche, 'When a Door is a Jar, or Out in the Theatre: Tennessee Williams and Queer Space,' *Theatre Journal*, 47 (1995), p. 261.

3 John M. Clum, '"Something Cloudy, Something Clear": Homophobic Discourse in Tennessee Williams,' *The South Atlantic Quarterly*, 88.1 (1989), pp. 162, 177.

4 John M. Clum, *Acting Gay: Male Homosexuality in Modern Drama* (New York: Columbia University Press, 1992), p. 150.

5 Clum, *Acting* (1992), pp. 186, 246.

6 Clum, *Acting* (1992), p. 153.

7 Clum, *Acting* (1992), p. 159.

8 Clum, *Acting* (1992), p. 158.

9 David Savran, *Communists, Cowboys, and Queers: The Politics of Masculinity in the Works of Arthur Miller and Tennessee Williams* (Minneapolis: University of Minnesota Press, 1992), pp. 115–16.

10 David Savran, '"By coming suddenly into a room I thought was empty": Mapping the Closet with Tennessee Williams,' *Studies in the Literary Imagination*, 24.2 (1991), p. 57.

11 Savran, *Communists* (1992), p. 83.

12 Savran, 'Closet' (1991), pp. 67–8.

13 Savran, 'Closet' (1991), p. 70.

14 Michael Paller, 'A Room Which Isn't Empty: *A Streetcar Named Desire* and the Question of Homophobia,' *Tennessee Williams Literary Journal*, 5.1(2003), p. 27.

15 Paller, 'Room' (2003), pp. 30–2.

16 Paller, 'Room' (2003), p. 35.

17 Michael Paller, *Gentlemen Callers: Tennessee Williams, Homosexuality, and Mid-Twentieth Century Broadway Drama* (New York: Palgrave Macmillan, 2005), p. 105.

18 Paller, *Callers* (2005), p. 113.

19 Paller, *Callers* (2005), p. 113.

20 Paller, 'Room' (2003), p. 36.

21 Dean Shackelford, '"The Ghost of a Man": The Quest for Self-Acceptance in Early Williams,' *Tennessee Williams Annual Review*, 4 (2001), p. 49.

22 Dean Shackelford, 'Is There a Gay Man in This Text?: Subverting the Closet in *A Streetcar Named Desire*,' in *Literature and Homosexuality*, ed. Michael J. Meyer (Amsterdam: Rodopi, 2000), p. 153.

23 Shackelford, 'Subverting' (2000), p. 150.

24 Dean Shackelford, 'The Truth That Must Be Told: Gay Subjectivity, Homophobia, and Social History in *Cat on a Hot Tin Roof*,' *Tennessee Williams Annual Review*, (1998), p. 107.

25 Shackelford, 'Truth' (1998), p. 108.

26 Shackelford, 'Truth' (1998), p. 109.

27 Shackelford, 'Truth' (1998), p. 114.

28 Roger Gross, 'The Pleasures of Brick: Eros and the Gay Spectator in *Cat on a Hot Tin Roof*,' *The Journal of American Drama and Theatre*, 9.1 (1997), p. 17.

29 Gross, 'Pleasures' (1997), p. 19.

30 Gross, 'Pleasures' (1997), p. 25.

31 Mark Royden Winchell, 'Come Back to the Locker Room Ag'in, Brick Honey!,' *Mississippi Quarterly*, 48 (1995), p. 702.

32 Winchell, 'Locker Room' (1995), p. 706.

33 Winchell, 'Locker Room' (1995), p. 711.

34 Georges-Michel Sarotte, *Like a Brother, Like a Lover: Male Homosexuality in the American Novel and Theater from Herman Melville to James Baldwin*, trans. Richard Miller (Garden City, NY: Doubleday Anchor, 1978), pp. 107–8.

35 Georges-Michel Sarotte, 'Fluidity and Differentiation in Three Plays by Tennessee Williams,' in *Staging Difference: Cultural Pluralism in American Drama and Theatre*, ed. Marc Maufort (New York: Peter Lang, 1995), p. 146.

36 Sarotte, 'Fluidity' (1995), p. 152.

37 Sarotte, *Brother* (1978), p. 114.

38 Sarotte, 'Fluidity' (1995), p. 152.

39 Michael P. Bibler, *Cotton's Queer Relations: Same-Sex Intimacy and the Literature of the Southern Plantation, 1936–1968* (Charlottesville: University of Virginia Press, 2009), p. 97.

40 Bibler, *Queer Relations* (2009), p. 107.

41 Bibler, *Queer Relations* (2009), p. 111.

42 Bibler, *Queer Relations* (2009), p. 117.

43 Bibler, *Queer Relations* (2009), pp. 118–19.

CHAPTER EIGHT

1 Michael Paller, 'A Room Which Isn't Empty: *A Streetcar Named Desire* and the Question of Homophobia,' *Tennessee Williams Literary Journal*, 5.1 (2003), p. 36.

2 Kathleen Hulley, 'The Fate of the Symbolic in *A Streetcar Named Desire*,' in *Drama and Symbolism*, ed. James Redmond (Cambridge: Cambridge University Press, 1982), p. 89.

3 Hulley, 'Symbolic' (1982), p. 90.

4 Hulley, 'Symbolic' (1982), p. 93.

5 Hulley, 'Symbolic' (1982), p. 95.

6 Hulley, 'Symbolic' (1982), p. 98.

7 John S. Bak, 'A Streetcar Named *Dies Irae*: Tennessee Williams and the Semiotics of Rape,' *The Tennessee Williams Annual Review*, (2009), p. 43.

8 Bak, 'Semiotics' (2009), p. 47.

9 Bak, 'Semiotics' (2009), pp. 49–50.

10 Bak, 'Semiotics' (2009), p. 62.

11 Bak, 'Semiotics' (2009), p. 63.

12 For extended considerations of the nature of closure in *Streetcar* see Jane Schlueter, '"We've had this date with each other from the beginning": Reading Toward Closure in *A Streetcar Named Desire*,' in *Confronting Tennessee Williams's 'A Streetcar Named Desire': Essays in Critical Pluralism*, ed. Philip C. Kolin (Westport, CT: Greenwood Press, 1993), pp. 71–82; and George Toles, 'Blanche DuBois and the Kindness of Endings,' *Raritan*, 14.4 (1995), pp. 115–43.

13 Nicholas Pagan, *Rethinking Literary Biography: A Postmodern Approach to Tennessee Williams* (Rutherford, NJ: Fairleigh Dickinson University Press, 1993), p. 107.

14 Pagan, *Rethinking* (1993), p. 124.

15 Philip C. Kolin, '"It's only a paper moon": The Paper Ontologies in Tennessee Williams's *A Streetcar Named Desire*,' *Modern Drama*, 40.4 (1997), p. 454.

16 Kolin, 'Paper' (1997), p. 460.

17 Kolin, 'Paper' (1997), p. 463.

18 Kolin, 'Paper' (1997), p. 464.

19 William Kleb, 'Marginalia, *Streetcar*, Williams and Foucault,' in *Confronting Tennessee Williams's 'A Streetcar Named Desire': Essays in Critical Pluralism*, ed. Philip C. Kolin (Westport, CT: Greenwood Press, 1993), p. 38.

20 Kleb, 'Marginalia' (1993), p. 29.

21 Kleb, 'Marginalia' (1993), p. 31.

22 Kleb, 'Marginalia' (1993), p. 36.

23 Kleb, 'Marginalia' (1993), p. 38.

24 Kleb, 'Marginalia' (1993), p. 41.

25 Philip C. Kolin, 'Roland Barthes, Tennessee Williams, and *A Streetcar Named Pleasure/Desire*,' *The Centennial Review*, 43.2 (1999), p. 298.

26 Nicholas O. Pagan, 'Tennessee Williams's Theater as Body,' *Philological Quarterly*, 22.1 (1993), p. 98.

27 Pagan, 'Body' (1993), p. 100.

28 Pagan, 'Body' (1993), p. 111.

29 Pagan, 'Body' (1993), pp. 111–12.

30 Laura Morrow and Edward Morrow, 'The Ontological Potentialities of Antichaos and Adaptation in *A Streetcar Named Desire*,' in *Confronting Tennessee Williams's 'A Streetcar Named Desire': Essays in Critical Pluralism*, ed. Philip C. Kolin (Westport, CT: Greenwood Press, 1993), p. 69.

31 Morrow and Morrow, 'Antichaos' (1993), p. 63.

32 Morrow and Morrow, 'Antichaos' (1993), p. 66.

33 Morrow and Morrow, 'Antichaos' (1993), p. 68.

34 Morrow and Morrow, 'Antichaos' (1993), p. 68.

CHAPTER NINE

1 For biographical data, consult Lyle Leverich, *Tom: The Unknown Tennessee Williams* (New York: Crown, 1995), pp. 483–4 and 495–526. For an extended treatment of the filmic techniques in *Streetcar*, see George Brandt, 'Cinematic Structure in the Work of Tennessee Williams,' in *American Theatre (Stratford-Upon-Avon Studies 10)*, ed. John Russell Brown and Bernard Harris (London: Edward Arnold, 1967), pp. 173–9; and for a general overview of Williams and the movies, see Albert E. Kalson, 'Tennessee Williams at the Delta Brilliant,' in *Tennessee Williams: 13 Essays*, ed. Jac Tharpe (Jackson: University Press of Mississippi, 1980), pp. 207–27.

2 Maurice Yacowar, *Tennessee Williams and Film* (New York: Frederick Ungar, 1977), p. 7.

3 Yacowar, *Film* (1977), p. 21.

4 Yacowar, *Film* (1977), p. 20.

5 Yacowar, *Film* (1977), p. 24.

6 Yacowar, *Film* (1977), p. 38.

7 Yacowar, *Film* (1977), pp. 46–7.

8 Yacowar, *Film* (1977), p. 43.

9 Gene D. Phillips, *The Films of Tennessee Williams* (Philadelphia, PA: Art Alliance Press, 1980), p. 18.

10 Phillips, *Films* (1980), p. 84.

11 In 1993, Warner Brothers rereleased the film of *Streetcar*, restoring the material that had been excised, including even a steamy portion of Alex North's musical score. See Gene D. Phillips, S.J., '*A Streetcar Named Desire*: The Restored Version of the Film,' *Tennessee Williams Literary Journal* V.1 (2003), pp. 39–46. For a photo essay of selected stills from the film that originally belonged to Vivien Leigh and are now in The Historic New Orleans Collection, see 'Rare Photographs from the Filming of *A Streetcar Named Desire*,' *The Tennessee Williams Annual Review* 10 (2009), pp. 6–15.

12 Phillips, *Films* (1980), p. 87.

13 Phillips, *Films* (1980), p. 144.

14 Nancy M. Tischler, 'Sanitizing the Streetcar,' *Louisiana Literature* 14 (Fall 1997), p. 50.

15 Nancy M. Tischler, '"Tiger—Tiger!": Blanche's Rape on Screen,' in *Magical Muse: Millennial Essays on Tennessee Williams*, ed. Ralph F. Voss (Tuscaloosa: University of Alabama Press, 2002), p. 67.

16 Christine Geraghty, *Now a Major Motion Picture: Film Adaptations of Literature and Drama* (Lanham, MD: Rowman & Littlefield, 2008), p. 75.

17 Geraghty, *Motion Picture* (2008), p. 76.

18 Geraghty, *Motion Picture* (2008), p. 81. For an alternative interpretation that associates Stanley's body with 'the beef-cake hero' from 1940s war movies whose 'bare torso or T-shirt … contributes to the image of victory won with an air of sexy bravado' and whose violence is an instrument the returning veteran uses to reassert patriarchal power on the domestic front, see John L Gronbeck-Tedesco's 'Absence and the Actor's Body: Marlon Brando's Performance in *A Streetcar Named Desire* on Stage and in Film,' *Studies in American Drama, 1945–Present* 8.2 (1993), pp. 115–26.

19 Geraghty, *Motion Picture* (2008), p. 93.

20 Geraghty, *Motion Picture* (2008), p. 94.

21 Geraghty, *Motion Picture* (2008), p. 99.

22 R. Barton Palmer and Robert Bray, *Hollywood's Tennessee: The Williams Films and Postwar America* (Austin: University of Texas Press, 2008), p. 85.

23 In his own exposition of the nature of this cinematic subgenre ('Tales of Sound and Fury: Observations on the Family Melodrama,' *Monogram* 4 [1972], pp. 2–15), Elsaesser comments tellingly that 'the element of interiorisation and personalisation of what are primarily ideological conflicts, together with the metaphorical interpretation of class-conflict as sexual exploitation and rape is important in all subsequent forms of melodrama, including that of the cinema. (The latter in America, of course, is a stock theme of novels and movies with a 'Southern' setting.)'

24 Palmer and Bray, *Hollywood's* (2008), p. 163.

25 Palmer and Bray, *Hollywood's* (2008), p. 166.

26 Palmer and Bray, *Hollywood's* (2008), p. 173.

27 Palmer and Bray, *Hollywood's* (2008), p. 169.

28 Palmer and Bray, *Hollywood's* (2008), pp. 178–9.

29 Pamela Anne Hanks, 'Must We Acknowledge What We Mean?: The Viewer's Role in the Filmed Versions of *A Streetcar Named Desire*,' *Journal of Popular Film and Television* 14.3 (Fall 1986), p. 116.

30 Hanks, 'Acknowledge' (1986), p. 116.

31 Hanks, 'Acknowledge' (1986), p. 117.

32 Hanks, 'Acknowledge' (1986), p. 117.

33 Hanks, 'Acknowledge' (1986), p. 120.

34 Hanks, 'Acknowledge' (1986), p. 121.

35 Hanks, 'Acknowledge' (1986), p. 120.

36 Jane Schlueter, 'Imitating an Icon: John Erman's Remake of Tennessee Williams's *A Streetcar Named Desire*,' *Modern Drama* 28 (1985), p. 139.

37 Schlueter, 'Icon' (1985), p. 141.

38 Schlueter, 'Icon' (1985), p. 144.

39 Schlueter, 'Icon' (1985), p. 143.

40 Schlueter, 'Icon' (1985), p. 147. The other television version of *Streetcar* that remains widely available on DVD, though much inferior to Erman's, is the 1995 'CBS Playhouse 90s' production, directed by Glenn Jordan. It stars Alec Baldwin as a young hotheaded Stanley, totally deficient in humor and sensitivity, and Jessica Lange as a calculating Blanche, displaying not a little of the worn-out gentility of Amanda from *Glass Menagerie;* the performance, though, is not without its effective moments, as when Blanche, remorsefully recalling her condemnation 'I know. I saw' to Allan, had acted in a way every bit as evidentiary and legalistic as Stanley. If the ending of Kazan's original film was imbalanced in one direction—with Stella taking the baby and vowing never to 'go back' to Stanley, the ending of Jordan's remake is just as imbalanced in another, with Stella and Stanley returning back inside their apartment, with no sign of the baby. For a review of Jordan's production that includes a brief recounting of other TV versions of Williams's plays see John Leonard, 'Crossover Artist,' *New York Magazine*, October 30, 1995, pp. 137–8.

41 Phillips, *Films* (1980), p. 153.

42 Phillips, *Films* (1980), p. 154. Olivier, of course, was very familiar with Williams's works, having directed the 1950 London premiere of *Streetcar*, starring his wife, Vivien Leigh, as Blanche. His conception of her character differed from Kazan's by being more naturalistic, reflecting Olivier's conviction that Williams's play, 'like other masterpieces, will continue to live and be fortified by new readings all the time.' See 'A Letter from Sir Laurence Olivier to Tennessee Williams,' intro. Philip C. Kolin, *The Missouri Review* 13.3 (1991), pp. 141–57.

CONCLUSION

1 Tennessee Williams, *A Streetcar Named Desire* (New York: New Directions, 1980), p. 83.

2 For a handling of 'parallels' between Williams and Shakespeare see Jacob H. Adler, 'Williams and the Bard,' *Tennessee Williams Literary Journal*, 2.1 (1990–91), pp. 37–49, which compares Blanche and Hamlet's idealism, their respective rejections of Allan and Ophelia, and their inability to act meaningfully in an 'imperfect world,' along with pointing out resemblances between Big Daddy and both Lear and Gloucester in their roles as fathers. Gary Harrington also points out Shakespearean resemblances and allusions in *Streetcar*: between Blanche and Ophelia, Lady Macbeth, and Cleopatra; between Mitch and Hamlet; and between the pairs of young lovers, Blanche and Allan and Romeo and Juliet. ('The Smashed Mirror: Blanche in *A Streetcar Named Desire*,' in *Staging a Cultural Paradigm: The Political and the Personal in American Drama*, eds. Barbara Ozieblo and Miriam Lopez-Rodriguez [Brussels: Peter Lang, 2002], pp. 67–78.) For a discussion of a likely 'intertextual connection' between Willliams's *Streetcar* and a classic American novel, F. Scott Fitzgerald's *The Great Gatsby*, see Jackson R. Bryer, '"Entitled to Write About Her Life": Tennessee Williams and F. Scott and Zelda Fitzgerald,' in *Magical Muse: Millennial Essays on Tennessee Williams*, ed. Ralph F. Voss (Tuscaloosa: University of Alabama Press, 2002), pp. 170–6.

3 Tennessee Williams, 'The Timeless World of a Play,' in *Where I Live: Selected Essays*, ed. Christine R. Day and Bob Woods (New York: New Directions, 1978), pp. 52, 54.

4 *A Streetcar Named Desire*, dir. Richard Sullivan Lee, Purdue University, West Lafayette, IN, September 25, 2009.

5 For examples of this scholarship of pedagogy, see Thomas P. Adler's essays, 'Setting as Meaning: A Scenic Approach to Teaching *The Glass Menagerie*,' *Alabama English*, 4.1 & 2

(1992), pp. 47–51; and 'Miller's Mindscape: A Scenic Approach to *Death of a Salesman*,' in *Approaches to Teaching Miller's 'Death of a Salesman,'* ed. Matthew C. Roudane (New York: Modern Language Association of America, 1995), pp. 45–51.

6 For brief remarks about the impact of *Streetcar* by nearly three dozen other dramatists, consult Philip C. Kolin (ed.), '*A Streetcar Named Desire*: A Playwrights' Forum,' *Michigan Quarterly Review*, 29.2 (1990), pp. 173–203.

7 John S. Bak, 'Criticism on *A Streetcar Named Desire*: A Bibliographical Survey, 1947–2003,' *Cercles* 10 (2004), p. 21, www.pdfdocspace.com/docs/5914/criticism-on-a-streetcar-named-desire (accessed on July 9, 2012).

Select Bibliography

EDITIONS

Cat on a Hot Tin Roof (New York: Signet, 1958).
Cat on a Hot Tin Roof (New York: New Directions, 2004).
A Streetcar Named Desire (New York: Dramatists Play Service, 1947).
A Streetcar Named Desire (New York: New Directions, 1980).
Tennessee Williams, 1937–1955, Mel Gussow and Kenneth Holditch (eds.) (New York: Library of America, 2000).
The Theatre of Tennessee Williams, Vols. 1 & 3 (New York: New Directions, 1971).

FILM AND TELEVISION ADAPTATIONS

Cat on a Hot Tin Roof. Directed by Richard Brooks (1958).
Cat on a Hot Tin Roof. Directed by Robert Moore (1976).
A Streetcar Named Desire. Directed by Elia Kazan (1951).
A Streetcar Named Desire. Directed by John Erman (1984).
A Streetcar Named Desire. Directed by Glenn Jordan (1995).

ESSAYS, LETTERS, JOURNALS, AND INTERVIEWS

Conversations with Tennessee Williams, Albert J. Devlin (ed.) (Jackson: University Press of Mississippi, 1986).
Five O'Clock Angel: Letters of Tennessee Williams to Maria St. Just, 1948–1982 (New York: Knopf, 1990).
Letters to Donald Windham, 1940–1965 (New York: Holt, Rinehart, 1977).
Notebooks, Margaret Bradham Thornton (ed.) (New Haven, CT: Yale University Press, 2006).
The Selected Letters of Tennessee Williams: Volume I, 1920–1945, Albert J. Devlin and Nancy M. Tischler (eds.) (New York: New Directions, 2000).
The Selected Letters of Tennessee Williams: Volume II, 1945–1957, Albert J. Devlin and Nancy M. Tischler (eds.) (New York: New Directions, 2004).
Where I Live: Selected Essays, Christine Day and Bob Woods (eds.) (New York: New Directions, 1978). Enlarged and expanded as *New Selected Essays: Where I Live*, John S. Bak (ed.) (New York: New Directions, 2009).

BIBLIOGRAPHIES AND REFERENCE GUIDES

Bak, John S., 'Criticism on *A Streetcar Named Desire*: A Bibliographical Survey, 1947–2003,' *Cercles* 10 (2004), www.pdfdocspace.com/docs/5914/criticism-on-a-streetcar-named-desire (accessed July 9, 2012).

Crandell, George W., *Tennessee Williams: A Descriptive Bibliography* (Pittsburgh: University of Pittsburgh Press, 1995).

Gunn, Drewey Wayne, *Tennessee Williams: A Bibliography* (Metuchen, NJ: Scarecrow Press, 1980; second edition, 1991).

Heintzelman, Greta and Alycia Smith Howard (eds.), *A Critical Companion to Tennessee Williams* (New York: Facts on File, 2005).

Kolin, Philip C. (ed.), *Tennessee Williams: A Guide to Research and Performance* (Westport, CT: Greenwood Press, 1998).

Kolin, Philip C. (ed.), *The Tennessee Williams Encyclopedia* (Westport, CT: Greenwood Press, 2004).

McCann, John S., *The Critical Reputation of Tennessee Williams: A Reference Guide* (Boston: G. K. Hall, 1983).

BIOGRAPHIES

Adler, Thomas P., 'Tennessee Williams,' *Dictionary of Literary Biography (Vol. 341: Twentieth-Century American Dramatists)*, Garrett Eisler (ed.) (Detroit, MI: Gale, 2008), pp. 276–97.

Hayman, Ronald, *Tennessee Williams: Everyone Else is an Audience* (New Haven, CT: Yale University Press, 1993).

Leverich, Lyle, *Tom: The Unknown Tennessee Williams* (New York: Crown, 1995).

Rader, Dotson, *Tennessee: Cry of the Heart* (New York: New American Library, 1985).

Rasky, Harry, *Tennessee Williams: A Portrait in Laughter and Lamentation* (New York: Dodd, Mead, 1986).

Spoto, Donald, *The Kindness of Strangers: The Life of Tennessee Williams* (Boston: Little, Brown, 1985).

Van Antwerp, Margaret and Sally Johns (eds.), *Tennessee Williams: Dictionary of Literary Biography, Documentary Series* (Detroit, MI: Gale, 1984).

Williams, Dakin and Shepard Mead, *Tennessee Williams: An Intimate Biography* (New York: Arbor House, 1983).

Williams, Edwina Dakin and Lucy Freeman, *Remember Me to Tom* (New York: Putnam's, 1963).

CRITICISM: COLLECTIONS OF ESSAYS

Bloom, Harold (ed.), *Tennessee Williams: Modern Critical Views* (New York: Chelsea, 2003).

Bloom, Harold (ed.), *Tennessee Williams's 'A Streetcar Named Desire'* (New York: Chelsea, 2005).

Crandell, George W. (ed.), *The Critical Response to Tennessee Williams* (Westport, CT: Greenwood Press, 1995).

Gross, Robert F. (ed.), *Tennessee Williams: A Casebook* (New York: Routledge, 2002).

Hurrell, John D. (ed.), *Two Modern American Tragedies: Reviews and Criticism of 'A Death of a Salesman' and 'A Streetcar Named Desire'* (New York: Scribner's, 1961).

Kolin, Philip C. (ed.), *Confronting Tennessee Williams's 'A Streetcar Named Desire': Essays in Critical Pluralism* (Westport, CT: Greenwood Press, 1993).

Martin, Robert A. (ed.), *Critical Essays on Tennessee Williams* (New York: G. K. Hall, 1997).

Miller, Jordan Y. (ed.), *Twentieth Century Interpretations of 'A Streetcar Named Desire': A Collection of Critical Essays* (Englewood Cliffs, NJ: Prentice-Hall, 1971).

Roudane, Matthew C. (ed.), *The Cambridge Companion to Tennessee Williams* (Cambridge: Cambridge University Press, 1997).

Stanton, Stephen S. (ed.), *Tennessee Williams: A Collection of Critical Essays* (Englewood Cliffs, NJ: Prentice-Hall, 1977).

Tharpe, Jac (ed.), *Tennessee Williams: A Tribute* (Jackson: University of Mississippi Press, 1977). Reprinted in abridged form as *Tennessee Williams: 13 Essays* (Jackson: University Press of Mississippi, 1980).

Vos, Ralph F. (ed.), *The Magical Muse: Millennial Essays on Tennessee Williams* (Tuscaloosa: University of Alabama Press. 2002).

CRITICISM: MONOGRAPHS AND ARTICLES

INTRODUCTION

Atkinson, Brooks, 'Streetcar Tragedy—Mr. Williams' Report on Life in New Orleans,' in Jordan Y. Miller (ed.), *Twentieth Century Interpretations of A Streetcar Named Desire* (Englewood Cliffs, NJ: Prentice-Hall, 1971), pp. 32–4.

Atkinson, Brooks, 'Theatre: Tennessee Williams' "Cat": Writer Depicts Some Restless Delta Folk,' *New York Times*, March 25, 1955, p. 18.

Becker, William, 'Reflections on Three New Plays,' *The Hudson Review*, 8.2 (1955), pp. 258–72.

Bentley, Eric, *In Search of Theatre* (New York: Vintage Books, 1959).

Bentley, Eric, *What is Theatre? Incorporating 'The Dramatic Event' and other Reviews, 1944–1967* (New York: Atheneum, 1968).

Chesler, S. Alan, '*A Streetcar Named Desire*: Twenty-Five Years of Criticism,' *Notes on Mississippi Writers*, 7 (1974), pp. 44–53.

Chesler, S. Alan, 'Tennessee Williams: Reassessment and Assessment,' in Jac Tharpe (ed.), *Tennessee Williams: A Tribute* (Jackson: University Press of Mississippi, 1977), pp. 848–80.

Clurman, Harold, *The Divine Pastime: Theatre Essays* (New York: Macmillan, 1974).

Kerr, Walter, *Journey to the Center of the Theatre* (New York: Knopf, 1970).

Kerr, Walter, 'A Secret is Half-Told in Fountains of Words,' in George W. Crandell (ed.), *The Critical Response to Tennessee Williams* (Westport, CT: Greenwood Press, 1996), pp. 118–20.

Kolin, Philip C., 'The First Critical Assessments of *A Streetcar Named Desire*: The *Streetcar* Tryouts and the Reviewers,' *Journal of Dramatic Theory and Criticism*, 6.1 (1991), pp. 45–67.

Margaronis, Maria, 'Blues for the True at Heart,' *Times Literary Supplement*, October 18, 2002, pp. 20–1.

McCarthy, Mary, 'Theatre Chronicle: Oh, Sweet Mystery of Life,' *Partisan Review*, 15.3 (1948), pp. 357–60.

Mendelsohn, Daniel, 'Victims on Broadway II,' *The New York Review of Books*, June 9, 2005, pp. 31–3.

CHAPTER ONE: PRODUCING PERFORMANCE TEXTS

Als, Hilton, 'The Theatre: Love and Disaster,' *The New Yorker*, March 17, 2008, pp. 88–9.

Brantley, Ben, 'A Fragile Flower Rooted to the Cruel Earth,' *New York Times*, December 3, 2009, pp. C1, C6.

Clay, Carolyn, 'Islands in the Storm,' *The Boston Phoenix*, March 4, 2011, p. 24.

Crandell, George W., '*Cat on a Hot Tin Roof*,' in Philip C. Kolin (ed.), *Tennessee Williams: A Guide to Research and Performance* (Westport, CT: Greenwood Press, 1998), pp. 109–25.

Funke, Lewis and Booth, John E., 'Williams on Williams,' in Albert J. Devlin (ed.), *Conversations with Tennessee Williams* (Jackson: University Press of Mississippi, 1986). pp. 97–106.

Jones, David Richard, *Great Directors at Work: Stanislavsky, Brecht, Kazan, Brook* (Berkeley: University of California Press, 1986), pp. 138–99.

Kazan, Elia, *A Life* (New York: Knopf, 1988).

Kazan, Elia, 'Notebook for *A Streetcar Named Desire*,' in Toby Cole and Helen Kritch Chinoy (eds.), *Directors on Directing: A Source Book of the Modern Theater* (Indianapolis, IN: Bobbs-Merrill, 1963), pp. 364–99.

Kolin, Philip C., *Williams: A Streetcar Named Desire* (Cambridge: Cambridge University Press, 2000).

McCarter, Jeremy, 'Upper Broadway,' *New York Magazine*, March 28, 2008, p. 67.

Murphy, Brenda, *Tennessee Williams and Elia Kazan: A Collaboration in the Theatre* (Cambridge: Cambridge University Press, 1992).

Parker, Brian, 'Bringing Back Big Daddy,' *The Tennessee Williams Annual Review*, 3 (2000), pp. 91–9.

Price, Marian, '*Cat on a Hot Tin Roof*: The Uneasy Marriage of Success and Idealism,' *Modern Drama*, 38 (1995), pp. 324–35.

Sacksteder, William, 'The Three Cats: A Study in Dramatic Structure,' *Drama Survey*, 53 (1966–67), pp. 252–66.

Terkel, Studs, 'Studs Terkel Talks with Tennessee Williams,' in Albert J. Devlin (ed.), *Conversations with Tennessee Williams* (Jackson: University Press of Mississippi, 1986), pp. 78–96.

CHAPTER TWO: MYTHIC PATTERNS—SOUTHERN, CLASSICAL, AND CHRISTIAN

Adler, Jacob H., 'The Rose and the Fox: Notes on the Southern Drama,' in Louis D. Rubin, Jr. and Robert D. Jacobs (eds.), *South: Modern Literature in its Cultural Setting* (Garden City, NY: Doubleday, 1961), pp. 349–75.

Barranger, Milly S. 'New Orleans as Theatrical Image in Plays by Tennessee Williams,' *The Southern Quarterly*, 23.2 (1985), pp. 38–54.

Bray, Robert, '*A Streetcar Named Desire*: The Political and Historical Subtext,' in Philip C. Kolin (ed.), *Confronting Tennessee Williams's 'A Streetcar Named Desire': Essays in Critical Pluralism* (Westport CT: Greenwood Press, 1993), pp. 183–97.

Crandell, George W., '"Echo Spring": Reflecting the Gaze of Narcissus in Tennessee Williams's *Cat on a Hot Tin Roof*,' *Modern Drama*, 42 (1999), pp. 427–41.

Hale, Alleen, 'How a Tiger Became the Cat,' *Tennessee Williams Literary Journal*, 2.1 (1990–91), pp. 33–6.

Holditch, W. Kenneth, 'The Last Frontier of Bohemia: Tennessee Williams in New Orleans, 1938–1983,' *The Southern Quarterly*, 23.2 (1985), pp. 1–37.

Holditch, W. Kenneth, 'South Toward Freedom: Tennessee Williams,' in Richard S. Kennedy (ed.), *Literary New Orleans* (Baton Rouge: Louisiana State University Press, 1992). pp. 61–75.

Holditch, W. Kenneth and Richard Freeman Leavitt, *Tennessee Williams and the South* (Jackson: University Press of Mississippi, 2002).

Jackson, Esther Merle, *The Broken World of Tennessee Williams* (Madison: University of Wisconsin Press, 1965).

King, Kimball, 'Tennessee Williams: A Southern Writer,' *The Mississippi Quarterly*, 48 (1995), pp. 627–47.

Mayfield, Panny, 'Mississippi's Tennessee,' *Mississippi*, 9.5 (1991), pp. 38–45.

Porter, Thomas E., *Myth and Modern American Drama* (Detroit, MI: Wayne State University Press, 1969), pp. 153–76.

Prenshaw, Peggy W., 'The Paradoxical World of Tennessee Williams,' in Jac Tharpe (ed.), *Tennessee Williams: 13 Essays* (Jackson: University Press of Mississippi, 1980), pp. 3–27.

Quirino, Leonard, 'The Cards Indicate a Voyage on *A Streetcar Named Desire*,' in Jac Tharpe (ed.), *Tennessee Williams: 13 Essays* (Jackson: University Press of Mississippi, 1980) pp. 29–48.

Thompson, Judith J., *Tennessee Williams' Plays: Memory, Myth, and Symbol*—University of Kansas Humanities Studies, 54 (New York: Peter Lang, 1987), pp. 25–51; 61–81.

Watson, Charles S., 'The Cultural Imagination of Tennessee Williams,' in *The History of Southern Drama* (Lexington: University Press of Kentucky, 1997), pp. 174–91.

CHAPTER THREE: POLITICAL, SOCIAL, AND CULTURAL CONTEXTS

Adler, Thomas P., 'Culture, Power, and the (En)gendering of Community: Tennessee Williams and Politics,' *The Mississippi Quarterly*, 48.4 (1995), pp. 649–65.

Bak, John S., '"sneakin' and spyin'" from Broadway to the Beltway: Cold War Masculinity, Brick, and Homosexual Existentialism,' *Theatre Journal*, 56.2 (2004), pp. 225–50.

Blades, Larry T., 'The Returning Vet's Experience in *A Streetcar Named Desire*: Stanley as the Decommissioned Warrior under Stress,' *The Tennessee Williams Annual Review*, 10 (2009), pp. 17–29.

Brewer, Mary F., *Staging Whiteness* (Middletown, CT: Wesleyan University Press, 2005), pp. 71–7.

Colanzi, Rita, 'Caged Birds: Bad Faith in Tennessee Williams's Drama,' *Modern Drama*, 35 (1992), pp. 451–64.

Corber, Robert J., *Homosexuality in Cold War America: Resistance and the Crisis of Masculinity* (Durham, NC: Duke University Press, 1997), pp. 1–43.

Crandell, George W., 'Misrepresentation and Miscegenation: Reading the Racialized Discourse of Tennessee Williams's *A Streetcar Named Desire*,' *Modern Drama*, 40 (1997), pp. 337–46.

Hurley, Paul J., 'Tennessee Williams: The Playwright as Social Critic,' reprinted in George W. Crandell (ed.), *The Critical Response to Tennessee Williams* (Westport CT: Greenwood Press, 1996), pp. 126–39.

Kelly, Lionel, 'The White Goddess, Ethnicity, and the Politics of Desire,' in Philip C. Kolin (ed.), *Confronting Tennessee Williams's 'A Streetcar Named Desire': Essays in Critical Pluralism* (Westport, CT: Greenwood Press, 1992), pp. 121–32.

McConachie, Bruce, '*Cat* and the Grotesque in the Cold War,' *Tennessee Williams Literary Journal*, 1 (1998), pp. 47–64.

Murphy, Brenda, *Congressional Theatre: Dramatizing McCarthyism on Stage, Film, and Television* (Cambridge: Cambridge University Press, 1999).

Paller, Michael, 'A Playwright with a Social Conscience,' *The Tennessee Williams Annual Review*, 10 (2009), pp. 105–10.

CHAPTER FOUR: WILLIAMS AND LITERARY CANONICITY

Adler, Thomas P., *American Drama 1940–1960: A Critical History* (New York: Twayne, 1994), pp. 131–80.

Adler, Thomas P., *Mirror on the Stage: The Pulitzer Plays as an Approach to American Drama* (West Lafayette, IN: Purdue University Press, 1987), pp. 17–22; 33–7.

Adler, Thomas P., *'A Streetcar Named Desire': The Moth and the Lantern* (New York: Twayne, 1990).

Bak, John S., '"Stanley made love to her!—by force": Blanche and the Evolution of a Rape,' *Journal of American Drama and Theatre*, 16.1 (2004), pp. 69–87.

Bigsby, C. W. E., *A Critical Introduction to Twentieth-Century American Drama 2: Tennessee Williams, Arthur Miller, Edward Albee* (Cambridge: Cambridge University Press, 1984), pp. 15–134.

Bigsby, C. W. E., *Modern American Drama: 1945–1990* (Cambridge: Cambridge University Press, 1992), pp. 32–71.

Boxill, Roger, *Tennessee Williams* (New York: St. Martin's, 1988).

Cluck, Nancy Anne, 'Showing or Telling: Narrators in the Drama of Tennessee Williams,' *American Literature*, 51.1 (1979), pp. 84–93.

Devlin, Albert J., 'Writing in "A Place of Stone": *Cat on a Hot Tin Roof*,' in Matthew C. Roudane (ed.), *The Cambridge Companion to Tennessee Williams* (Cambridge: Cambridge University Press, 1997), pp. 95–113.

Donahue, Francis, *The Dramatic World of Tennessee Williams* (New York: Frederick Ungar, 1964).

Falk, Signi, *Tennessee Williams*, 2nd edn. (Boston, MA: Twayne, 1978).

Ganz, Arthur, 'The Desperate Morality of the Plays of Tennessee Williams,' *The American Scholar*, 31.2 (1962), pp. 278–90.

Griffin, Alice, *Understanding Tennessee Williams* (Columbia: University of South Carolina Press, 1995).

Hirsch, Foster, *A Portrait of the Artist: The Plays of Tennessee Williams* (Port Washington, NY: Kennikat, 1979).

Isaac, Dan, 'No Past to Think In: Who Wins in *A Streetcar Named Desire?*,' *Louisiana Literature*, 14.2 (1997), pp. 8–35.

Kalem, T. E., 'The Laureate of the Outcast,' *Time*, March 7, 1983, p. 88.

Krasner, David, *American Drama 1945–2000: An Introduction* (Malden, MA: Blackwell, 2006), pp. 40–8; 51–5.

Kullman, Colby, 'Ruled by Power: "Big Daddyism" in the World of Tennessee Williams Plays,' *The Mississippi Quarterly*, 48 (1995), pp. 667–76.

Londre, Felicia Hardison, 'A Streetcar Running Fifty Years,' in Mathew C. Roudane (ed.), *The Cambridge Companion to Tennessee Williams* (Cambridge: Cambridge University Press, 1997), pp. 45–66.

Londre, Felicia Hardison, *Tennessee Williams* (New York: Frederick Ungar, 1970).

Murphy, Brenda A., 'Tennessee Williams,' in David Krasner (ed.), *A Companion to Twentieth-Century American Drama* (Malden, MA: Blackwell, 2005), pp. 175–91.

Nelson, Benjamin, *Tennessee Williams: The Man and His Work* (New York: Ivan Obolensky, 1961).

Robinson, Marc, *The Other American Drama* (Cambridge: Cambridge University Press, 1994), pp. 29–59.

Sievers, W. David, *Freud on Broadway: A History of Psychoanalysis and the American Drama* (New York: Hermitage, 1955).

Smith, Susan Harris, 'Generic Hegemony: American Drama and the Canon,' *American Quarterly*, 41 (1989), pp. 112–22.

Tischler, Nancy M., *Tennessee Williams: Rebellious Puritan* (New York: Citadel Press, 1961).

CHAPTER FIVE: DRAMATIC FORM, STYLE AND GENRE

Adler, Thomas P., 'Tennessee Williams's "Personal Lyricism": Towards an Androgynous Form,' in William W. Demastes (ed.), *Realism and the American Dramatic Tradition* (Tuscaloosa: University of Alabama Press, 1996), pp. 152–77.

Berkman, Leonard, 'The Tragic Downfall of Blanche DuBois,' *Modern Drama*, 10.3 (1967), pp. 249–57.

Cardullo, Bert, 'Birth and Death in *A Streetcar Named Desire*,' in Philip C. Kolin (ed.), *Confronting Tennessee Williams's A Streetcar Named Desire: Essays in Critical Pluralism* (Westport CT: Greenwood Press, 1993), pp. 167–80.

Cardullo, Bert, "The Blind Mexican Woman in Williams's *A Streetcar Named Desire*", *Notes on Modern American Literature*, 7.2 (1983), item 14.

Cardullo, Bert, "Drama of Intimacy and Tragedy of Incomprehension: *A Streetcar Named Desire* Reconsidered", in Jac Tharpe (ed.), *Tennessee Williams: A Tribute* (Jackson: University Press of Mississippi, 1977), pp. 137–53.

Cardullo, Bert, "The Role of the Baby in *A Streetcar Named Desire*", *Notes on Contemporary Literature*, 14.2 (1984), 4–5.

Corrigan, Mary Ann, "Realism and Theatricalism in *A Streetcar Named Desire*", *Modern Drama*, 19.4 (1976), 385–96.

Fleche, Anne, *Mimetic Disillusion: Eugene O'Neill, Tennessee Williams, and U. S. Dramatic Realism* (Tuscaloosa: University of Alabama Press, 1997), pp. 1–24; 89–106.

Harwood, Britton J., "Tragedy as Habit: *A Streetcar Named Desire*", in Jac Tharpe (ed.) *Tennessee Williams: A Tribute* (Jackson: University Press of Mississippi, 1977), pp. 104–15.

Heilman, Robert B., *The Iceman, the Arsonist and the Troubled Agent: Tragedy and Melodrama on the Modern Stage* (Seattle: University of Washington Press, 1973) pp. 115–41.

Jackson, Esther Merle, *The Broken World of Tennessee Williams* (Madison: University of Wisconsin Press, 1965).

Kolin, Philip C., "Williams's *Cat on a Hot Tin Roof*", *The Explicator*, 60.4 (2002), 215–16.

Mielziner, Jo, *Designing for the Theatre: A Memoir and a Portfolio* (New York: Bramhall, 1965).

Riddell, Joseph N., "*A Streetcar Named Desire*—Nietzsche Descending", reprinted in Jordan Y. Miller (ed.), *Twentieth Century Interpretations of "A Streetcar Named Desire"* (Englewood Cliffs, NJ: Prentice-Hall, 1971), pp. 80–9.

Roderick, John M., "From 'Tarantula Arms' to 'Della Robbia Blue': The Tennessee Williams Transit Authority", in Jac Tharpe (ed.) *Tennessee Williams: A Tribute* (Jackson: University Press of Mississippi, 1977), pp. 116–25.

Schvey, Henry I., "Madonna at the Poker Night: Pictorial Elements in Tennessee Williams's *A Streetcar Named Desire*", in J. Bakker and D. R. M. Wilkinson (eds.), *From Cooper to Philip Roth: Essays in American Literature* (Amsterdam: Rodopi, 1980), pp. 70–7.

Von Szeliski, John, *Tragedy and Fear: Why Modern Tragic Drama Fails* (Chapel Hill: University of North Carolina Press, 1971).

Vowles, Richard B., "Tennessee Williams: The World of His Imagery", *Tulane Drama Review*, 3.2 (1958), 51–6.

CHAPTER SIX: FEMINIST PERSPECTIVES

Blackwell, Louise, "Tennessee Williams and the Predicament of Women", reprinted in Robert A. Martin (ed.) *Critical Essays on Tennessee Williams* (New York: G. K. Hall & Co., 1997), pp. 243–8.

Bordo, Susan, *The Male Body: A New Look at Men in Public and Private* (New York: Farrar, Straus and Giroux, 1999), pp. 134–49.

Da Ponte, Durant, "Tennessee Williams' Gallery of Feminine Characters", reprinted in Robert A. Martin (ed.) *Critical Essays on Tennessee Williams* (New York: G. K. Hall & Co., 1997), pp. 259–75.

Dworkin, Andrea, *Intercourse* (New York: The Free Press, 1973), pp. 35–45.

Gilbert, Susan M. and Susan Gubar, *No Man's Land: The Place of the Woman Writer in the Twentieth Century, Volume 1: The War of the Words* (New Haven CT: Yale University Press, 1988), pp. 46–52.

Harris, Laurilyn J., "Perceptual Conflict and the Perversion of Creativity in *A Streetcar Named Desire*", in Philip C. Kolin (ed.) *Confronting Tennessee Williams's A Streetcar Named Desire: Essays in Critical Pluralism* (Westport CT: Greenwood Press, 1993), pp. 83–103.

Kataria, Gulshan Rai, "A Hetaira of Tennessee Williams: Maggie", *Indian Journal of American Studies*, 7.1 (1982), 45–55.

Kolin, Philip C. "Eunice Hubbell and the Feminist Thematics of *A Streetcar Named Desire*", in Philip C. Kolin (ed.) *Confronting Tennessee Williams's A Streetcar Named Desire: Essays in Critical Pluralism* (Westport CT: Greenwood Press, 1993), pp. 105–20.

Kundert-Gibbs, John, "Barren Ground: Female Strength and Male Impotence in *Who's Afraid of Virginia Woolf?* and *Cat on a Hot Tin Roof*", in Katherine M. Burkman and Judith Roof (eds.), *Staging the Rage: The Web of Misogyny in Modern Drama* (Cranbury NJ: Fairleigh Dickinson University Press, 1998), pp. 230–47.

Lant, Kathleen Margaret, "A Streetcar Named Misogyny", in James Redmond (ed.), *Violence in Drama* (Cambridge: Cambridge University Press, 1991), pp. 225–38.

O'Connor, Jacqueline, *Dramatizing Dementia: Madness in the Plays of Tennessee Williams* (Bowling Green, OH: Bowling Green State University Press, 1997).

Vlasopolos, Anca, "Authorizing History: Victimization in *A Streetcar Named Desire*", *Theatre Journal*, 38 (1985), 322–38.

CHAPTER SEVEN: QUEER THEORY AS LENS

Bibler, Michael P., *Cotton's Queer Relations: Same-Sex Intimacy and the Literature of the Southern Plantation, 1936-1968* (Charlottesville: University of Virginia Press, 2009).

Bibler, Michael P., "'A Tenderness which was Uncommon': Homosexuality, Narrative, and the Southern Plantation in Tennessee Williams's *Cat on a Hot Tin Roof*", *The Mississippi Quarterly*, 55.3 (2002), 380–400.

Clum, John M., "'Something Cloudy, Something Clear': Homophobic Discourse in Tennessee Williams", *The South Atlantic Quarterly*, 88.1 (1989), pp. 161–79.

De Jongh, Nicholas. *Not in Front of an Audience: Homosexuality on Stage* (London: Routledge, 1992).

Fleche, Anne, "When the Door is a Jar, or Out in the Theatre: Tennessee Williams and Queer Space", *Theatre Journal*, 47 (1995), 253–67.

Gindt, Dirk, "Torn between the 'Swedish Sin' and 'Homosexual Freemasonry': Tennessee Williams, Sexual Morals, and the Closet in 1950s Sweden", *Tennessee Williams Annual Review*, 11 (2010), 19–39.

Gross, Roger, "The Pleasures of Brick: Eros and the Gay Spectator in *Cat on a Hot Tin Roof*", *The Journal of American Drama and Theatre*, 9.1 (1997), 11–25.

Lilly, Mark, "The Plays of Tennessee Williams", *Gay Men's Literature in the Twentieth Century* (Washington Square: New York University Press, 1993), pp. 105–26.

Paller, Michael, *Gentlemen Callers: Tennessee Williams, Homosexuality, and Mid-Twentieth Century Broadway Drama* (New York: Palgrave Macmillan, 2005).

Paller, Michael, "A Room Which Isn't Empty: *A Streetcar Named Desire* and the Question of Homophobia", *Tennessee Williams Literary Journal*, 5 (2003), 21–37.

Sarotte, Georges-Michel, "Fluidity and Differentiation in Three Plays by Tennessee Williams", in Marc Maufort (ed.), *Staging Difference: Cultural Pluralism in American Drama and Theatre* (New York: Peter Lang, 1995), pp. 141–56.

Sarotte, Georges-Michel, Tennessee Williams: Theatre as Psychotherapy", in *Like a Brother, Like a Lover: Male Homosexuality in the American Novel and Theater from Herman Melville to James Baldwin*, Richard Miller (trans.) (Garden City, NY: Doubleday Anchor, 1978), pp. 108–20.

Savran, David, "'By coming suddenly into a room I thought was empty': Mapping the Closet with Tennessee Williams", *Studies in the Literary Imagination*, 24.2 (1991), 57–74.

Savran, David, *Communists, Cowboys, and Queers: The Politics of Masculinity in the Works of Arthur Miller and Tennessee Williams* (Minneapolis: University of Minnesota Press, 1992), pp. 76–174.

Shackelford, Dean, "'The Ghost of a Man': The Quest for Self-Acceptance in Early Williams", *Tennessee Williams Annual Review*, 4 (2001), 49–58.

Shackelford, Dean, "Is There a Gay Man in This Text?: Subverting the Closet in *A Streetcar Named Desire*", in Michael J. Meyer (ed.), *Literature and Homosexuality* (Amsterdam: Rodopi, 2000), pp. 135–55.

Shackelford, Dean, "The Truth Must be Told: Gay Subjectivity, Homophobia, and Social History in *Cat on a Hot Tin Roof*", *Tennessee Williams Annual Review*, (1998), 103–24.

Sinfield, Alan. *Cultural Politics—Queer Reading* (Philadelphia: University of Pennsylvania Press, 1994), pp. 40–59.

Sinfield, Alan, "Reading Tennessee Williams", *Out on Stage: Lesbian and Gay Theatre in the Twentieth Century* (New Haven: Yale University Press, 1999), pp. 186–207.

Winchell, Mark Royden, "Come Back to the Locker Room Ag'in, Brick Honey!", *The Mississippi Quarterly*, 48 (1995), 701–12.

CHAPTER EIGHT: CONTEMPORARY CRITICAL THEORY AND *STREETCAR*

Bak, John S., "A Streetcar Named *Dies Irae*: Tennessee Williams and the Semiotics of Rape", *The Tennessee Williams Annual Review*, (2009), 42–72.

Bedient, Calvin, "There Are Lives that Desire Does Not Sustain: *A Streetcar Named Desire*", in Philip C. Kolin (ed.), *Confronting Tennessee Williams's A Streetcar Named Desire: Essays in Critical Pluralism* (Westport CT: Greenwood Press, 1993), pp. 45–58.

Fleche, Anne, "The Space of Madness and Desire: Tennessee Williams and *Streetcar*", *Modern Drama*, 38 (1995), 496–508.

Hulley, Kathleen, "The Fate of the Symbolic in *A Streetcar Named Desire*", in James Redmond (ed.), *Drama and Symbolism* (Cambridge: Cambridge University Press, 1982), pp. 89–99.

Kleb, William, "Marginalia, *Streetcar*, Williams and Foucault, in Philip C. Kolin (ed.), *Confronting Tennessee Williams's A Streetcar Named Desire: Essays in Critical Pluralism* (Westport CT: Greenwood Press, 1993), pp. 29–43.

Kolin, Philip C., "Roland Barthes, Tennessee Williams, and *A Streetcar Named Pleasure/Desire*", *The Centennial Review*, 43.2 (1999), 289–304.

Kolin, Philip C., "'It's only a paper moon': The Paper Ontologies in Tennessee Williams's *A Streetcar Named Desire*", *Modern Drama*, 40.4 (1997), 454–67.

Morrow, Laura and Edward Morrow, "The Ontological Potentialities of Antichaos and Adaptation in *A Streetcar Named Desire*", in Philip C. Kolin (ed.), *Confronting Tennessee Williams's A Streetcar Named Desire: Essays in Critical Pluralism* (Westport CT: Greenwood Press, 1993), pp. 59–70.

Pagan, Nicholas, *Rethinking Literary Biography: A Postmodern Approach to Tennessee Williams* (Rutherford, NJ: Fairleigh Dickinson University Press, 1993).

Pagan, Nicholas O., "Tennessee Williams's Theater as Body", *Philological Quarterly*, 22.1 (1993), 97–115.

Schlueter, Jane, "'We've had this date with each other from the beginning': Reading Toward Closure in *A Streetcar Named Desire*", in Philip C. Kolin (ed.), *Confronting Tennessee Williams's A Streetcar Named Desire: Essays in Critical Pluralism* (Westport CT: Greenwood Press, 1993), pp. 71–82.

Toles, George, "Blanche Dubois and the Kindness of Endings", *Raritan*, 14.4 (1995), 115–43.

CHAPTER NINE: FILM AND TELEVISION ADAPTATIONS

Benshoff, Harry M. and Sean Griffin, *Queer Images: A History of Gay and Lesbian Film in America* (Lanham, MD: Rowman & Littlefield, 2006).

Brandt, George, "Cinematic Structure in the Work of Tennessee Williams", in John Russell Brown and Bernard Harris, (eds.) *American Theatre (Stratford-Upon-Avon Studies 10)* (London: Edward Arnold, 1967), pp. 173–9.

Byars, Jackie, *All that Hollywood Allows: Re-reading Gender in the 1950s* (Chapel Hill: University of North Carolina Press, 1991).

Cahir, Linda Costanzo, "The Artful Rerouting of *A Streetcar Named Desire*", *Literature/Film Quarterly*, 22 (1994), 72–7.

Ciment, Michel (ed.), *Kazan on Kazan* (New York: Viking, 1974).

Cohan, Steven, *Masked Men: Masculinity and the Movies in the Fifties* (Bloomington: Indiana University Press, 1997).

Geraghty, Christine, *Now a Major Motion Picture: Film Adaptations of Literature and Drama* (Lanham, MD: Rowman & Littlefield, 2008), pp. 77–84; 92–101.

Gronbeck-Tedesco, John L., "Absence and the Actor's Body: Marlon Brando's Performance in *A Streetcar Named Desire* on Stage and in Film", *Studies in American Drama, 1945-Present*, 8 (1993), 115–26.

Hanks, Pamela Anne, "Must We Acknowledge What We Mean?: The Viewer's Role in the Filmed Versions of *A Streetcar Named Desire*", *Journal of Popular Film and Television*, 14 (1986), 114–22.

Kalson, Albert E., "Tennessee Williams at the Delta Brilliant," in Jac Tharpe (ed.), *Tennessee Williams: 13 Essays*, (Jackson: University Press of Mississippi, 1980), pp. 207–27.

Leff, Leonard J., "And Transfer to Cemeteries: The *Streetcars Named Desire*", *Film Quarterly*, 55 (2002), 29–37.

Leonard, John, "Crossover Artist," *New York*, 30 October 1995, pp. 137–8.

Palmer, R. Barton, "Hollywood in Crisis: Tennessee Williams and the Evolution of the Adult Film", in Matthew C. Roudane (ed.), *The Cambridge Companion to Tennessee Williams* (Cambridge: Cambridge University Press, 1997), pp. 204–31.

Palmer, R. Barton and Robert Bray, *Hollywood's Tennessee: The Williams Films and Postwar America* (Austin: University of Texas Press, 2008).

Phillips, Gene D., *The Films of Tennessee Williams* (Philadelphia, PA: Art Alliance Press, 1980).

Phillips, Gene D., S.J., *A Streetcar Named Desire*: Play and Film", in Philip C. Kolin (ed.), *Confronting Tennessee Williams's A Streetcar Named Desire: Essays in Critical Pluralism* (Westport, CT: Greenwood, 1993), pp. 223–35.

Phillips, Gene D., S. J., '*A Streetcar Named Desire*: The Restored Version of the Film,' *Tennessee Williams Literary Journal*, 5 (2003), pp. 39–46.

Schlueter, June, 'Imitating an Icon: John Erman's Remake of Tennessee Williams's *A Streetcar Named Desire*,' *Modern Drama*, 28 (1985), pp. 139–47.

Schumach, Murray, *The Face on the Cutting Room Floor: The Story of Movie and Television Censorship* (New York: DeCapo Press, 1974).

Tischler, Nancy M., 'Sanitizing the Streetcar,' *Louisiana Literature*, 14 (1997), pp. 48–56.

Tischler, Nancy M., '"Tiger—Tiger": Blanche's Rape on Screen,' in Ralph F. Voss (ed.), *Magical Muse: Millennial Essays on Tennessee Williams* (Tuscaloosa: University of Alabama Press, 2002), pp. 50–69.

Yacowar, Maurice, *Tennessee Williams and Film* (New York: Frederick Ungar, 1977).

Young, Jeff (ed.), *Kazan, The Master Director Discusses His Films: Interviews with Elia Kazan* (New York: Newmarket Press, 1999).

CONCLUSION

Adler, Jacob H., 'Williams and the Bard,' *Tennessee Williams Literary Journal*, 2 (1990–91), pp. 37–49.

Adler, Thomas P., 'Setting as Meaning: A Scenic Approach to Teaching *The Glass Menagerie*,' *Alabama English*, 4 (1982), pp. 47–51.

Bak, John S., 'Criticism on *A Streetcar Named Desire*: A Bibliographical Survey, 1947–2003,' *Cercles* 10 (2004), www.pdfdocspace.com/docs/5914/criticism-on-a-streetcar-named-desire (accessed on July 9, 2012).

Bryer, Jackson R., '"Entitled to Write About Her Life": Tennessee Williams and F. Scott and Zelda Fitzgerald,' in Ralph F. Voss (ed.), *Magical Muse: Millennial Essays on Tennessee Williams* (Tuscaloosa: University Press of Alabama, 2002), pp. 163–77.

Harrington, Gary, 'The Smashed Mirror: Blanche in *A Streetcar Named Desire*,' in Barbara Ozieblo and Miriam Lopez-Rodriguez (eds.), *Staging a Cultural Paradigm: The Political and the Personal in American Drama* (Brussels: Peter Lang, 2002), pp. 67–78.

Kolin, Philip C. (ed.), '*A Streetcar Named Desire*: A Playwrights' Forum,' *Michigan Quarterly Review*, 29 (1990), pp. 173–203.

INDEX